# Public Opinion and Constitution Making in Pakistan 1958–1962

# PUBLIC OPINION
# AND CONSTITUTION
# MAKING IN PAKISTAN
# 1958–1962

*by*

EDGAR A. AND KATHRYN R. SCHULER

MICHIGAN STATE UNIVERSITY PRESS
1966

# CONTENTS

Preface . . . . . . . . . . . . . . . . . . 1

I. Introduction . . . . . . . . . . . . . . . 4

II. The First Year of Martial Law
(October 1958-October 1959) . . . . . . . . . 14

III. Basic Democracies (October 1959-February 1960) . . . 40

IV. The Constitution Commission I (February-May 1960) . . 49

V. The Bar and the Bench (April-June 1960) . . . . . . 55

VI. Public Response to the Constitution Commission
Questionnaire (May-August 1960) . . . . . . . . 61

VII. The Government's Reaction (June-August 1960) . . . 74

VIII. The Constitution Commission II
(June 1960-May 1961) . . . . . . . . . . . . 83

IX. The Cabinet Subcommittee (May-September 1961) . . . 105

X. The Turning Point (October 1961-January 1962) . . . 123

XI. Action and Reaction (February 1962) . . . . . . . 152

XII. The Announcement of the Constitution and the
(Report of the Constitution Commission
(March 1, 1962) . . . . . . . . . . . . . . 170

XIII. Analysis . . . . . . . . . . . . . . . . 181

XIV. Gainers and Losers Under the New Constitution . . . 198

Epilogue . . . . . . . . . . . . . . . . . 211

Appendices . . . . . . . . . . . . . . . . 217

Index . . . . . . . . . . . . . . . . . . 275

# Public Opinion and
# Constitution Making
# in Pakistan 1958–1962

# PREFACE

THIS WORK attempts to tell the story of the drafting of Pakistan's Constitution of 1962. What went on in the committee meetings and the actual drafting sessions has not been made public. The sub-title is intended to make clear that, with few exceptions, only newspaper sources were used in making this study. Actually only two of the four major Pakistani English-language daily newspapers were consulted systematically. Under these circumstances—since we were not able to use either Urdu or Bengali newspapers—we recognize that it may be regarded as presumptuous to call this a study of public opinion. However, we are not inclined to undervalue the importance of the English language press or of the role it plays in Pakistan.

We did not have access to original documents nor were we in a position to interview the leading personalities involved in the drafting of the new constitution. Furthermore, although we lived in Pakistan during thirty-four of the forty-four months of martial law, we resided in the *mofussil*—the picturesque Bengali term referring to the outlying districts or hinterland—of East Pakistan rather than in any large city. Access to such informed public opinion as may then have existed in the major urban centers was thus seriously restricted. Except in a very few instances, it has not been possible to verify the accuracy of the alleged facts as published in the daily press.

But in our view this study, despite its limitations, makes a contribution to the emerging literature on the development of Pakistan's constitution by bringing to light an unexpectedly large body of public opinion data as reported in the press during the period when the constitution was being formulated. The wealth of this information is "unexpectedly large" because during this entire process Pakistan was under martial law—and martial law administrations generally are notorious for their incompatibility with freedom of the press.

The plan of the study is chronological and is based on relevant events

1

and published expressions of public opinion from the first promise made by the Chief Martial Law Administrator, General Mohammad Ayub Khan, through the setting up of the constitution commission, the study of the Constitution Commission Report by the cabinet sub-committee, the drafting of the constitution, and finally to the announcement and promulgation of the constitution by President Ayub Khan.

A word about spelling, footnotes and index is in order. When direct quotations from newspapers are woven into the text, we have changed the spelling of such words as labour, programme and organise to conform to American usage. However, in quotations from journal articles, pamphlets and books the original spelling has been retained. In citations of newspaper sources it has not always been possible to include page numbers.

The procedure used in order to avoid direct attribution to President Ayub Khan or government officials of their remarks as printed in newspapers in cases where the original newspaper account used only indirect quotations should be explained here. In such cases the text of the source is often reproduced without quotation marks. It has seemed preferable to us to indulge in such acknowledged plagiarism rather than to give the misleading impression that we are directly quoting the person involved. Another reason for our preferring to copy the indirect quotations from the newspaper text rather than to rephrase the material is our opinion that in most cases the attributed remarks were actually the direct quotations.

In the index an attempt has been made to list the major issues involved in the drafting of the constitution such as the presidential system of government, unitary form, Islamic principles and others.

Many people have helped us in a wide variety of ways in the preparation of this manuscript. So far as possible we want to be explicit in our acknowledgments and expressions of appreciation but if any omissions are apparent to the reader we hope this general statement of indebtedness and gratitude will be taken as the sincere expression of appreciation we mean it to be. We would, however, particularly like to thank the following: Professor Donald S. Hecock of Wayne State University for his initial encouragement and moral support as well as for his critical reading and valuable suggestions for improvement of an early draft of the manuscript; Mr. John Thomas Herriman for competent editorial assistance; Professors Charles P. Loomis and Lyle Blair who gave valued counsel on bringing the manuscript to its present form; the Pakistan Embassy in Washington, D.C., which provided a copy of the *Report of the Constitution Commission, 1961*.

Members of the staff of the Michigan State University Library have been invariably helpful, especially Professor Eugene de Benko, Head, International Division; Mrs. H. Alubowicz, Reference Librarian, and her assistants in the Reference Department; and Mr. Frank C. Mc-Dougall, Community Development Librarian, in charge of the Microfilm Department, and his assistants. It is of course understood that we take full responsibility for any errors of fact or judgment.

We are most appreciative of the help rendered by the Publications Committee of the Asian Studies Center.

Our special thanks go to Dr. William T. Ross who, as Director of the Asian Studies Center of Michigan State University, gave us not only needed encouragement but the financial support which enabled us to complete the manuscript.

CHAPTER I

# INTRODUCTION

PAKISTAN was created on the premise that the Muslims of India required an independent political state.[1] From 1940, when the Muslim League of India formalized its demand for the creation of an independent Pakistan in the Lahore Resolution, until 1947, when India and Pakistan were granted independence, little thought had been given to the precise nature of the future state of Pakistan or to the policies it should pursue. Mohammad Ali Jinnah, leader of the Muslim League and first Governor-General of Pakistan, and the Constituent Assembly set up in August 1947 immediately faced the necessity of providing a government to unify the nation and an Islamic constitution to justify the existence of Pakistan.

The greatest hindrance to unity was the variety and number of components which made up this new state, each with its own language, culture, and traditions. An almost insurmountable barrier was the fact that Pakistan consisted of two areas separated by a thousand miles of Indian territory. The province of East Bengal (later called East Pakistan) which formed the east wing was a cultural entity and contained more than half of the total population of Pakistan in less than one-sixth of the total area. Urdu, Punjabi, Pushto, and Sindhi, as well as several minor languages were spoken in the west wing made up of three provinces, various tribal areas and ten princely states. (The provinces were Sind, Punjab and the Northwest Frontier; the states were Makran, Kalat, Las Bala and Kharan in the south, grouped together as the Baluchistan States Union; Khairpur and Bahawalpur in the east, and Chitral, Dir, Swat and Amb in the northwest.) In September 1955 the provinces of the west wing were merged into One Unit, West Pakistan, but the estrangement between West Pakistan and East Pakistan increased. Islam, with all its economic and political implications, was the only binding force between the two wings. The effect of this situation was a strongly developed provincial and parochial

feeling which has been called "the biggest single factor which the leadership found difficult to overcome."²

Drafting an Islamic constitution revealed the sharp differences between the orthodox religious teachers *(ulema)* and the more secular Western-educated Muslims. The former believed the constitution should follow a pattern laid down thirteen centuries ago in Arabia, while the latter believed "that the requirements of Islam [could] be met without departing from the essentials of a modern democratic state."³ Whether the government should be parliamentary or presidential, unitary or federal, were also highly controversial issues. In 1949 the agreement by the Assembly that the structure of government should be federal led to conflicts as to the share of each province in administration and in the legislature, the distribution of powers between the federal government and the provinces and the question of a national language or languages.

These problems alone would not have delayed the writing of the constitution for as many as nine years had the Constituent Assembly not been also a legislative body. To stay in power became the chief concern of the politicians. Following Jinnah's death a year after independence, his Prime Minister, Liaquat Ali Khan, carried on as best he could but his power and influence were never equal to that of Jinnah. After Liaquat Ali Khan's assassination in 1951 "Pakistan drifted towards impotence and disruption."⁴ Factional rivalries became more intense; governors-general and prime ministers differed about their share of power. As a draft constitution neared completion in 1954 Governor-General Ghulam Mohammad dismissed the Assembly for political reasons. In 1955 the provincial assemblies elected a new Constituent Assembly which convened in July. However, Governor-General Ghulam Mohammad did not ask the second Assembly to draft a constitution. Under Iskander Mirza, who became governor-general in September, a draft constitution was presented by the government to the Assembly in January 1956. Approved on February 29, the Constitution officially went into effect on March 23, 1956, and brought into being the Islamic Republic of Pakistan.⁵ The Constitution changed the title of the nation's head of state from Governor-General to President, although there was little perceptible change in the function of the office. Thus Iskander Mirza became the first and only President under the 1956 Constitution.

The politicians who had been in and out of power for nine years were determined to prevent, if possible, elections from taking place, for they feared loss of power and privileges. On October 7, 1958, after four prime ministers had come and gone and the possibility of achiev-

ing political stability through holding the long-deferred elections seemed unlikely, President Iskander Mirza proclaimed martial law. He abrogated the 1956 Constitution, dismissed the Central and provincial governments and assemblies, abolished political parties, and named Commander-in-Chief of the Army General Mohammad Ayub Khan Chief Martial Law Administrator.[6]

The purpose of this study is to detail the steps, as published chiefly in two Pakistani English-language daily newspapers, the *Pakistan Observer* (Dacca) and *Dawn* (Karachi), and in an Indian paper, the *Statesman* (Calcutta), by which a new constitution was created to replace that abrogated in 1958.

Fifty daily newspapers were published in Pakistan in 1953 including eleven English-language dailies, three Bengali, two Gujerati, three Sindhi and thirty-five Urdu.[7] At the beginning of martial law only four of the English-language daily newspapers in Pakistan were classified as of major importance: *Dawn, Pakistan Observer, Morning News* (Dacca and Karachi) and *Pakistan Times* (Lahore and Rawalpindi).[8] Neither *Dawn* nor the *Pakistan Times,* considered the two leading daily newspapers, can claim to be a truly national paper, for each caters mainly to the small, Westernized urban group. *Dawn* was founded in New Delhi in 1943 by Mohammad Ali Jinnah to propagate the demand of the Muslim League for the creation of Pakistan and was supported by the Aga Khan and other influential Muslims. *Dawn* was first published in Karachi on Pakistani Independence Day, August 14, 1947. By 1959 it was said to have the largest circulation and the highest prestige among the newspapers of Pakistan. Whether or not it was always the spokesman for the government, certainly under the editorship of Altaf Hussain it played a supportive role to martial law. The *Pakistan Times* of Lahore was owned by Mian Iftikharuddin, "a millionaire with leftist leanings" and "a crypto-Communist politician," under whose aegis it strongly opposed Pakistan's pro-Western policy.[9]

The *Morning News,* the only newspaper published simultaneously in Dacca and Karachi, apparently made some attempt to bridge the gap by calling itself the "Voice of the Nation." Founded in 1942, according to its masthead, it actually began as a weekly in Dacca in 1948 and soon changed to a daily.[10] Its circulation remained higher in Dacca than in Karachi.[11] The policies of the two editions are not necessarily similar.[12] Because the *Morning News* circulated in both provinces, it tended to strive for objectivity by avoiding controversial subjects[13] and therefore seemed colorless. In contrast, the *Pakistan Observer*—founded in 1949 and the oldest English-language daily in

East Pakistan—rarely left the reader in doubt as to where its sympathies lay and more nearly represented the point of view of the East Pakistani intellectuals. It was owned by Hamidul Huq Choudhury, a former minister and lieutenant of Fazlul Haq.[14] Within the ambit of martial law the *Pakistan Observer* did take a stand, and while its stand often appeared to represent economic, social and political betterment of East Pakistan vis-à-vis West Pakistan, in reality its policy was based on a strong conviction that Pakistan could become a great nation only if both wings were politically stable, economically strong and equitably developed. Under the pretext of writing about Korea or Egypt or Turkey, the editor was sometimes able to express vigorously his belief in democracy as represented by the parliamentary system, fundamental rights and the freedom of the press.

What then determined the selection of the two newspapers on which this study is based? The *Pakistan Observer* was originally chosen simply on the advice of local Pakistani friends and associates who were asked to recommend one of the East Pakistani daily English-language newspapers. Subsequently this choice was felt to be justified because of our growing conviction that here was to be found the best expression of the opinion of educated East Pakistanis. *Dawn* was chosen as a representative West Pakistani newspaper to maintain a balanced point of view.

The third newspaper consulted in this study was the *Statesman* of Calcutta which was "recognized as the outstanding journal in the whole subcontinent."[15] Informed Pakistanis pointed out that to learn what was going on in Pakistan even before martial law it was almost obligatory to read the *Statesman*. Frequently from one or two to as many as five or six stories relating to Pakistan, originating either from resident correspondents or the Press Trust of India (PTI), would appear. Editorials on Pakistan appeared rarely in the *Statesman* but from time to time lengthy and enlightening analyses of significant developments in Pakistan appeared under the byline of the *Statesman*'s political correspondent. For our purposes the chief contribution of the *Statesman* lay in its disclosure of public opinion in Dacca, opinion which could not be printed in the local press. Undoubtedly, this largely accounted for the fact that the *Statesman* was often seen in the offices of high-level government officials in Dacca.

The situation of the press in Pakistan under martial law was not comfortable. A standard technique in a political takeover is the imposition of drastic censorship. In Pakistan the pre-publication censorship of local newspapers lasted only one week and Indian newspapers were banned for two weeks.[16] Freedom of the press was then consider-

ably reduced by the following regulations of the Chief Martial Law Administrator, General Ayub Khan.

> Martial Law Regulation No. 20: No person shall commit any act or be guilty of an omission or make a speech
>
> (A) which is to the prejudice of good order or the public safety, or
>
> (B) which is calculated to mislead or hamper movements of or imperil the success of or tamper with the loyalty of forces under my command.
>
> Martial Law Regulation No. 24: No one by word of mouth or in writing or by signals or otherwise will spread reports calculated to create alarm or despondency amongst the public or calculated to create dissatisfaction toward the Armed Forces and Police or any members thereof.[17]

In early December further restrictions were placed on the press by Martial Law Regulation No. 51:

> No person shall publish, print, circulate or cause to be published, printed, or circulated or otherwise be in possession of any pamphlet, poster, publication or any type of literature calculated to promote or attempt to promote feelings of enmity or hatred against the Government or between different classes, sects or religious orders.[18]

The arrests of several newsmen further dismayed the press. Detained in Lahore under the Safety Act were the editors of two Urdu-language papers,[19] while six journalists were arrested under the East Pakistan Prevention of Prejudicial Acts Ordinance: the editor of the English weekly, *New World;* the assistant editor of the leftist Bengali *Sangbad;* two assistant editors of the Bengali *Ittefaq;* the editor of another Bengali weekly; and the chief reporter for the *Pakistan Observer.* In Lahore the editor of the Urdu daily *Imroze*[20] and the editor of the *Pakistan Times* were arrested.[21]

The anxiety of the press caused by the martial law regulations and the arrests of journalists in the early days of the military regime was compounded on April 17, 1959, by the seizure of the *Pakistan Times* under the Security of Pakistan Act.[22] The Pakistan Government named an administrator to take charge of the paper. The shares owned by Mian Iftikharuddin and his son, with a face value of Rs. 1,614,000, were sold at auction by the government on August 30, 1959, to Ahmad Dawood, an industrial magnate, for Rs. 6,440,000. Legal recourse was attempted in vain because Martial Law Regulation No. 72, issued prior to the auction, barred suits against the government by anyone held under the Security of Pakistan Act.[23] Later Manzur Qadir, the Foreign Minister, asserted that the regime had not misused the Security Act and that the action was necessary in the larger interests of the country. He

also pointed out that no other newspaper had been dealt with under this law.[24]

The press had thus been thoroughly intimidated.[25] *Dawn* enthusiastically supported the new regime's policies and the martial law administration in its October 10 editorial relating to the military takeover.[26] In contrast the *Pakistan Times* and the *Pakistan Observer* proceeded with caution. Their first editorials on the new government did not appear until October 12. Although they did not actually welcome martial law, they did recognize the necessity for it and approved of the reforms promised by the new regime. The *Pakistan Observer* maintained the policy of commenting editorially only when it agreed with the Government's policies. At times the *Pakistan Observer* showed a great deal of courage. For instance, it printed the testimony of several East Pakistanis before the Constitution Commission and it editorially contradicted Zakir Husain, the Interior Minister, on whether the form of government or the people who ran it was the more important. Merely to refrain from criticizing the military regime, however, was not sufficient to put a newspaper in the good graces of the officials and the Government could use its advertising budget in a way less crude than censorship to express its attitude toward specific publications. The Minister for Information and Broadcasting, Fazlur Qadir Choudhury, answering a question in the National Assembly in March 1963, pointed out that from July 1959 through December 1962 the central government's expenditures for newspaper and journal advertising in West Pakistan was almost five times greater than the amount spent in East Pakistan. Commenting on the recent blacklisting of three East Pakistan dailies, the *Pakistan Observer*, *Ittefaq* and *Sangbad*, Choudhury said,

> The newspapers in question had maintained a uniformly unethical attitude on all matters including even national security. . . . Obviously the Government would not be justified in extending patronage to those newspapers which do not observe proper journalistic standards or which follow a demonstrably anti-national policy.[27]

Despite the climate of repression in which the press worked, some intimations of public opinion, however fragmentary and indirect, may be gleaned from these newspapers. The kinds of questions to government officials posed by reporters point to matters the public wanted to know more about. Additional sources of public opinion are the publications of non-Pakistanis—reports by foreign correspondents, articles by informed visitors and scholarly studies.

Unlike many military coups, the action by General Ayub Khan in taking over the government of Pakistan was based on a long-term

plan for the rehabilitation and reform of every phase of national life— political, economic, social and religious. As early as October 1954, according to his biographer, he had written out his views about the problems of Pakistan and had considered methods of coping with them. The plan was not written for public consumption and was not made available to the public until 1960 when General Ayub Khan's diagnosis and blueprint for action were published in *My Chief,* a short biography of the General from 1947 to 1958 by Colonel Mohammad Ahmad.[28] Colonel Ahmad's association with the future President began in East Pakistan in 1948 when he was on the General's staff. When Ayub Khan became the first Pakistani Commander-in-Chief in 1951, Ahmad became his private secretary.

General Ayub's plan called first for an integrated West Pakistan. When that was achieved, East Pakistan and West Pakistan were to have their own legislatures. After emphasizing the fact that the "eventual aim must be to develop democracy in Pakistan, but of a type that suits the genius of the people," he said it was necessary to have "a controlled form of democracy with checks and counter-checks." The people would choose an electoral college which in turn would elect a president and the members of the provincial and central legislatures. Each legislature, he believed, should have about 150 members. The membership of the central legislature should be equally divided between the two units and headed by a cabinet with executive powers subject to effective control by the president.

Because he was concerned that the provinces have as close a partnership as possible, General Ayub thought communications (except interprovincial), industries, commerce, health and other such subjects should be the responsibility of the provinces while the Center would retain control of inter-wing communications, defense, foreign affairs and currency. He felt that for development purposes administration should be decentralized down to the divisional level. He believed that development boards should be set up for education, cottage industries and other fields on the pattern of the Pakistan Industrial Development Corporation. Land reform was a prerequisite to other phases of development and an overhauling of the legal system was necessary.

The president, "the repository of power" according to his plan, should appoint the supreme commander of the armed forces and should have "overriding powers to assume control should things go wrong in the Provinces or the Centre." General Ayub further said that the term Islamic Democracy was a "dangerous cliché" which no one had ever defined. "Would it, therefore, not be correct to say that any variety of democracy when worked in the spirit of the Quran [could] be called an Islamic Democracy?" he asked.[29]

His plan concluded with a hope and prayer that if "this Constitution is worked in the spirit of the Quran . . . our solidarity, strength and future is assured."

## NOTES

1. The treatment of this subject is based on the first chapter of G. W. Choudhury, *Constitutional Development in Pakistan* (Lahore: Longmans Green, 1959) and the second chapter of Keith Callard, *Political Forces in Pakistan, 1947-1959* (New York: Institute of Pacific Relations, 1959).

2. Choudhury, *op. cit.*, p. 2.

3. *Ibid.*, p. 3.

4. Callard, *op. cit.*, p. 5.

5. Callard, *Pakistan, A Political Study* (London: George Allen & Unwin Ltd., 1957), pp. 3-32, 118-121.

6. *Pakistan Observer*, October 8, 1958.

7. A. Moid and Akhtar H. Siddiqui, *A Guide to Periodical Publications and Newspapers of Pakistan* (Karachi: Pakistan Bibliographical Working Group, 1953).

8. The other seven are *Civil and Military Gazette,* famous for Kipling's association with it and published in Lahore since 1870; *Comment* (Karachi); *Evening Star* (Karachi); *Khyber Mail* (Peshawar), a weekly founded in 1932 which became a "drab daily" in 1951; *Leader* (Karachi); *Pakistan Sentinel* (Karachi); and *Times of Karachi*. This list was compiled from two sources: *A Select Pakistan Bibliography* (Karachi: Department of Advertising, Films and Publications, Government of Pakistan, 1958), pp. 27-29 and "The Press in Pakistan," *Eastern World*, XIII (March 1959), pp. 27-28. The classification of the four English-language daily newspapers mentioned is from the Text of the Journalists' Wage Board Award announced in a *Gazette Extraordinary* by the Government of Pakistan on January 31, 1961, and published in the *Pakistan Observer*, February 2, 1961. All daily newspapers were divided into (1) metropolitan and (2) regional. The metropolitan papers were divided into Section A, which included, besides the four already mentioned, *Anjam* (Urdu—Karachi and Peshawar), *Jang* (Urdu—Karachi and Rawalpindi), *Nawa-i-Waq* (Urdu—Lahore, Rawalpindi and Multan), *Imroze* (Urdu—Lahore, Multan and Karachi), *Kohistan* (Urdu—Rawalpindi, Lahore and Multan), *Daily Azad* (Bengali—Dacca), and *Ittefaq* (Bengali—Dacca), and Section B, which included all other dailies published in metropolitan centers not included in the above list. No regional papers were listed by name.

9. Material for this paragraph is taken from "The Press in Pakistan," *op. cit.*, p. 27 and Hugh Tinker, *India and Pakistan, A Political Analysis* (New York: Praeger, 1962), pp. 179-181 and 186-187.

10. Majid Nizami, *The Press in Pakistan* (Lahore: University of the Punjab, 1958), p. 24.

11. "The Press in Pakistan," *loc. cit.*

12. Nizami, *op. cit.*, p. 15.

13. Tinker, *op. cit.*, p. 186, said it had "a right-wing non-Bengali policy."

14. *Ibid.*, p. 187. Fazlul Haq was a politician of undivided Bengal and founder of the Krishak Sramik Party in East Pakistan.

15. *Ibid.*, p. 179.

16. *Statesman* (Calcutta), October 16, p. 1; October 23, 1958, p. 5.
17. *Dawn* (Karachi), October 19, 1958, p. 1.
18. *Ibid.*, December 5, 1958, p. 1.
19. *Statesman*, October 17, 1958, p. 1.
20. *Ibid.*, October 27, 1958, p. 7.
21. On December 15, 1958. "The Press in Pakistan," *loc. cit.* A partial list of arrests of journalists in 1959 includes: a *Khairpur Press* reporter (*Dawn,* January 21, 1959, p. 8); editor of a Chittagong daily, charged under Section 54 with "suspicion of movement" (*ibid.,* January 31, 1959, p. 8); the editor and publisher of the English weekly *Freedom* of Karachi, under Martial Law Regulation No. 24 (*ibid.,* March 4, 1959, p. 4); and the editor of the Feni (Noakhali district) weekly *Sangram* and former member of the East Pakistan assembly, charged under Martial Law Regulation No. 24 and sentenced to six months rigorous imprisonment by a summary military court (*ibid.,* May 22, 1959, p. 6). Tafazzal Hussain, editor of the Bengali *Ittefaq* and once acknowledged as the right-hand man of a former Prime Minister, Suhrawardy, was arrested September 28, 1959, under Martial Law Regulation No. 24. The charges related to a series of articles beginning the previous February which, it was claimed, created despondency and dissatisfaction toward the armed forces (*Pakistan Observer,* September 30, October 16, 18, 20, 30, 1959; *Statesman,* October 14, 20, 1959. The Indian newspaper pointed out that this was the first action by the military against a newspaper proprietor in East Pakistan). Cases were also started against the Lahore daily *Hilal-e-Pakistan* and the weekly *Iqdaam* under Martial Law Regulations Nos. 23, 24, and 51 (*Pakistan Observer,* October 15, 1959); the house of a Pabna Hindu journalist was searched (*ibid.,* November 11, 1959) and two months later he was arrested under Martial Law Regulation No. 51 (*ibid.,* January 19, 1960).
22. *Dawn,* April 19, 1959, p. 1.
23. *Ibid.*, July 30, 1959, p. 1.
24. *Ibid.*, April 11, 1960, p. 1. Later the original sale of Mian Iftikharuddin's and his son's shares was cancelled and a resale was held by the government. Choudhury Mohammad Husain, Vice-Chairman of the Lahore Municipal Corporation, and his "unofficial partners" offered the highest bid of Rs. 4,700,000 (*ibid.,* October 15, 1961, p. 8; November 22, 1961, p. 9). Three years following the seizure of the paper after much litigation and severe heart trouble on the part of Mian Iftikharuddin, he and his son were paid Rs. 3,306,000 (*Pakistan Times,* April 26, 1962, p. 1). The following week directors were elected and the newspaper came under new control (*ibid.,* May 3, 1962, p. 1).

*The Times* (London) writing about the case at the time of the second auction, was quoted in the *Pakistan Observer* (October 31, 1961): "In fact, it was the measures taken in the early days of President Ayub's Government that effectively silenced criticism. Journalists were arrested and sentenced under Martial Law Regulations. An influential opposition paper, the *Pakistan Times,* was taken over by the Government. This proved enough to cow journalists, and fear has hung over newspaper offices ever since, reducing much of the press to a pale reflection of Government opinion."
25. Despite the insistence of Z. A. Bhutto, a cabinet minister, that the action against the *Pakistan Times* did not in any way affect the freedom of the press. *Dawn,* April 29, 1960, p. 1.
26. The political correspondent of the *Statesman* explained it this way:

"After an initial phase of hesitation, the leading newspapers, it seems, have fallen in line with the essential objectives of the new regime. After *Dawn* had turned a spectacular somersault, the *Pakistan Times* came out with a strong editorial in support of the Martial Law Administration" (October 15, 1958, p. 7).

27. *Dawn,* March 10, 1963, p. 10.

28. Mohammad Ahmad, *My Chief* (Lahore: Longmans, Green, and Co., 1960).

29. *Ibid.,* pp. 86-93. See Appendix B for text of this plan.

# THE FIRST YEAR OF MARTIAL LAW
## (October 1958—October 1959)

WHILE a new constitution was promised in President Iskander Mirza's proclamation of October 7, 1958[1] abrogating the 1956 Constitution, sixteen months passed before the first official step—the appointment of a constitution commission—was taken. Talk about the constitution began, however, at General Ayub Khan's first press conference as Chief Martial Law Administrator even before President Mirza was ousted. General Ayub, in answer to questions by reporters, replied that the 1956 Constitution was abrogated and not merely suspended because it was "unworkable" and "full of compromises." He said his first job was to clear up the mess—"mess" was the term used almost invariably by Ayub Khan for hoarding, black-marketing, smuggling, adulteration of food and overcharging, as well as the inefficiency and corruption at all levels in the government. Once this had been accomplished, the most appropriate persons in the country would be consulted on the drafting of a constitution which would then be presented to the people in a referendum. He could not say how much time this process would take. His personal views on the constitution were not quite formed but he definitely preferred the unitary structure of government. In view of the eighty-five percent illiteracy prevailing in the country, his conviction was that the people should be allowed to choose the electoral college which in turn would elect the assemblies and the president.[2]

Both President Iskander Mirza and General Ayub issued statements that Pakistan was "not forsaking democracy permanently." President Mirza told foreign correspondents that after corruption was abolished they would get "about 30 or 40 good men to frame a constitution." It would be "examined by people of international repute" and then submitted to the people in a referendum. He also preferred a unitary form of government with a strong center, but decentralized administration.[3] There were hints that the diplomatic missions in Karachi had

already been approached for copies of the constitutions of their respective governments.[4]

Two weeks after becoming Chief Martial Law Administrator, General Ayub visited East Pakistan to promote unity between the two sections. He spoke of the importance of a "sense of single nationhood." He admitted that there might be differences of opinion but all must be agreed on the basic issues important to the country.[5] Not the least of East Pakistan's complaints was that West Pakistanis dominated the government, the civil services and the army and that most of the officials of East Pakistan were from the western wing.[6] General Ayub promised that East Pakistan would be run as the people wanted it and that the central government was prepared to render all possible assistance toward that end. No official would be sent there of whom they did not approve. Nothing should be done, he warned, that would jeopardize the security of Pakistan. At times unscrupulous politicians had exploited students for their own selfish purposes, he said, but students should not allow themselves to be exploited and should not ruin their lives. General Ayub also recognized that in the past certain mischievous people had tried to sow seeds of disruption between East and West Pakistan, but these people had never made any constructive suggestions for the betterment of the country. He acknowledged that everyone from West Pakistan was not necessarily an "angel" but the army had come "only to serve the people and the country." He assured the press that his administration would maintain parity in the services and other spheres.[7]

On October 25 came the announcement that President Mirza had constituted a twelve-man cabinet with General Mohammad Ayub Khan as Prime Minister with the portfolios of Defense and Kashmir Affairs. The cabinet was sworn in on the morning of the 27th and that very night President Mirza was deposed. He and his wife left for England a few days later.[8] On October 28 the cabinet assumed office. General Ayub, assuming the presidency, abolished the post of prime minister, and promulgated a Presidential Cabinet Order.[9] The government was now organized along the lines on which it was to function, with very few changes, for the following forty-four months.[10]

President Ayub Khan said in a press interview, "Politics caused Mirza's ouster. . . . He had vague ideas. I have definite ideas. I say that what we are practicing is also democracy." He asserted that Pakistan definitely needed the presidential system. The previous system had gone wrong because of division of power between the president and the prime minister. "It is much better having one man," he stated, and that man had to be "really powerful."[11]

A series of editorials in the Karachi *Dawn* dealing with the revolution gave the impression that this newspaper might wish to out-militarize the military. The titles dealt not with the subject matter of the editorials but with the paper's reaction to it. The first editorial in this series on October 10 was called "The New Look." On the subject of President Mirza's and General Ayub's promises to restore democracy *Dawn* said that, although this announcement of ultimate purpose was necessary for sustaining morale at home and prestige abroad, there was "no need to hurry." It suggested, "Now that a break has been made with the past system and a new one has been ushered in under which it is much more easy to take quick decisions on the country's urgent problems, it may not be desirable to make another early change. . . ." In "A Sane Revolution" on October 12, *Dawn* stated, "For all practical purposes the executive and judicial machinery of the State will continue to function as if there had been no change at all. Of course, Ministers and Legislatures will be lacking—but the country can well do without them for some time to come." *Dawn* greeted the announcement of President Mirza's new cabinet as "a pleasant surprise" in its editorial "A Welcome Step." Repeating the assurances of both President Mirza and Chief Martial Law Administrator Ayub that "steps would be taken at the appropriate time to set up a suitable body to frame a new constitution," *Dawn* made the ironical statement on October 26, the day before President Mirza was ousted, that, "It is difficult to see how long the new arrangement will last." This change of power brought forth "An End and a Beginning" on October 29 and "We Can Raise Our Heads Again" on November 1. "A Gigantic Task" on November 9 was a laudatory review of the first month of martial law, as was the editorial of December 25, Mohammad Ali Jinnah's birthday, "Anniversary with a Difference."

The *Pakistan Observer* waited two days longer than *Dawn* before taking editorial notice of the new regime. This silence might have meant that the *Pakistan Observer* disapproved of martial law. At least it represented a wait-and-see attitude. On October 12 in "Not an Easy Job," the Dacca paper began:

> What has happened was not unexpected. As we have said so often during the last three years, we have passed through a crisis of character. Our economic and civil administrations were on the point of complete breakdown; both morals and morale were at a very low ebb; patriotism was at a discount; self-interest was predominant.

After commenting that martial law was not to be a permanent feature of the government and that the courts and civil administration were to be geared in with the military regime, the editorial concluded:

> This will not be an easy job; and we have no doubt that the Admin-
> istration is quite aware that it is not an easy job. Corruption, chican-
> ery, anti-social proclivities have permeated all levels of society. The
> problem is one of a mass re-education of a whole nation.

Further observations by the *Pakistan Observer* on the new regime took
a pragmatic approach. In the ensuing months certain elements of the
program of the revolutionary government were considered, one at a
time, and evaluated. The editor's yardstick was defined: "The merit
of a principle or a course of action is to be judged by its utility in
practice."[12] Written for the most part on economic subjects, these
editorials also considered the moral issues involved, health conditions,
and the role of newspapers.

Of greatest concern to the people had been the upward trend in
the prices of necessities. Less than two weeks after the abrogation of
the constitution the *Pakistan Observer* on October 19 in "A Wise
Step" pointed out:

> For a long time the bulk of the population has lived through extreme
> difficulties due to the abnormally high cost of living. . . . No sign of
> remedy and redress from continued distress was anywhere in sight.
> The present decline in the prices of the essential commodities is,
> therefore, very gratifying. . . . The notable feature of the situation is,
> however, that not only has the upswing been arrested, but the present
> trend is definitely downward. And this seemed nearly impossible only
> a little while ago. . . .

On the determination of the government to root out corruption, an
editorial on October 22 entitled "A Moral Crusade" observed:

> It must be the fervent prayer of all patriotic elements in the country
> that the Administration succeed in doing what they set out to do,
> namely, putting the country 'on an even keel.' The task bristles
> with difficulties. . . .

The remainder of the editorial considered the widespread corruption
in the country.

"The Turning Point" on October 24 probably came as near to ex-
tolling the martial law regime as a *Pakistan Observer* editorial was
capable of. The effusive words did not praise the administration but
the changes already accomplished:

> An honest observer visiting Pakistan will unmistakably find that the
> country today is astir with emotion and action. Vibrating with a new
> life it is becoming increasingly busy. In business, in social life and in
> public affairs the sign of animation is too glaringly evident to escape
> notice. The markets, better described as black markets, are apparently
> turning fair and the consumers are rushing in where till recently they
> feared to tread. Towns, residences, roads and lanes—so long littered

with dirt, filth and garbage—are wearing a clean look. . . . The indifferent citizens seem to be developing the hitherto unknown civic sense, and the municipalities are practically demonstrating a sudden awareness of their normal responsibilities. . . . Water supply, electric supply, railways, telephone exchange, post offices and all other public service organisations are making honest efforts to increase their efficiency. Public servants have begun to control their superior temper and behave like public servants. . . . Files, that were gathering dust and moss . . . have started to roll and move from their hide-outs. . . . A sense of urgency has dawned on all; and inaction, procrastination, lethargy and laziness that were paralysing our national life are giving place to visibly increasing preparedness for work, greater alertness and promptitude.

Are these outward manifestations a portent of new glories and do they reflect a national re-awakening stirring and stimulating the minds of the people? The answer must be in the affirmative. It has got to be proved that what is in evidence now is not merely a temporary phase but a turning point in the history of the country.

With its emphasis on the economic aspects of life, it was natural for the *Pakistan Observer* on October 30 to think it was "heartening" and "The Right Thing" for the new cabinet "to take stock of the economic situation in the country in its first meeting." It felt that the new President's statement would "create a sense of security in the minds of the people . . . as well as allay the uneasiness and fear that [might] be troubling the business and industrial community regarding their future."

The *Pakistan Observer* had declared on October 15 that to achieve increased food production was "The Basic Problem." The editorial "Food—the First Target" on November 5 is significant for its expressed belief that the new administration would actually do what it had set itself to do: "That the present regime has given food the topmost place in its program should infuse new hope in the public mind." After discussing the details of the program to increase food production, the editorial concluded:

These are admittedly not new measures. What inspires hope is the belief that their implementation, previously delayed, will now be expeditious and that the money available for the purpose will be fully and quickly utilized.

"The Battle Cry" on December 28 indicated approval of the administration for its efforts to increase food production without delay. Not only the Minister for Food and Agriculture but every one of the cabinet members was exhorting the public to take part in a "grow-more-food" campaign. Subjects on which the *Pakistan Observer* expressed great hope for improvement were industrial production, cottage industries and the jute industry.[13]

The program for improving health conditions and for providing essential medical care as explained by General W. A. Burki, the Minister for Health and Social Welfare, elicited a November 1 editorial "The New Approach" which stated:

> It must be admitted that the policy is aimed at practically promoting the real welfare of the people and not merely holding out promises of such welfare. . . . His determination to ensure the availability of essential and life-saving drugs at all times . . . is reassuring and will infuse new confidence into the public mind. One hopes that the neglected people in the rural areas will now reap the full benefit of a more efficiently administered health service. . . .

Another discussion of the health care situation on November 10 said, "We believe the present administration has the determination and the imagination to take charge of the situation and treat this matter of life and death with all the seriousness it deserves."

The high costs and endless delays of legal proceedings were particular irritants to President Ayub Khan. He repeatedly stressed the need for quick and inexpensive justice. The *Pakistan Observer* admitted on November 13 that the "accumulated arrears of cases in the law courts of the country constitute a convincing argument for the simplification of judicial and legal procedures advocated by General Ayub Khan." Again hope was expressed that the new regime would do the right thing—in this case that a process of law would be evolved that would "safeguard both justice and the rights of individual freedom."

A glimpse of the reaction in East Pakistan to the military regime was brought out clearly on November 12 by the editor's comment called "Taken at the Flood" on the letters received from the public:

> From the tone of the letters we are receiving daily, it would appear that the common man is much more optimistic in airing his complaints and grievances nowadays than he has been in the past. Previously they added in riders saying such things as, 'of course, nothing will be done about it,' or 'it is probably a waste of time for me to bring this matter to the attention of the Authorities through your columns,' etc. . . . It remained a fact, however, that their pessimism was justified since, in almost every case, no action whatsoever was taken to rectify things.
> Nowadays it is different. Most of the grievances of the people aired so often in the past, have been put right practically overnight, or else they are in the process of being put right.

As President Ayub Khan and his cabinet got down to the tasks to which they had given top priority, there was not much time devoted to speeches or press interviews on the nature of the future constitution. In a filmed interview which was telecast in London, President Ayub

said he envisaged creation of a commission to draft a new constitution which "suited the country's conditions and circumstances and which her people [could] understand and work." He thought his regime would be able to complete the tasks it had taken in hand within about a year's time. After the present phase was over the regime could get on with the task of preparing, with the help of a constitution commission, the blueprint for the political future of Pakistan. President Ayub said that due to widespread illiteracy his country could not successfully operate a parliamentary type of democracy based on the Westminster model. The interview as quoted by *Dawn* on December 3 concluded:

> General Ayub Khan rejected the suggestion that a general election might have solved Pakistan's political malady. The recent conduct of Pakistani politicians and their parties had convinced him that a general election would have only produced more political instability and many more parties all jockeying for offices and self-aggrandizement.

Although many subjects were touched on in this report, "New Constitution After a Year" was the headline in *Dawn*.

In an airport interview the President asserted the constitution would be "a very good constitution indeed," but he urged, "Have patience and let us solve the basic problems of the country first of all."[14] These basic problems he had identified earlier as resettlement of refugees, land reform and modification of the educational and legal systems. After these problems were solved he planned to "consult the best brains and ascertain the feelings of the people in order to draw up a constitution" suited to the needs of Pakistan and not a copy of any other constitution. The people should elect a president through an electoral college and he should be given fairly wide powers. The legislatures should only frame laws and not interfere with the administration of the country.[15]

The greatest concerns of the bar and the judiciary were fundamental rights, the rule of law and the independence of the judiciary. Within three days after the imposition of Martial Law, all the civil courts had been reinstated. The Supreme Court and High Courts were given the power to issue writs of *habeas corpus, mandamus,* prohibition, *quo warranto* and *certiorari.* The rights of the civil courts were, however, limited by the provisions that no writ could be issued against the Chief Martial Law Administrator and his deputies and that the civil courts could not question any finding, judgment or order of any special or summary military court, any presidential proclamation, or any martial law order or regulation.[16]

During December the West Pakistan High Court discussed fundamental rights as provided for in the 1956 Constitution.[17] Later, Chief

Justice M. R. Kayani of the West Pakistan High Court, in a speech on martial law and the separation of the judiciary, pointed out that healthy criticism was necessary for good government.[18]

At a public meeting in Karachi on December 25, 1958, the birth anniversary of Mohammad Ali Jinnah, President Ayub Khan reviewed the events leading up to the "peaceful revolution." He pointed to Kashmir and the canal waters dispute with India as the two biggest issues facing Pakistan. With regard to the possibility of a constitution he said,

> Almost everyone must be anxious to know the constitutional future of this Country. Our aim is to introduce a representative form of government, such as can be understood and worked by our people. We shall have to ensure that such a representative government is so designed that its working is not marred by political instability. As soon as the major problems facing the country have been solved, the reforms have been put into operation and the administration rehabilitated, the best constitutional brains in our country will be asked to apply themselves to the question of framing a constitution. When doing so, the wishes and desires of the people of Pakistan will be fully respected.[19]

In response to President Ayub Khan's message, the *Pakistan Observer*'s editorial of December 27 on "Rediscovering Values" declared: "A new dedication is called for; and the President's speech in Karachi on the Quaid-e-Azam's birthday should usher in this period of dedication." The editorial called it a "great relief" to be assured by the President that it "was not the lure of power but a sense of duty to save the country from ruination" that prompted him to take over the "present administrative responsibilities." Especially gratifying was President Ayub Khan's promise "that representative government would be restored as soon as the immediate problems"—food, land reform and educational reforms—had been solved. "What stimulates hope of success," the editorial of December 30 stated, "is the undeniable fact that this regime has already got down to business and has displayed a real sense of urgency and devotion."

Ayub Khan made his second visit to East Pakistan (his first as President) December 26. In Dacca he exhorted the university students "to study during the ten years of student life" to prepare themselves for the "important role" they would have to play as leaders of "a nation of 80 millions, the bulk of which lies here [in East Pakistan]." The President assured the students, "We can be good Bengalis and Punjabis, but above all we must be first-class Pakistanis." He stated that the "bigger loyalty to Pakistan" was necessary "in order to protect the local loyalty to different languages and customs."[20]

In Chittagong President Ayub spoke to members and presidents of the local union boards on the importance he placed on local self-government and the *panchayat* system (the traditional system of village councils, literally meaning "composed of five persons"). The members of the *panchayats* were to lead the masses and keep them informed of the daily affairs of the administration. He said that justice should be more readily available and much cheaper and explained that the new Law Commission was to recommend ways and means of bringing this about.[21]

In January 1959 President Ayub Khan addressed the Karachi High Court Bar Association. He repeated his assurance of December 25 that as soon as his various reform commissions were well under way he would set up a constitution commission. The President estimated that this program might take two years. He also promised that free elections would be held under the constitution. President Ayub stated that the rule of law prevailed in Pakistan and that the independence of the judiciary was observed and protected. With regard to the concern of the Bar Association over the new regime's powers to suspend High Court judges, he said the statutory power to appoint included the power to suspend but any suspension would be made only in consultation with the Chief Justice of Pakistan.[22]

The *Pakistan Observer* of January 18 commented on the "frankness" of President Ayub's speech to the Karachi High Court Bar Association. By repeating "his assurance about the early formulation of a suitable constitution" and "a fair and unfettered election," the President "once again emphatically asserted that the object of the peaceful revolution [was] to end the confusion in administration." The editorial continued:

> These are benefits which cannot be enjoyed except in an atmosphere of political and economic stability. . . . The present regime is determined to enable the people to enjoy this freedom. . . . It is working vigorously in that direction instead of indulging in tall talk and extravagant fables and promises. . . . We hope [the government] is fully conscious of the heavy burdens it has undertaken and of the need to ensure that the exalted hopes entertained by the people today are not followed by creeping disillusionment tomorrow.

This speech to the Bar Association in January together with his Pakistan Day message in March, an interview with a British correspondent of the London *Observer* in April and his first full-dress press conference in August, all discussed below, comprise the major statements of the President on the constitution during the first nine months of 1959. The President had a plan clearly in mind. First, he wanted to

eliminate corruption. Martial Law courts and various screening committees and other bodies had been set up to complete this job in the shortest possible time. Second, he wanted the numerous commissions which he had appointed on land reforms, education, press, law and other aspects of national life to make their recommendations so that reforms could be initiated in all these fields. Third and finally, he wanted to get his plan for local self-government, called Basic Democracies, so firmly rooted that it would inevitably be incorporated into the new constitution. Until substantial headway could be made in these three areas, there was no likelihood that any commission to draft a constitution would be set up. The President's preoccupation with other matters, especially with Basic Democracies, explains why the public heard so little during the first year of martial law on the nature of the future constitution. The four major statements identified above had as much to do with Basic Democracies as with the constitution.

On January 14, 1959 the government of Pakistan with little fanfare established a significant new central branch called the Bureau of National Reconstruction. The new bureau was announced by means of a press note:

> Among the objectives the new regime has in view are, above all, the need for ensuring and maintaining the unity of Pakistan and her independence, bringing home to the people inhabiting the various parts of the country the concept of one Pakistani people, and by eradicating parochial tendencies, to coalesce all the divergent linguistic, sectarian and social groups into a single cohesive nation.
>
> Side by side, with the development of our economic resources, the new regime is determined also to accord high priority to the important task of the development of our social and cultural institutions, and to give the country an educational system suited to its needs. . . .
>
> Another important task facing the new regime is to give the country an honest and impartial administration and the creation of honest and rational business and professional methods. . . .
>
> It will be a part of the responsibility of the Bureau to explain the policies of the Government to the people with a view to gaining their understanding and fullest possible cooperation and support. For this purpose the Bureau will undertake to study and assess the impact of Government policies and bring it to the notice of the appropriate authorities for suitable action.[23]

A *Dawn* editorial called the decision to set up the Bureau of National Reconstruction "a logical corollary of the Revolution."[24]

At about the same time as this new agency was set up, the Public Conduct Scrutiny Ordinance was announced. This ordinance provided for screening committees and defined their powers.[25] Department by

department, all civil administration personnel were to be investigated and punishment was to be meted out to those found guilty of corruption and abuse of power. The process was to take about six months.

After three months' experience with the military regime the tradesmen and businessmen began to realize that, despite the threats of the martial law administration, nothing very serious had happened to most of them. They began to revert to their old practices of hoarding food and other goods and creating artificial shortages in order to raise prices. In three editorials, "Commodity Market" on January 29, "The Problem of Prices" on February 15 and "The Black Market" on February 27, the *Pakistan Observer* called rising prices "a disturbing fact" and directed the government's attention to the "soaring house-rents."

President Ayub Khan was already well aware of the inflationary trends. At a large public meeting in Lahore in February he warned the business community to keep "to the fixed prices and not sell their conscience for monetary gains." The President briefly recounted the events leading to the revolution and added, "As a matter of principle, we should start looking forward instead of backward." National progress, he told his audience, could not be achieved by miracles. "There is only one miracle that can change the destiny of our nation," he asserted, "and that miracle is hard work, honest work, clean work." Material development was not enough in itself, the President emphasized: "A nation's advancement is incomplete without moral and spiritual progress. . . . Without the Islamic way of life, Pakistan is no more than a mere wasteland."[26]

In order to explain government policies and assess public opinion, cabinet ministers were called on to make speeches and encourage questions. The Law Minister, Mohammad Ibrahim, told lawyers of the Dacca District Bar Association early in January they would have to make constructive suggestions for the constitution when the proper time came, for the present situation could not be expected to continue forever. He emphasized that to become a well-knit nation the people must be animated by a common national outlook and share a common culture.[27] Z. A. Bhutto, Minister of Commerce, addressing students at Islamia College in Lahore in February, told them that the unitary form of government was the best for Pakistan. He said that people should get rid of the sense of frustration and cynicism which had crept into them in the past.[28]

Manzur Qadir, the Foreign Affairs Minister, and Lieutenant General K. M. Sheikh, the Interior Minister, made a "reaction assessment tour" in West Pakistan during the second week in March. In Lyallpur Qadir said that as soon as the views of the people were ascertained

not a moment would be lost in giving the country a constitution. The reason for the failure of the last constitution was that it did not enjoy the confidence of the people. This time the government wanted to have a really workable constitution but unless people were properly educated and their correct views ascertained, the mistakes of the past were bound to be repeated. For this reason the Bureau of National Reconstruction had been established. He said that people should be given guidance in selecting honest men to run the country. The new bureau would explain whatever was done by the government and seek the people's opinions and suggestions.[29]

Moving on to Jaranwala, Qadir explained that it was not easy to frame an Islamic constitution; the greatest obstacle was the existence of seventy-two sects among the Muslims and their seventy-two interpretations of the Holy Quran and the Sunnah. He stated that complete unity of the nation was a prerequisite for the framing of the constitution and asked for the fullest cooperation with the new regime.[30] In Lahore the ministers discussed the revival or creation of political parties and consolidation of the country. They explained that the Bureau of National Reconstruction was trying to make the people aware that the government had no intention of creating a one-party system itself or of allowing the establishment of other parties.[31]

In Lahore the Foreign Affairs Minister was asked more forthright questions than were reported elsewhere. He took exception to the suggestion that the people were restive and anxious for the early adoption of a constitution. He said that in most of the rural areas he had recently toured the people abhorred the very name of "elected assemblies." However, he was forced to acknowledge that there "might be a few people in the cities" who wanted an early constitution. Another listener suggested that by giving the impression that the future constitution would not be Islamic, the present regime was bound to lose an enormous wealth of popular support. The Foreign Minister denied having implied this. Only elected representatives of the people, he said, were to work out the details of the future constitution. On this point, obviously, Qadir spoke too hastily for it had been said many times that an appointed commission would draft the constitution. A final question dealt with the purpose of the National Bureau of Reconstruction. Qadir replied that it was to bring about an awareness of the nation as an entity, explain to the people the consideration that led the government to adopt certain policies and assess the requirements of the people. The bureau would also educate the masses to use their right of franchise in electing their representatives.[32]

On Pakistan Day,[33] March 23, 1959, President Ayub summarized his

thoughts on the future constitution. He told the nation that the form of the constitution concerned him constantly, that he had come to certain conclusions and definitely felt that a representative form of government was vital if Pakistan were to achieve its destiny. He said that when the vital reforms were under way, he would then appoint a constitutional commission. When the draft constitution was ready it would be put to a vote of the people in a suitable manner and then put into effect. He said he did not foresee that this would take an undue amount of time.[34]

The *Pakistan Observer* made no immediate comment on the President's Pakistan Day speech. In a two-paragraph editorial on March 23 it referred to the Lahore resolution of 1940 and decided the time was appropriate to make another resolution, "to do our best to make Pakistan a really strong, progressive and prosperous country and to safeguard the dignity and fundamental rights of every Pakistani." It was not until March 28 that the Dacca newspaper, commenting on the President's announcement concerning the constitution commission, called it "welcome news." The *Pakistan Observer* felt that it "reflect[ed] great credit on the present regime that it [was] aware that the country [could] not remain without a constitution for long." It lamented the fact that even a perfect constitution was not a guarantee of success if the people in charge of governing the country "lacked either the ability or the intention" of observing the spirit of "the laws of the game."

*Dawn*'s editorial of March 25 on the President's speech said that, while democracy would be welcomed back, a return to the chaotic multi-party system was "unthinkable." It suggested that perhaps "the new democratic order that [was] in the offing [would] have room only for a single nation-wide organization." President Ayub promptly refuted the idea of a one-party system for Pakistan. "I don't see why there should be only one party," he told reporters in Lahore. "So long as there are no parties to disrupt the country, it is not our function to say which party should come and which should go. Anyway, I am not starting a party of my own." When asked to share his views on the constitution, the President replied, "No sharing at this stage." He did, however, reiterate the need for political stability as fundamental to sound planning.[35] Later, in Hyderabad, President Ayub told journalists the same thing: all that was needed was that "the constitution should be good enough to give the people assurance and pride and help us to create a sense of one nationhood." Regarding political parties, they would be permitted to function after the constitution was launched.[36]

The *Pakistan Observer* in a first-page article on April 9 discussed editorially "Six Months of the New Regime." After commenting on the situation prior to the revolution, the article considered the achievements of the military regime—land reforms, rehabilitation of Muslim refugees from India, economic policies, social reforms and the use of commissions whose recommendations would lead to further improvements. The concluding paragraph was in bold face:

> The new regime . . . is not oblivious of the genuine feelings of the people for a democratic system of government in the country. The President and his colleagues have time and again assured the people that they did not want to continue to rule for all time to come and that democracy was going to be restored in the near future. A constitution would be framed as soon as circumstances permitted. The President has repeatedly assured [the country] that people would be given the chance of choosing their own representatives. But before it is done the mess has to be cleared so that the people can get the chance of choosing their representatives in a congenial atmosphere and under a system which suited their own genius.

An editorial on April 18 in the same newspaper spoke out strongly against "certain ill-advised statements made by non-official persons" who were alleging that the country would not require a constitution "for many years to come." Admitting that the present stage was perhaps necessary, the *Pakistan Observer* contended that there should not be "any difference [of opinion] about the desirability of a constitution without any avoidable delay." Perhaps the masses were not educated; perhaps politicians and political parties had made a mess of things; then perhaps constitution-making should be turned over to "persons who will not be expected to work it or to take a direct part in the government later." In any event, the editorial concluded, whatever form was provided, if it "ensure[d] the flowering of our national genius," it would be "preferable to no constitution at all."

The Law Minister, Mohammad Ibrahim, in an address to the Dacca District Board assured the members that a democratic constitution would be provided for Pakistan. He declared that the district boards and union boards had an important role to play as they were the "cradles of democracy." Ibrahim also said that the future constitution would safeguard the interests of East Pakistan.[37]

An article in the *Observer* (London) reported in *Dawn* on April 20, gave the details of the President's program for establishing constitutional government. President Ayub, in an interview with Guy Wint, said that he hoped to be able to set up by November 1959 a constitution commission of about a dozen members. In about six months this group should produce a constitution which the President intended

should provide for a presidential rather than a parliamentary form of democracy. Then the draft constitution would be submitted to a two-stage plebiscite. "The plan," according to the article, "is to divide the entire population into groups of about 1,000 voters.[38] . . . Each unit will elect a single representative. Then these representatives will vote 'yes' or 'no' upon the Constitution." The article concluded,

> President Ayub believes that a population such as Pakistan's can best express itself indirectly rather than by direct balloting.
>   'What is the point of going back to the old parliamentary system?' asks President Ayub. 'Pakistan needs an executive which is popularly elected—and re-elected at fixed intervals—but which cannot be overturned constantly by changing party combinations in the legislature.'

Early in May the Karachi Bar Association had as its guest Manzur Qadir. The President of the Association, Z. H. Lari, in welcoming the Foreign Minister said that Qadir had repeatedly expressed his desire to be acquainted with "the feelings and aspirations of the people in regard to the fundamental problems facing the nation." He went on, speaking on the "absence of a constitution and the resultant delay in the establishment of a representative democratic government," to compare a state without a constitution to "a boat without an oar." Lari refuted the two main arguments put forth by the government in explaining the delay. On the first—that certain reforms should be completed before a constitution was adopted—he said this implied that political activity impeded reform. To this he took exception. The second objection—that early elections would enable the discredited politicians to stage a comeback—underestimated the common man's intelligence. He pointed out that the discredited politicians had held power through "machinations and intrigues," and not as a result of direct elections on the basis of adult suffrage. At any rate, he was glad to note that due to one reform by the present regime there would be "no feudal lords to intimidate the voters."[39] Other suggestions made by Lari included a directly elected constituent assembly with an imposed time limit rather than an appointed commission and trial of offenders of martial law regulations by regular courts. He also mentioned the effect on fundamental rights of some of the orders now in force.

Qadir responded to this address by saying that, since the constitution-making body had yet to be set up, any official expression of opinion by him on the issues raised by Lari would be premature. In an individual capacity, however, the Minister gave his general reaction to some of the problems mentioned. On the need for a constitution he stated,

In so far as the underlying idea stressed in your address, namely the need for a constitution, is concerned, let me say at once that no one is more acutely conscious of that need and more earnestly desirous of fulfilling it than those on whose shoulders rests the responsibility of Government today.

On the rule of law the Foreign Minister said,

I join you also in hoping that the rule of law will permeate every institution that flourishes in this land of ours.

On representative government he observed,

That the power of the State must be derived from the people to be exercised through institutions of a representative character, I would regard as axiomatic. The question, however, of choosing the representatives is something which requires careful consideration and a realistic approach. . . . While some sections of our society are enlightened . . . there are others living in villages . . . who are not even aware of the meaning of a vote.[40]

In editorially discussing these two speeches *Dawn* apparently feared that Qadir had not been firm enough in his efforts to convince Lari of the present regime's point of view. The editorial of May 7 went over each of Lari's statements point by point and refuted them. It concluded, "Meanwhile the Revolution, which all patriots have hailed with such relief and even joy, must be given time to fulfill itself."

At a press interview where he revealed that the union board system of local self-government was to be introduced into West Pakistan (a system that had existed in Bengal since 1919) President Ayub repeated that the country needed a constitution and it would be provided at the proper time. "We are working in that direction," he said. "The task [would] be entrusted to a commission to thrash out the details," but he was sure that the presidential form was best suited for Pakistan.[41] Later, on the question of a time limit for the drafting of the constitution, the President said that the commission would be set up before the year was out, but constitution-making was a delicate job and the commission would not be expected to do things in a hurry. The major reforms had to be introduced and working and the commission had to "gauge the wishes of the people" before starting on the constitution.[42]

President Ayub Khan made a strong appeal to the *ulema* and scholars of Pakistan to infuse the masses with the dynamic life of Islam and to make it simple and understandable to the common man. In a speech to the Darul Uloom Islamia, an educational institution attached to a mosque, the President spoke of the emergence of Islam more than thirteen hundred years ago as "a dynamic and progressive movement"

which "gave a new meaning and purpose to man's endeavors." "Unfortunately," he explained, "with the passage of time, the Muslims at large sought to concentrate more on the dogmatic aspects of Islam and less on its inherent greatness as a movement." The chief emphasis which the President made was that in time every innovation came to be considered un-Islamic and the innovators as non-believers, while "those who clung to mere formality and dogma and remained static claimed to be true Muslims."

Maulana Ihteshamul Haq Thanvi, head of the Darul Uloom Islamia, in welcoming the President, said:

> No magnificent mansion can be erected until its foundations are laid on sound footings. Politicians not only tried to alter this mansion's outward appearance but also began to change its very basis. God be praised that the foundations, laid by Quaid-e-Azam's hands, have proved [to be] like a rock and none has been able to shake them. It is gratifying to note that you are determined to launch a national reconstruction movement on the same lines.[43]

In a two-column editorial on May 6 *Dawn* discussed some aspects of the "confused thinking" and "endless debate" of the past decade on how Islam should be interpreted and applied in the context of the social, economic and political development of the new nation of Pakistan. It concluded:

> It is now for President Ayub and his regime to follow up themselves the lead that he has given on this vital question. In revising the system of education, in reforming the legal and other systems that are at present under examination, and in evolving the new Constitution the keynote of State policy should be to strike the much needed balance between the religious and the secular, wherever necessary. . . . The Government should also take its own steps to rid the houses of worship of the ignorance, reaction and obscurantism which characterize so much of what is "preached" in them on Fridays—as well as on other occasions. It is in the mosques that truth and knowledge can be most effectively inculcated among the vast masses of our people. . . .

But for the insistent questions of the newspaper correspondents, June and July of 1959 might have passed without any pronouncements by officials on the future constitution or the constitution commission. Mohammad Ibrahim, the Law Minister, said that the Pakistani constitution would be democratic, whatever its form. When pressed by the newsmen he stated that it was still too early to say anything further than what he had already told them. He added, however, that in the forthcoming governors' conference at Nathiagali, it was not likely the commission would be discussed although matters bearing on the constitution might come up. In the course of this same interview Manzur

Qadir said Basic Democracies would be discussed at the governors' conference but refused to comment on the future pattern of the constitution. He also parried a question on the rumored limited terms of reference of the proposed constitution commission by saying, "You will come to know of the terms of reference in the near future."[44]

Zakir Husain, the Governor of East Pakistan, said that the constitution commission would be announced before the year was out and its report could be expected before the end of 1960. Existing electoral rolls, prepared in 1957, would be used in the elections to the east wing *panchayats* in October after the rains.[45] The next day the Governor issued a statement correcting press reports which ascribed to him the remark that, with the exception of defense, foreign affairs and currency, all powers were likely to be transferred to the provinces. "The correct position is," he stated, "that the distribution of subjects between the Centre and the Provinces will depend on the shape of the future Constitution."[46]

Ibrahim said as little as possible in replying to the reporters' questions in Dacca. The people's approval would be necessary for the constitution, the actual procedure of obtaining the opinion of the people had not been decided upon and the shape of the future constitution was gradually being reflected in the administration. He said that no decision had yet been taken on the composition of the commission but the appointees would be experienced men capable of dealing with the constitutional problems of the country. Nothing, he warned, should be inferred from what he said regarding the scope and terms of reference of the proposed constitution commission.[47] A month later, again in Dacca, Ibrahim told reporters that both Basic Democracies and the constitution commission were expected to be set up before the end of the year. He reminded them that, although the government was doing everything with the greatest dispatch, careful thought had to be given to each matter, for they were all serious and decisions were intended to be permanent.[48]

Lieutenant General W. A. Burki, Minister of Health and Social Welfare, although he had not spoken publicly in Pakistan on political matters, granted an interview to the press during a visit to London. He said that elected representatives of the people would take over political power after adoption of the new constitution in about two years' time:

> A commission of jurists will produce a workable constitution for Pakistan. A referendum will then be held to ascertain the wishes of the people about the new constitution. If they say yes, we shall have elections, and the four Generals now in power [Ayub Khan, Burki, Sheikh and Azam Khan] will probably go back to their duties.

Before adoption of the constitution, General Burki continued, special courts would "weed out those politicians from public life who had misbehaved while in office." The Minister added dryly that the generals would probably prefer to go back to their old jobs: "I for one had a very good job and had a good sleep at night before I became a Minister. It is of course difficult to say what may happen if the people force us to continue in office."[49]

In an interview granted to a French correspondent in July 1959 the President was asked to comment on plans to introduce a new constitution in Pakistan. He said,

> I never wanted to make any exact promise on that subject but I can announce today that before the end of next year a new constitution will be in force in Pakistan and that general elections, with universal suffrage, will take place in the country.
>
> The Constitution will be of Islamic inspiration—the only ideology capable of halting Communism. Western materialism is out of date and no longer offers an attraction to the masses.
>
> The electoral choice will take place on a pyramid system, and the Parliament as well as the President will be designated by an Electoral College chosen at the base by the people.[50]

On August 10, 1959, in Karachi, General Ayub held his first press conference as President. It was attended by over one hundred local and foreign correspondents. The statements that martial law would remain in force until the constitution was launched, that there would be no hasty revival of political parties, and that Basic Democracies would be under way by the end of the year were featured in the headlines. President Ayub assured the journalists that elections to Basic Democracies would be held in utter and complete freedom. When he was asked whether politicians would be associated with the promised constitution commission, the President said he wanted commission members who possessed qualities of both statesmanship and constitutional sense. They would have to study the causes of the political and constitutional ills from which Pakistan had suffered and suggest remedies for the future. The President said that the basic requirement for newly independent countries was a strong government—not a dictatorship, but a benevolent government run by determined people.[51] In its editorial "A Promising Start" on August 13 *Dawn* said that the press conference showed "a heartening picture of a leader deeply conscious of his responsibilities and anxious to approach the great task with which destiny [had] entrusted him in a true spirit of humility and patriotic service. . . . Robust realism was the keynote of the statements."

When Lieutenant General Sheikh, the Minister of the Interior, was

asked whether the government would use former politicians in helping to draft the constitution, he too parried the question by replying that since the government "wanted to give the country a constitution best suited to its needs, for the purpose certainly the best qualified people would be consulted."[52] Habibur Rahman, the Minister of Education, Information and Broadcasting, stated in Lahore that the constitution commission which was to be appointed "before the year [was] out" would be given a time limit not exceeding six months for drafting the constitution. He said a year would be too long; no other commission set up by this regime had been given more than six months to complete its work, except possibly the Commission of Agriculture. He re-emphasized that the government wanted a strong Center.[53]

President Ayub Khan and the members of the cabinet visited East Pakistan during the first week of September to attend an important governors' conference at which it was expected that the finishing touches would be put on the Basic Democracies plan. In addition, the President was scheduled to visit Rajshahi, Jessore, Khulna and Mymensingh and to address public meetings at Khulna and Dacca. President Ayub had clearly shown that he wanted to win the goodwill and cooperation of East Pakistan by visiting that province within two weeks of becoming Chief Martial Law Administrator and again as President in the latter part of December 1958. His government had also taken action to show that efforts were being made to reduce the disparity between the two wings; for instance, the chairman of the Pakistan Industrial Development Corporation (PIDC) promised another cement factory for East Pakistan to be situated in Chittagong.[54] Lieutenant General K. M. Sheikh had also told newsmen in late 1958 that the new regime wanted East Pakistan to develop economically and culturally according to its own genius; while certain politicians in the past had tried to exploit friction between the two wings, he stated, this regime wanted to introduce "harmonious cooperation."[55] An example of the government's desire for harmony was the promptness with which it put down an attempt of a West Pakistan women's group to revive the language issue by promoting Urdu as the only national language. Even before an expression of disapproval by the comparable east wing society could be published, the government had firmly announced that Urdu and Bengali were the national languages, that this issue had been finally settled in 1956 and that it would not permit the revival of bitter controversies.[56]

Specific plans to promote the idea of unity and of "single nationhood" included the sponsorship by the central government of an exchange of visits every month by East and West Pakistan journalists[57]

and the setting up of a council to promote cultural unity.[58] National unity was the theme of President Ayub's Id-ul-Fitr message.[59] At the governors' conference in June it had been announced that Pakistan's new capital would be located near Rawalpindi and a subsidiary capital would be established in East Pakistan.[60] The Planning Commission which met early in August discussed an increase in industries for East Pakistan "in order to reduce economic disparities between East and West Pakistan. This [was] in fulfillment of one of the objectives of the Second Five-Year Plan (1960-1965)."[61] The Finance Minister, Mohammad Shoaib, also spoke of the need for a faster rate of development for East Pakistan.[62]

During his second visit to East Pakistan as President, Ayub Khan paid particular attention not only to government officials but also to lawyers, union board presidents, students and chairmen of district boards. The central ministers also had itineraries tailored to meet their respective interests. The emphasis during this tour was not on the constitution or the form of the future government but rather on the initiation of reforms and an inspirational appeal for the future. A record-breaking crowd at the Dacca stadium heard the President review the achievements of the present regime and describe his hopes for the future. The *Pakistan Observer* of September 6 saw him as "a man who meant what he said and who was fired with the desire to bring the country out of the morass into which it had fallen." His address "was a message of hope, and a beacon call to the people to bestir themselves, to shake off the frustration and hopelessness of the past. . . . After two centuries of subjection . . . we have the opportunity of building a new nation of our own." Before leaving the east wing President Ayub told his audience in Mymensingh that elections to Basic Democracies would be held by the middle of December and that Pakistan would get a constitution by the end of the next year.[63]

Early in October there were rumors in Karachi, as reported in the *Pakistan Observer* on October 7, that the proposed constitution commission would be announced on Revolution Day. The press even guessed at the names of the members. This gossiping was quashed when, a week later, Law Minister Ibrahim said the commission would not be set up until the first quarter of 1960. It could not be done at once because, he said, there was another stage to be passed through before the formation of the body to draft the constitution.[64] His meaning was not clear at the time. Then President Ayub Khan told newspaper correspondents at an airport interview in Rawalpindi that elections to Basic Democracies would be held in the middle of December 1959 after which a constitution commission would be set up and

Pakistan would have a new constitution by the end of 1960. He explained that the commission would travel throughout the country soliciting public opinion and educating the people as to what was in the best interest of Pakistan.[65] The latter function, a perfect example of so-called "controlled democracy," was at some time quietly dropped. Apparently someone realized that one commission would have difficulty educating the public as to what it should think and, at the same time, seeking to discover what it actually did think.

In Sylhet the Governor of East Pakistan, Zakir Husain, addressed a group of local officials on Basic Democracies and the need to "go back to the villages." He said that a commission would be set up in due course to draft a constitution. However, the government did not want to prepare a constitution hastily and repent of it later.[66] Shortly before the first anniversary of the revolution President Ayub Khan declared himself in favor of a unitary form of government with a presidential system and said he believed this would best suit the country's requirements, provided there was decentralization of power in favor of the provincial governors. By "unitary government" the President explained that he meant one with a central government and no separate provincial legislatures.[67]

Nothing apparently was published in the Pakistani papers on the real explanation for the delay in the establishment of the promised constitution commission or on the people's reaction to the postponement. As early as April 1959 the President had said he hoped to be able to set up the commission by November; in May, "before the year was out." Three ministers in the next few months also assured the naming of the commission "before the end of the year." Suddenly, in mid-October, it was announced that it would be put off for a few more months.

What can be learned about the East Pakistani people's feelings on this matter comes from the Dacca correspondent of the Calcutta *Statesman* in a dispatch dated October 24 and printed three days later:

> Delay in the setting up of the Constitutional Commission and Basic Democracies has . . . of late caused bewilderment. Elections to Union Panchayats were originally scheduled for October but have been postponed to December, while reports from some ministerial sources have indicated that the Constitution Commission might be delayed till the end of the first quarter of next year though the President himself reiterated that the end of December is the deadline. The delay in this connection was put down to the need for acquiring experience with the Basic Democracies' working to see if they could be incorporated into the Constitution.

The article summed up the first year of the military regime in Pakistan, listing the outstanding achievements of the government and also mentioning the points on which it had received criticism. The accomplishments included accord with India on certain border problems, restoration of political stability and the rebuilding of the country's economic foundations, as shown by the almost one hundred percent rise in foreign exchange reserves, the new interest shown in investment by foreign firms, the advance made in the sphere of industrial production and the appreciation in value of the Pakistani rupee. The problem which plagued the new regime in its first year was East Pakistan's perennial question of an adequate food supply. Some misgivings were expressed quite early during the military regime. According to the same article in the *Statesman,* "The first murmur of dissatisfaction arose against the system of Basic Democracies and the decision to shift the capital." The grounds for complaint against Basic Democracies were that

> through its provisions for nominations to otherwise elected councils, it virtually amounts to 'putting the clock back politically', at least as far as [East Pakistan] is concerned. This is unfortunate, and, as has been explained officially, is the result of a desire not to differentiate between East Pakistan and West Pakistan, where the people just released from feudal landlordism, are not yet politically conscious to a degree prevalent in the eastern wing. This determination to root out the evil of disparity has been amply borne out in the weightage proposed to be given East Pakistan in the latest proposals for the second Five Year Plan to pull her [up to] a level with her sister province in terms of economic and industrial development.

In spite of the intensive screening that eliminated many corrupt and inefficient staff members, the *Statesman* article continued, even the President acknowledged that there was a "note of dissatisfaction that not all deserving of it had felt the axe." He explained that corruption was so widespread that too drastic screening would have rendered the country "devoid of administrators." Rumors about some noticeable exceptions apparently indicated

> that perhaps the regime might have been motivated by consideration of the need to retain some who are obviously in a position to assist it in the propagation of its ideological aims, which latter have been described as a return to the ideology that inspired the creation of Pakistan.

*Dawn* and the *Pakistan Observer* marked the first anniversary of the revolution by looking over the year which began October 27, 1958, with the takeover by General Ayub Khan. Writing on "The Meaning of Today" in a three-column editorial, *Dawn* said:

. . . The twelve months since [the revolution's real architect emerged fully into view and took firm control of our drifting ship of state] have been crowded with achievements which are there for all to see, and it is now acknowledged throughout the free world that Pakistan —which had become the sickliest nation in the region due to the mishandling of her affairs by the inept and corrupt political elements who successively seized power since the demise of the Quaid-i-Millat —is today a stronger, healthier and worthier member of the comity of nations than perhaps ever before. . . .

If the progress already made in the past one year under the leadership of President Ayub is so heartening, the coming twelve months hold forth the prospect of even greater things. . . .

In contrast with the enthusiasm of *Dawn,* a more cautious optimism was exhibited by the *Pakistan Observer:*

Much has happened since [General Mohammad Ayub Khan took over the reins of the country's administration] to raise hope that some day soon the revolution, unprecedented in its bloodlessness, will successfully complete its task.

Summarizing the achievements of the regime in the fields of weeding out corruption, streamlining the administration for efficiency and honesty, encouraging productive efforts, strengthening the rupee and especially "the long overdue land reforms in West Pakistan," the editorial concluded:

It may be too early yet to assess the final results; but already there are ample indications that they will be good. . . . We start, therefore, the second year of the revolutionary era with much greater optimism than a year ago.

### NOTES

1. For text of the proclamation see *Pakistan Horizon,* XI (1958), 303-307.
2. *Dawn* (Karachi), October 11, 1958, p. 1.
3. *Ibid.,* October 16, 1958, pp. 1, 10.
4. *Statesman* (Calcutta), October 18, 1958, p. 7.
5. *Dawn,* October 21, 1958, p. 1.
6. For a thoroughgoing statement on the grievances of East Pakistan and their causes, see Richard D. Lambert, "Factors in Bengali Regionalism in Pakistan," *Far Eastern Survey,* 28 (April 1959), 49-58.
7. *Pakistan Observer* (Dacca), October 22, p. 1 and *Dawn,* October 23, 1958, p. 8.
8. *Dawn,* October 30, 1958, p. 1.
9. *Ibid.,* October 29, 1958, p. 1.
10. See Appendix A for names of cabinet members and other important officers.
11. *Dawn,* October 31, 1958, pp. 1, 10.

12. This was not written about the military regime but in an editorial on the United Nations on March 6, 1959.

13. November 6, p. 2; December 4, p. 2; December 14, p. 2; December 29, 1958, p. 2.

14. *Dawn,* December 15, 1958, p. 1.

15. *Statesman,* December 4, 1958, p. 1.

16. *Dawn,* October 11, 1958, p. 1.

17. *Ibid.,* December 4, 1958, p. 4.

18. *Ibid.,* December 16, 1958, p. 7.

19. *Pakistan Observer,* December 27, 1958, p. 3.

20. *Ibid.,* December 27, 1958, p. 1.

21. *Ibid.,* December 28, 1958, p. 1.

22. *Dawn,* January 16, 1959, pp. 1, 6.

23. *Ibid.,* January 14, p. 1.

24. January 16, 1959, p. 5. Even before the creation of this admittedly propagandistic agency, the *Statesman* had recognized by the assignment of portfolios in the new cabinet that propaganda would be a serious effort of the military regime: "Among other features of the new Pakistani Cabinet is the combination of the portfolios of Education [with] Information and Broadcasting. Apparently education and propaganda will now march hand in hand under the new regime" (October 26, 1958, p. 1).

25. *Pakistan Observer,* January 8, 1959, p. 1.

26. *Dawn,* February 26, p. 1; *Pakistan Observer,* February 27, 1959, p. 3.

27. *Dawn,* January 6, 1959, p. 1.

28. *Ibid.,* February 14, 1959, p. 1. For further discussion on this "sense of frustration" see Orville Linck, *Passage through Pakistan* (Detroit: Wayne State University Press, 1959), pp. 192-233.

29. *Dawn,* March 8, p. 1; March 9, 1959, p. 1.

30. *Ibid.,* March 10, 1959, p. 1.

31. *Ibid.,* March 12, 1959, p. 1.

32. *Ibid.,* March 15, 1959, p. 1.

33. Pakistan Day commemorates the passage on March 23, 1940, of the Lahore resolution by the Muslim League under Mohammad Ali Jinnah in which the Muslims resolved to work for a separate Islamic nation. As a national holiday Pakistan Day provides an occasion not only for patriotic speeches but also for significant acts of government. The 1956 Constitution, for example, was adopted on March 23.

34. *Dawn,* March 25, 1959, p. 1.

35. *Ibid.,* March 28, 1959, p. 1.

36. *Ibid.,* April 17, 1959, p. 1.

37. *Pakistan Observer,* April 24, 1959, p. 1.

38. The writer apparently erred, for Ayub meant "persons" instead of "voters".

39. The subject of "the support that politicians derive from their tenants and tribes" is touched lightly in Khalid Bin Sayeed, "Collapse of Parliamentary Democracy in Pakistan," *Middle East Journal,* 13 (1959), 389-406. The author said he was "not aware of any study of Pakistan which throws any light on this highly important aspect of Pakistan's politics" (p. 393).

40. *Dawn,* May 3, 1959, p. 1.

41. *Ibid.,* May 11, 1959, pp. 1, 6.

42. *Ibid.,* May 27, 1959, p. 1.

43. *Ibid.,* May 4, 1959, pp. 1, 3.

44. *Ibid.,* June 11, 1959, p. 1.

45. *Ibid.,* June 16, 1959, p. 1.

46. *Ibid.,* June 17, 1959, p. 1.

47. *Ibid.,* June 18, 1959, p. 1.

48. *Ibid.,* July 25, 1959, p. 1.

49. *Ibid.,* July 3, 1959, p. 1.

50. *Le Monde* (Paris), June 31, 1959, reported in *Pakistan Observer,* August 2, 1959, p. 4.

51. *Dawn* and *Pakistan Observer,* August 11, 1959, p. 1.

52. *Pakistan Observer,* August 19, 1959, p. 1.

53. *Dawn,* August 23, p. 1; August 25, 1959, p. 1.

54. *Ibid.,* October 24, 1958, p. 1.

55. *Ibid.,* November 21, 1958, p. 1.

56. *Ibid.,* January 3, p. 4; January 7, 1959, pp. 3, 8.

57. *Ibid.,* February 15, 1959, p. 5.

58. *Ibid.,* March 12, 1959, p. 4.

59. *Ibid.,* April 12, 1959, p. 1. Id-ul-Fitr is the religious feast day which occurs the first day after the holy month of Ramazan during which sunrise-to-sunset fasting and other special religious practices are observed.

60. *Ibid.,* June 13, 1959, p. 1.

61. *Ibid.,* August 2, 1959, p. 6.

62. *Ibid.,* August 19, 1959, p. 1.

63. *Pakistan Observer,* September 7, 1959.

64. *Ibid.,* October 14, 1959.

65. *Ibid.,* October 16, 1959, p. 1.

66. *Ibid.,* October 26, 1959.

67. *Dawn,* October 24, 1959.

# CHAPTER III

# BASIC DEMOCRACIES
### (October 1959—February 1960)

THE first anniversary of the revolution, October 27, 1959, was a momentous occasion for Pakistan for several reasons. First, the government was moved to the new interim capital at Rawalpindi and from there President Ayub broadcast his Revolution Day message. Second, the cabinet conferred the rank of Field Marshal on President Ayub Khan "as a token of the nation's gratitude." In addition, the President announced that elections to the union councils would be held within the next few weeks. Most important of all was the Basic Democracies Order.[1]

The Basic Democracies Order provided for a five-tier scheme of councils partly elected and partly appointed: union councils, *thana* and *tehsil* councils, district councils, divisional councils and two provincial development advisory councils. A union consisted of a number of villages whose populations totaled about 10,000. According to the Order one representative was to be elected by adult franchise for each 1,000 of the population, thus yielding a total of 80,000 elected union council members.[2] Each union council was to consist of the elected members plus not more than half as many appointed or "nominated" members. The chairmen of the union councils plus up to an equal number of official and nominated members formed the second tier—*thana* councils in East Pakistan and *tehsil* councils in West Pakistan. The third tier, district councils, consisted half of official members and half of nominated members; and half of the nominated members had to be chosen from among the chairmen of the union councils. The divisional councils were formed by the chairmen of the district councils, certain government officials and nominated members whose number was to equal the number of official members, and at least one-half of whom were to be chosen from among the chairmen of union councils. As the tiers neared the top, the proportion of elected members dropped from two-thirds for union councils to one-half for *thana* and *tehsil* councils and to only one-fourth for district and divi-

sional councils. In the provincial development advisory councils only one-sixth of the membership were union council chairmen.[3]

Then began a hectic period of preparing for the elections to Basic Democracies. Mohammad Ibrahim, the Law Minister, assured a news conference that the constitution commission would be set up after the union council elections. Whether the Basic Democracies Order would form a part of the future constitution was a matter for the proposed commission to decide, he stated, but it was meant to be a permanent institution. At a one-day governors' conference held in Rawalpindi November 2 the groundwork was laid for setting up the elections. Scheduled to begin the last week of December 1959, the elections were expected to be completed by the middle of January 1960.

Preoccupation with Basic Democracies did not, of course, preclude interest in the constitution. At a press conference Manzur Qadir, the Foreign Minister, said that the basic conception of the future constitution would be the welfare of the people. Qadir's reply to the question, "Don't you think that the present Government of Pakistan . . . is one of the most democratic governments in the whole of Asia?" is quoted here in full:

> Yes, from the practical point of view but sound governments need the government of rules in institutions. Government by men, however good they may be, is dependent upon the quality of the man. Pakistan at the moment is fortunate in having a man who has within him the necessary qualities of self-restraint and self-imposed restrictions which are indispensable for a good government. But for a perpetual system, it is necessary that institutions must be devised which ensure it.
>
> I would agree with you that the present Government of Pakistan under the guidance of a very popular President has the backing, consent and support of the people but unless there is a machinery by which the people can express their approval or disapproval of measures the requirement of sound institutions will not be fulfilled. It is for that reason that the President himself is very anxious to introduce in the country sound institutions which will be suitable to the genius of the people, which would be capable of being understood by the people and which would be capable of being worked by them. When he has done that I think, without drawing any comparisons, it will be a real democracy functioning in the country.[4]

On another occasion Qadir said it was likely that the elected members of the 8,000 union councils would form an electoral college for choosing the national assembly and the president. But of course, he added, it would be up to the constitution commission to decide the future pattern of elections.[5] The Foreign Minister was the first to indicate that the commission was already constituted and that it would start

work immediately after the Basic Democracies elections were held.[6] On the same day in the *Pakistan Observer* a correspondent in Rawalpindi wrote that the composition and terms of reference of the proposed constitution commission would be announced on January 4. He said that the selection of the group had already been completed and it was believed that it would take not more than six months to finish its work. The constitution might be launched by the end of 1960.

President Ayub Khan spoke of Basic Democracies wherever he went and, in fact, created opportunities to explain his new system and to educate the people regarding its benefits. On such occasions the subject of the future constitution was always brought up. During a state visit to Iran in the middle of November he told the Pakistani community in Teheran that he hoped the constitution would be formed by the middle of 1961. He said it would be a constitution that would ensure the stability of government, for it was on this that Pakistan's future primarily depended. He reiterated that he believed the presidential system would best ensure the nation against the shifting political scenes which had brought it to the brink of ruin.[7]

Manzur Qadir told reporters at the Lahore airport that "no such move" as lifting the ban on political parties was at present "under contemplation." He added, "It is possible and even anticipated that after the Basic Democracies begin functioning, new parties . . . may emerge." The Foreign Minister announced that Martial Law Regulation No. 55 which prohibited political activity would be amended shortly in order to allow public meetings and canvassing for the Basic Democracies election. But he stressed the fact that elections were to be on an individual non-party basis.[8]

The meet-the-people tour of West Pakistan undertaken by the President December 14-21, 1959, provided many opportunities for speeches, informal talks and question-answer meetings.[9] He told a public meeting in Hyderabad that the union councils might be entrusted with the responsibility of electing members of the assembly and the president of the country, therefore it was important to elect the right people to Basic Democracies. He also stated that he believed indirect elections were best suited for this country. The President re-affirmed that the constitution commission, which would be announced by the end of March, would consist of able and experienced men who had a thorough knowledge of constitutional and administrative problems. He made it clear that this would be a commission and not a constituent assembly. "We have had enough experience of such bodies which only delayed constitution-making and caused confusion and disunity," he said. He repeated that Pakistan needed democracy without political

parties. If the party system was not abolished, the country would never have peace.

The President suggested that the future constitution might have a provision authorizing the assembly to pass amendments with a two-thirds majority. Again he stressed that the unitary form of government was preferable for Pakistan because a country in a formative stage has to develop a common outlook, and the federal form of government does not help in doing that. He envisaged a central government with considerable delegation of authority to governors who, in turn, were to delegate their authority to commissioners and deputy commissioners in order to find remedies for local problems without encountering "red-tapism."

At other places during the tour President Ayub explained that past events had, in his view, made it abundantly clear that direct elections in a parliamentary form of government were unsuitable for Pakistan. He was asked whether the 80,000 members of union councils would elect members to the national assembly or whether the election would be by adult franchise. At first the President hedged by saying that it would depend on the reports of the election commission and the constitution commission. When he was reminded of Mr. Qadir's statement that the government favored indirect elections through an electoral college he admitted that he did not favor adult franchise for elections to the assembly. After twelve years of sad experience, he said, it was now known what the country needed; even if the constitution commission recommended the adoption of direct elections the cabinet would never accept it. He stated, "I shall never accept any wrong recommendation of any Commission." The President felt that candidates for election to a national assembly might be required to meet certain educational qualifications. He drove home his point that there should be no provincial assemblies by calling them the "cause of disruption." He reassured another questioner that the constitution would reflect the glorious principles of Islam while, at the same time, methods and details would have to be in consonance with conditions prevailing in the world today. "We must go forward, keeping pace with the modern scientific world; we cannot be backwards by thousands of years," he added.

The *Pakistan Observer* of December 25 called President Ayub Khan's "triumphal progress in West Pakistan . . . a measure of the hopes and the aspirations generated by the new regime." A "sense of direction and purpose had been created" by the President's statesman-like announcement that he was determined to find a "democratic system" suited to Pakistan's needs and one which would include the

fundamental rights of the people. "Never since the Quaid-e-Azam . . . left us for his heavenly home," declared the editorial, "has there been so much reason to feel so assured of our future." If the President succeeded in his determination, he would "deserve to be reckoned as among the dozen or so of the great nation-builders of history."

In a twenty-minute speech before a large public meeting in Rawalpindi celebrating the Quaid-e-Azam's birth anniversary, President Ayub Khan outlined the principles on which he believed any plan for the future government of Pakistan should be based: (1) the presidential form is best suited to the country; (2) legislative bodies should be entrusted with the function of law-making only; (3) electoral colleges with appropriate breadth of vision should be provided for; (4) only those questions should be placed before the people for purposes of election which were within their purview and which they could answer from their own understanding and intelligence. President Ayub said he believed that if the future constitutional structure were governed by these basic principles there would be no reason for the country to fail to attain a high degree of political stability.[10]

Early in January an outstanding Pakistani economist, Dr. Anwar Iqbal Qureshi, who later became the economic adviser to the government of Pakistan, issued a statement which closely paralleled the President's suggestions for the future government. First he explained that even in the best of democracies the party system fails to work during emergencies. Pakistan was experiencing an emergency and needed a "non-party government." Among Dr. Qureshi's suggestions were: any well-qualified candidate should be allowed to run for the presidency; the president should select his cabinet from the best talent available; the ministers should be responsible to the president and the president should be responsible to the nation; there should be only one legislature for the whole country; the president should have the veto power; a free and independent judiciary should be established; there should be freedom of the press and no person should be detained without a proper trial.[11]

Elections to Basic Democracies began on December 26, 1959. During the next two weeks all official efforts were concentrated on persuading the voters to select honest, selfless men. Just before the balloting was completed two announcements were made. The first was that the President would make a meet-the-people tour in East Pakistan during the last week in January similar to the tour he had made in West Pakistan a month earlier. The second and more important announcement was the Presidential (Election and Constitution) Order 1960. According to a press communiqué issued on January 8, 1960 by the

cabinet division of the President's secretariat, the cabinet under the chairmanship of Lieutenant General Mohammad Azam Khan passed a resolution requesting that "as soon as conveniently may be upon the completion of the first elections under the Basic Democracies Order 1959 the persons who are declared to have been elected as members . . . be asked . . . to vote in respect of their confidence in the present President of Pakistan." Should the majority vote in the affirmative, then "it would be treated as a mandate for the President . . . to make provision for establishing a constitutional machinery in Pakistan." Furthermore, "he should also be deemed to have been elected as the President of Pakistan for the first term of office under the constitution to be so made." The communiqué concluded: "Subsequently this resolution was submitted to the President who was pleased to accept the proposals made therein."

This then was the hitherto unexplained reason for the postponement of the announcement of the constitution commission. The resolution meant that the representatives of the people by expressing their confidence in the President were giving him authority to set up the constitution commission. Now it could be said that this authority came from the people. The second part of the communiqué—that "he should also be deemed to have been elected President . . . under the constitution to be so made"—probably dictated the timing of its being made public. It is conceivable that the cabinet thought that while the people would go along with the vote of confidence in order to set up a constitution commission, they might not have been so agreeable to the idea of naming in advance the head of state under a government whose structure was yet unknown.

During President Ayub's meet-the-people tour of East Pakistan, January 21-29, 1960, the chief subjects of his speeches were Basic Democracies, the proposed constitution and Indo-Pakistan relations. At his first press interview in Dacca he expressed satisfaction with the elections, which had been completed by mid-January, and said the next step would be for the people to say whether or not they wanted him. If they expressed confidence in him, he would set up a constitutional commission which would be able to complete its work in six or eight months.[12]

At various stops along the way, President Ayub Khan brought out points that he felt should be included in the future constitution.[13] In his first major speech the President declared, "If democracy is not firmly established, the people will not get the fruits of their freedom." At one place he said he preferred one legislature for the whole country, probably with about 150 members, each with a constituency of

500 elected members of union councils. He defended his choice of 150 members for the national assembly on the ground that a few wise persons were better than a crowd of stupid people. As for the electorate, the President felt that the newly elected union council members, because they had a broader vision than the mass of voters, would be the right people to choose a national parliament and the president. At another place he said the elected union council members would form an electoral college for the vote of confidence, while decisions about future elections, the number of members of the national assembly and other questions would be made by the constitution commission. However, he promised that, even though the Basic Democracies councils included nominated or appointed members, the legislature would include only elected representatives of the people. The President also wanted the future constitution to contain provisions to ensure that the politicians would not indulge in malpractices—preventive measures, not punitive. The President again stated his belief that a unitary form of government with powers decentralized down to provinces, divisions and districts would best suit the country. There would be no provincial legislatures because they would only cause confusion, as they had in the past. The central government would be the policy-making and supervisory machinery for its representatives to the provinces, divisions and districts. President Ayub expressed the opinion that the executive should be given considerable power in the new constitution in order to "get something done." The national legislature should confine itself to law-making. In answer to the question of whether sovereignty would lie with the legislature or in the head of state, he responded that they should share sovereignty jointly. The President said the constitution commission would include in addition to lawyers, right-thinking people from various walks of life, such as administrators and financial experts. The commission would issue a questionnaire to elicit public opinion, tabulate and collate the replies and then draft the constitution. He did not agree with the suggestion that the draft constitution be circulated before adoption. He felt a popular referendum would cause confusion, although later he said it might not be a bad idea if a referendum were held in the electoral college concerning any amendment called for in the future constitution. It was perhaps inevitable that some reporter should inquire whether the constitution commission would be asked to work along predetermined lines. This question was not reported in the Pakistan press but by the Dacca correspondent of the Calcutta *Statesman,* on January 25; his version stated that the President seemed to side-step the question.

On this tour of East Pakistan a recurring question from the public dealt with political parties. The President expressed the hope that re-emergence of political parties after the establishment of parliamentary government would not cause the same chaos as had led the country to the verge of ruin in the past. He realized that a parliamentary system implied political parties, whether one liked it or not. However, the constitution should provide that political parties be kept from destroying the nation. The President assured his audiences that the proposed constitution, while it would be Islamic in spirit and true to the basic ideology of Pakistan, would not be dogmatic nor would it discriminate against any sect.[14]

Editorializing on President Ayub's tour of East Pakistan, the *Pakistan Observer* of January 28 said that, by answering the questions of the people, he had shown "his appreciation of the spirit of democracy which implies the right of the man in the street to demand replies to his queries . . . from the highest policy-maker of the State." This newspaper commented further:

> His replies to questions concerning the future constitution were almost always prefaced by the remark that the details would be worked out by the Constitution Commission, although in his forthright manner, he never hesitated to give his own personal view in regard to specific points of the constitution. On two points he however laid special stress; and there can be very few indeed who will question this stress. The State exists for the individuals. . . . The second point he emphasized was that democracy, in the sense of the will of the people ultimately prevailing, will come in any case; but it does not necessarily imply a particular form of Government. . . .
> It will be for the Commission to invent the machinery that will ensure the maintenance of the two criteria mentioned above.

Even before the President had finished this tour the Foreign Minister took the stump to explain the nature of the future constitution and the membership of the commission. Mr. Qadir said the commission would not be limited to legal experts. Any person disqualified under the Elective Bodies Disqualification Order (EBDO) would not be considered for membership, but all other citizens, even former politicians, were eligible. He hastened to add that this did not mean that any former office-holders were likely to be included. The commission's job, he stated, was to study and make recommendations; the cabinet would then make the final decisions. The President, he said, had some ideas of his own on the future constitution but should the commission put forward better ideas they would surely be accepted.[15]

The first two weeks in February were devoted to setting up the machinery for the vote of confidence and instructing the electoral

college members in the voting procedures. The election took place on February 14, 1960. When the results were known—95% voting yes—President Ayub addressed the nation over Radio Pakistan. He said it was now obligatory for him to give the country a constitution—one which was democratic, easily understandable and workable, not too expensive to run and "above all a constitution which enables us to live the life of good Muslims."[16] Three days after the vote of confidence President Ayub Khan was inducted into office.

## NOTES

1. *Pakistan Observer* (Dacca), October 27, p. 1; October 29, 1959, p. 1; Khan, Md. Ayub, *Speeches and Statements* (Karachi: Pakistan Publications), II (July 1959—June 1960), pp. 44-47.

2. The Census of 1951 gave 75,800,000 as the population of Pakistan. The population in 1961 was 94,600,000 as given by *Pakistan Statistical Yearbook 1962*, issued by Central Statistical Office, Economic Affairs Division, President's Secretariat, Government of Pakistan, Karachi (Karachi: Manager of Publications, 1962), p. 2.

3. See *Gazette of Pakistan Extraordinary,* October 27, 1959, for the complete Basic Democracies Order. See Harry J. Friedman, "Basic Democracies: A Pakistan Experiment," *Pacific Affairs,* XXXIII (June 1960), 107-125, for an analysis and explanation of the Order.

4. *Pakistan Observer,* November 7, 1959, p. 1.

5. *Ibid.,* November 13, p. 1; November 17, 1959, p. 1.

6. *Ibid.,* November 21, 1959, p. 1.

7. *Ibid.,* November 14, 1959, p. 1.

8. *Dawn* (Karachi), November 18, 1959, p. 1.

9. *Ibid.,* December 15-22, 1959.

10. *Pakistan Observer,* December 27, 1959, p. 1; Khan, *op. cit.,* II, 74-80.

11. *Dawn,* January 9, 1960, p. 10.

12. *Pakistan Observer,* January 22, 1960, p. 1.

13. *Ibid.,* January 22-30, 1960.

14. *Statesman* (Calcutta), January 26, 1960, p. 1.

15. *Pakistan Observer,* January 25, 1960, p. 1.

16. *Ibid.,* February 16, 1960, p. 1; Khan, *op. cit.,* II, 111-113.

# THE CONSTITUTION COMMISSION I
(February—May 1960)

AFTER the swearing-in ceremony of President Ayub Khan on February 17, 1960, and re-induction of his cabinet, the appointment of an eleven-man Constitution Commission was announced. Headed by Justice Muhammad Shahabuddin, Senior Judge of the Supreme Court, the Commission included five members from each wing representing such diverse interests as trade, industry, the judiciary and minorities. The members from East Pakistan were Azizuddin Ahmad, a former central minister; D. N. Barori, a representative of minorities; Abu Sayeed Chowdhury, barrister-at-law and Advocate General of East Pakistan; Obeidur Rahman Nizam, a representative of commerce, and Aftabuddin Ahmed, a representative of agriculturists. Those named to the Commission from West Pakistan were Muhammad Sharif, a former judge of the Supreme Court of Pakistan; Naseer A. Shaikh, an industrialist; Arbab Ahmad Ali Jan, a retired judge of the former North-west Frontier Province; Sardar Habibullah, a representative of agriculturists and Tufailali A. Rahman, an advocate from the former province of Sind. The Commission's secretary was A. Majid, formerly secretary of the Election Commission. In April Shafiuddin Pirzada, a prominent Karachi lawyer who had appeared in a number of important cases dealing with the constitution, was appointed as honorary adviser to the Constitution Commission.[1] Subsequently other honorary advisers added to the Commission included G. W. Choudhury, K. Sawar Hasan, Begum Jahanara Shah Nawaz and Begum Shamsunnaha Mahmud.[2]

The terms of reference for the Constitution Commission were:

> To examine the progressive failure of parliamentary government in Pakistan leading to the abrogation of the Constitution of 1956 and to determine the causes and the nature of the failure;
> To consider how best the said or like causes may be identified and their recurrence prevented;
> And, having further taken account of the genius of the people,

the general standard of education and of political judgment in the country, the present state of a sense of nationhood, the prime need for sustained development, and the effect of the constitutional and administrative changes brought into being in recent months, to submit constitutional proposals in the form of a report advising how best the following ends may be secured:—a democracy adapted to changing circumstances and based on the Islamic principles of justice, equality and tolerance; the consolidation of national unity; and a firm and stable system of government.[3]

The members of this Commission differed widely from those mentioned by newsmen only four months earlier as most likely to be selected for the post. On October 7, 1959, the *Pakistan Observer* reported a rumor that Chief Justice Mohammad Munir was the obvious choice to head the commission since he had decided some of the most famous constitutional cases in Pakistan's history. Possible members suggested were Khwaja Nazimuddin, a former governor-general (September 1948 to October 1951); Chaudhri Mohamad Ali, a former prime minister (August 1955 to September 1956); I. I. Chundrigar, a former prime minister (who had held that office for the shortest term, October 1957 to December 1957);[4] A. K. Brohi, a former law minister; Altaf Hussain, editor of *Dawn;* Maulvi Ebrahim Khan; Tamizuddin Khan, president of the first Constituent Assembly; and Nurul Amin, a former chief minister of East Pakistan. The article assumed that the following men would undoubtedly be appointed to the commission: Manzur Qadir, Lieutenant General Sheikh, Governor Akhtar Hussain of West Pakistan and Governor Zakir Husain of East Pakistan.[5]

At the time, of course, no criticism of the personnel chosen for the Commission appeared in the press. Later a prominent lawyer indicated that the bar had not been entirely pleased with the appointments. Mr. Z. H. Lari, President of the West Pakistan High Court Bar Association, in a speech of welcome to Mr. Ibrahim, the Law Minister, said,

> We welcome the appointment of a Constitution Commission and we are glad that one of us is there and another is associated with it. But we are not satisfied with its composition as a whole. We would, however, suspend our judgment till we have seen its recommendations.[6]

In the letters-to-the-editor column of the *Pakistan Observer* on March 4, a spokesman for certain traditional points of view reminded readers that, since one of the terms of reference was the drawing up of a constitution based on Islamic principles, it was "very necessary that Islamic ideology should have adequate representation on the Commission." He felt that representatives of trade, commerce and agriculture were unequal to that task.

Within a month after its appointment the Constitution Commission got down to work. Too many years of Pakistan's short history had already been devoted to constitutional problems and consequently the Commission had a body of precedent and past experience on which to draw. The issues involved had been argued and discussed both for the draft constitution of 1954 and the accepted constitution of 1956. As the report of the Commission was to bring out later, it was the abrogated 1956 Pakistan Constitution and the 1949 Indian Constitution to which the Commission turned for guidance.[7] At the first meeting held in Lahore on March 19 Justice Shahabuddin, chairman, denied that the pattern of the constitution had already been decided upon and that the Commission was there only to rubber-stamp it. He asserted that the Commission would be unfettered in the discharge of its functions within the limits of the terms of reference.[8]

On succeeding days the Commission decided on its procedure and evolved a draft questionnaire to elicit public opinion on various aspects of the new constitution. The questionnaire was to be printed and distributed in April.[9] Copies were to be sent to bar associations, universities, central and provincial secretariats, headquarters of the armed forces, chambers of commerce, commissioners of divisions, deputy commissioners (called district magistrates in East Pakistan at that time), district judges and to the press. Other interested individuals and organizations were free to express their views and could obtain copies from their deputy commissioners.[10] The final date for receipt of replies had first been set at May 20 but when the questionnaire was released this date was fixed at May 31. All replies were to be sent to Lahore for analysis.[11]

On April 15 the questionnaire was released to the press.[12] It was a booklet of about seventy-five pages; the first part was devoted to forty questions with spaces for answers; the second part consisted of sixteen annexures including the terms of reference of the Commission, notes on various forms of democratic government and selected parts of the 1956 Constitution. The questions were designed to find out what, in the respondent's judgment, had caused the failure of parliamentary democracy in Pakistan, how this could be prevented from happening again, whether a parliamentary or a presidential form was preferable and whether a unitary or a federal system should be adopted. Other questions asked whether checks and balances should be provided, as in the American Constitution, how the president and legislature should be elected, whether human rights should be precisely formulated, what the functions of the election commission should be, and how the constitution should be amended.

A schedule was set by the Commission for its meetings and interviews. Its next session was to take place in Dacca toward the end of May. In June a two-month-long interviewing program in East Pakistan would be begun at Dacca, then Chittagong and Rajshahi, the three divisional headquarters. By the middle of August the Commission expected to move on to West Pakistan. When interviews had been completed there, work on the final report would be speedily carried through and the completion of the draft constitution was anticipated by January 1961.[13]

In mid-May the final date for receiving replies from the questionnaire was once again postponed to June 30, 1960, because of the demand for official Urdu and Bengali translations which had not been made available promptly.[14] At about this time the prospective schedule was also slightly changed: the Commission would meet in Dacca June 4 or 5 and additional interviews would be held in Sylhet and Khulna. Interviews at the divisional headquarters of West Pakistan would take place in September and October. It was stressed that complete secrecy of replies to the questionnaire was guaranteed and that no one need fear administrative action for any suggestions made concerning the future constitution.[15]

At first it appeared that when the Commission began its work public pronouncements by the government on the nature of the future constitution would end. From the middle of February until the end of April nothing on that subject appeared in the newspapers. Then the President, in London to attend a Commonwealth meeting, spoke on May 1 to a rally of over 7,000 Pakistanis living in Britain. In the course of his ninety-minute speech he dwelt on the history of Pakistan, the necessity for the revolution, the achievements of the military regime and the work that lay ahead. He declared, "The first task is to unify the people. Unification . . . comes through a sound constitution, a common legal system, a common educational system and a common administrative system." He felt that Pakistan was not ready for the British type of democracy which had taken centuries to evolve but needed a democratic system which came from a strong, sound, solid, stable government. He said that the Commission would be reporting in about six months and that by the end of the year the government would be in a position to say when they could launch the new constitution.[16]

Later the President, still in London, emphasized in a radio speech the independent character of the Commission. When he was asked what he would do if the Commission recommended revival of the old political order, he replied that he would accept the Commission's recom-

mendations, provided they were an improvement on his own ideas about the future constitution. "Both the past constitution of Pakistan and the people who were entrusted with the nation's political machinery," he said, "were to blame for the situation that prevailed. After the Quaid-e-Azam [Mr. Jinnah] and the Quaid-e-Millat [Liaquat Ali Khan] there was no man of caliber to lead Pakistan. Men of honesty and character were lacking. The new [1956] Constitution was such that our people did not understand it. It benefited the politicians, the thieves and the self-seekers."[17] In his second London broadcast the President said he thought the future government of Pakistan would be more along the lines of the American presidential system than of the Westminster type. Asked if there would be an "official opposition," President Ayub Khan replied, "It has to be. There cannot be a parliament without political parties."[18]

These London addresses of President Ayub were the only statements about the future constitution made before the general public by a high official from February 17 until the middle of June. What was said before certain bar associations is discussed in the following chapter.

## NOTES

1. *Dawn* (Karachi), April 1, 1960, p. 4.
2. *Report of the Constitution Commission 1961*, (Karachi: Manager of Publications, Government of Pakistan Press, 1962), p. 1.
3. *Ibid.*
4. Except for Ayub Khan who was prime minister for about 12 hours, from the morning of October 27, 1958, when he was inducted into office, until ten o'clock in the evening of the same day when President Iskander Mirza handed over all powers to the Chief Martial Law Administrator.
5. A Lahore daily described this unconfirmed report as "kite-flying."
6. *Dawn*, May 15, 1960, p. 1.
7. Some of the more important and difficult problems to be considered were the form of government, the federal structure and provincial controversy, the "special case of East Pakistan" and Islamic concept of the state. For discussions of various aspects of the development of the 1956 Constitution see: for a general work, G. W. Choudhury, *Constitutional Development in Pakistan* (Lahore: Longmans Green, 1959). For the political aspects, see Keith Callard, *Pakistan: A Political Study* (London: George Allen and Unwin, 1957). For the unification of West Pakistan, Wayne A. Wilcox, *Pakistan: The Consolidation of a Nation* (New York: Columbia University Press, 1963). For the almost insoluble difficulties involved in writing an Islamic constitution, Leonard Binder, *Religion and Politics in Pakistan* (Berkeley: University of California Press, 1961). For the problems of East Pakistan, Choudhury, *op. cit.*, Callard, *op. cit.*, Richard D. Lambert, "Factors in Bengali

Regionalism in Pakistan," *Far Eastern Survey*, 28 (April 1959), 49-58; Richard L. Park, "East Bengal: Pakistan's Troubled Province," *Far Eastern Survey*, 23 (May 1954), 70-75; Khalid Bin Sayced, "Federalism and Pakistan," *Far Eastern Survey*, 23 (September 1954), 139-143; Stanley Maron, "The Problem of East Pakistan," *Pacific Affairs*, 28 (June 1955), 132-144.

8. *Pakistan Observer*, March 20, 1960.

9. *Ibid.*, March 22-25, 1960.

10. *Ibid.*, April 3, 1960, p. 9.

11. *Ibid.*, April 17, 1960, p. 3.

12. See Appendix B for the text of the questionnaire.

13. *Pakistan Observer*, April 20, p. 8; April 25, 1960, p. 8.

14. *Ibid.*, May 15, 1960, p. 5.

15. *Ibid.*, May 19, 1960.

16. *Ibid.*, May 5; May 9, 1960, p. 3.

17. *Dawn*, May 12, 1960, p. 1.

18. *Ibid.*, May 21, 1960, p. 1.

CHAPTER V

# THE BAR AND THE BENCH
## (April—June 1960)

JUDGES and lawyers were deeply concerned that independence of the judiciary, the rule of law and the justiciability of fundamental human rights be embodied in the new constitution. Members of the military regime refrained from volunteering any statement on these subjects; even when addressing meetings of bar associations they usually managed to avoid such issues. Only the President made any relevant remark and that was to declare to the Karachi High Court Bar Association in January 1959 that the rule of law did prevail in Pakistan and the independence of the judiciary was observed and protected.

By April 1960 Martial Law had been in effect for one and one half years. On April 14, just one day before the release of the Commission's questionnaire, Chief Justice M. R. Kayani of the West Pakistan High Court made a speech before the Pakistan Bar Association in which he touched on martial law, the legalizing of the revolution by the Supreme Court, the independence of the judiciary, fundamental human rights, the rule of law, the assurance by the chairman of the Commission that the document had not already been drafted and the "delightful surprise" of the vice president of the Pakistan Bar Association "at the discovery that even two practising lawyers" had been appointed to the commission. Chief Justice Kayani was one of the most sought-after speakers in West Pakistan because of his delightful and unusual style. He quoted easily from the Quran, the Bible and Shakespeare. His remarks might seem at first glance to be only a sly dig in the ribs but proved to be a mortal thrust. To demonstrate why this speech was probably electrifying, refreshing and inspiring to Pakistani citizens, his remarks on martial law are quoted at length:

> I said that you should look for fundamental rights in man. Look for them in the President. Did he not tell you in Dacca that you should speak freely, even though he may not agree with you in your views? In a regime of Martial Law you might call that a charter of freedom. You must make use of it, and if you come to harm, Mr. Chundrigar

55

[President of the Pakistan Bar Association] will go to the President and tell him that his officers do not share his practical idealism. There are quite a few thousand men who would rather have the freedom of speech than a new pair of clothes and it is these that form a nation, not the office-hunters, the license-hunters, even the tillers of the soil and the drawers of water. It is good to have an honest police and an efficient magistracy, and to improve the peasant's lot and to make the laborer cheerful. It is good that Jack should have his Jill. . . . But the feeling that you can give expression to a sincere conscience without restraint is on a much higher level. And I appreciate that, notwithstanding the President's charter of Dacca, you have a feeling that while Martial Law lasts, it is not safe to practise sword-play in speech.

Perhaps it would not be unsafe to suggest that in preparation for the Constitution and to create an atmosphere of confidence, Martial Law may gradually be lifted; perhaps some military courts could be retained for specified purposes and the relevant Martial Law Regulations converted into a law entitled some such thing as the Military Courts Ordinance. . . .

Although I cannot distinguish a star from a crown, and my ignorance of military affairs must be colossal, I sometimes have apprehensions about the Army. An efficient Army, unsophisticated by the doctrine of civil necessity is the first need of a country like Pakistan. And people said with pride, before ever Martial Law came, that the Army and the Judiciary were the saving graces of Pakistan. The Martial Law of General Azam in 1953 had created additional confidence, though even there we had begun feeling the strain after a couple of months.

After these remarks on martial law, the Justice said, "That hackneyed expression, 'a strong public opinion,' comes back to me from some distant past, from some distant land. But I have not seen that strong public opinion, and I do not know if I can hope to see it in the future."

Despite his light touch, Justice Kayani's words revealed his deep depression over the state of the rule of law and the independence of the judiciary.[1] After eighteen months of reading only what the government wanted or permitted people to read—and that meant nothing controversial or unfavorable to itself—the publication of the Chief Justice's speech was quite shocking. A very cautiously worded letter-to-the-editor in the *Pakistan Observer* of April 21 found it "refreshing to go through the speech of Chief Justice Mr. Kayani. . . . These days we rarely see such depth in lightness." As a result of the speech, some army officers were reported to have felt "that their work [had] not been appreciated." Justice Kayani apologized, "It should have been unnecessary for me to say that on the whole, the Army has so conducted itself that an outsider visiting this country would not know that there was Martial Law here. . . . The Army, like the President,

... should always be above controversy." He assured the officers that he had "a deep and abiding affection for them."[2]

Two weeks later Chief Justice Mohammad Munir of the Supreme Court of Pakistan made his farewell address before the Lahore High Court Bar Association. He spoke on democracy and the rule of law—terms, he said, that represent a philosophical conception of the purpose of a state: "In a democratic state where the rule of law prevails, the emphasis is on certain values of life, namely, freedom of thought, freedom of action, which includes freedom of expression . . . , and freedom of association." The outgoing Chief Justice pointed out that Mohammad Ali Jinnah, the creator of Pakistan, "never defined or emphasized the philosophical purposes of the new state beyond its independence. . . . The words 'independent democratic state' and 'Islamic socialism' occur in some of his speeches but while the conception of an independent democratic state could be easily understood, 'Islamic socialism' never appears to have been defined or explained by him." Justice Munir closed his speech on a very pessimistic note: with everything swept away, "the Constitution, the Islamic Republic, the law, the Courts and all legal authority, we stand where we were almost thirteen years back, perhaps in a position of greater uncertainty. . . . The fundamental law by which we for the rest of our lives and our children are to live is still undefined and there still exist differences of opinion as to the end of the State and the form of government. . . . We cannot afford to make any further mistake without inviting utter disaster."[3]

A few days later, during the ceremony in which Chief Justice Munir relinquished the office he had held since June 1954, he said the judiciary "stands crippled today but that is due to the factors of which we are not the judge and I have no doubt that when the Constitution comes to be promulgated, and I think it is not a long way off, the independence and importance of the judiciary will be properly secured." The retiring Chief Justice referred to a current rumor that the seat of the Supreme Court might be transferred from Lahore. He felt that such action would be a misfortune since it would deprive the Supreme Court of the "valuable assistance of the Lahore Bar." He said, "Of course, it will be for the Constitution Commission to express its opinion on the subject after giving a hearing to the Bars interested."[4]

The office of Chief Justice was held on the basis of seniority, and succeeding Chief Justice Munir was Justice Muhammad Shahabuddin, the chairman of the Constitution Commission, who reached retirement age within nine days of assuming office. In laying down his robes

after seven years on the Supreme Court, Shahabuddin promised that the Commission would consider all the matters relating to the future constitution presented to it by interested persons.[5]

At the annual meeting of the Karachi High Court Bar Association, Mr. Z. H. Lari, President, in his welcome address to the Law Minister, Mohammad Ibrahim, said that according to a pronouncement by the Supreme Court, the Laws (Continuance in Force) Order 1958, which was now the charter of the rights of the people, had taken away "our fundamental rights and the powers of the courts to enforce these basic human rights." Mr. Lari pointed out that to assure the people of their freedom of expression, the only course was to give legislative recognition to that right and to the right of the courts to enforce it. He also complained of two objectionable trends in recent legislation: the exclusion of jurisdiction of courts and the prohibition of lawyers from participation in judicial or quasi-judicial proceedings.[6]

Mr. Lari observed that the future constitution should come into existence as promised before the year ran out. And he said no constitution would have "willing acceptance unless it provided for: (a) fundamental rights enforceable through courts, (b) independent judiciary, (c) supremacy of parliament subject to results of referendum if any, (d) direct elections based on adult franchise, (e) elections to all offices and legislature to be held after withdrawal of Martial Law and (f) authority to Parliament and Parliament alone to change the constitution."[7] On this occasion Lari voiced his disappointment in the commission's personnel.

It is interesting to note that it was exactly a year earlier that Mr. Lari had addressed the bar association's complaints to Mr. Manzur Qadir. Now Mr. Ibrahim, replying to Mr. Lari's speech of welcome, after a polite introduction said he shared the Karachi High Court Bar Association's feeling about the necessity of guaranteeing fundamental freedoms. He pointed out that, considered out of context, many measures taken by the military regime might "produce a very wrong impression." He therefore gave background details of the October revolution and justified the necessity for these steps. "Whatever the measures this Government has taken have been not to cripple or extinguish civil liberties," he concluded, "but to create conditions in which civil liberties can be fully restored and enjoyed equally by the common man."

Without mentioning Chief Justice Kayani, Ibrahim referred to his remarks and their relevance to the independence of the judiciary. "The Judges are not free," he said, "to give vent to their own feelings on any matter publicly that may embarrass the relations between the

Government and the people. . . . The very rule of law whose importance you have so rightly emphasized may suffer if Judges project their
views publicly on matters relating to government and administration."[8]

Continuing the dialogue between the government and the lawyers,
Habibur Rahman, the Minister for Education and Minority Affairs,
visited the Rawalpindi Bar Library and talked informally with the
members. Rahman asserted that the present regime had never inter-
fered with the independence of the judiciary and was anxious that this
independence be maintained. In response to questions about the constitution, he reminded the lawyers that the President had said that
Pakistan would have a parliament by February 1961. The Minister repeated that the government wanted a presidential form of government,
but that the Commission would submit its report on this question according to its terms of reference. He said that expert constitutionalists
both in Pakistan and from abroad would be consulted before the final
writing of the constitution. He also said the government wanted everyone interested to reply to the questionnaire in order to help the Commission determine the type of constitution the country needed.[9]

Next to speak on the rule of law was Pakistan's new Chief Justice
A. R. Cornelius. At a Dacca High Court Bar Association dinner in his
honor, he said that the rule of law must aim at maintaining the
integrity of the central organism, in which "a strong executive, working
in accordance with the will of the people and the laws they have accepted for themselves, holds the first place." He said that the rule of
law was usually understood "in relation to the duty falling upon the
legal profession and on the Courts of keeping the powers of the State
within their true bounds."[10]

The new Chief Justice of East Pakistan, Imam Hossain Chowdhury,
stated that it was the duty of the judges to uphold the rule of law
and maintain the independence of the judiciary which was the aim
and object of the present government.[11]

## NOTES

1. The speech appeared in four parts in the *Pakistan Observer*, (Dacca),
April 16, p. 6; April 17, p. 8; April 18, p. 3; April 21, 1960, p. 5 and in five
parts in *Dawn* (Karachi), April 15-19, 1960.

2. *Pakistan Observer*, April 18, 1960, p. 8.

3. *Ibid.*, April 30, 1960, p. 6.

4. *Ibid.*, May 3, 1960.

5. *Ibid.*, May 13, 1960.

6. In referring to the prohibition of lawyers in certain judicial proceedings,
Lari was referring to the Elective Bodies Disqualification Tribunals and to

the Industrial Disputes Ordinance. *Ibid.,* August 8, 1959, and October 22, 1959, respectively.

7. *Ibid.,* May 15, 1960, p. 1.

8. *Pakistan Observer,* May 17, 1960, p. 5.

9. *Ibid.,* May 29, 1960, p. 5.

10. *Ibid.,* June 3, 1960, p. 1.

11. *Ibid.,* June 16, 1960, p. 8.

CHAPTER VI

# PUBLIC RESPONSE TO THE CONSTITUTION
# COMMISSION QUESTIONNAIRE
(May—August 1960)

DURING the months of talk about the nature of the future constitution, the *Pakistan Observer* was editorially silent. When it spoke on the subject on May 26 it confined itself to a consideration of principles of government rather than of structure. The editorial writer pointed out that the form of government was less important than the spirit in which it was worked:

> It is the lesson of history that the only effective safeguard [against political disintegration] can be a fairly high level of public morality and a general sense of pride and self-respect among the people at large. Every one of us . . . should contribute . . . by helping in the creation of those conditions which shall make a Pakistani proud of his country and proud of himself as a Pakistani.

Democracy, the editor concluded, is the most difficult form of government. It cannot begin fully grown. "What is essential is that the system should be such as to be able to absorb strains and stresses safely without damage and be capable of growing with the growing nation."

Within two weeks after the questionnaire had been released to the press various organizations began to assess the opinions of their memberships about the future constitution. The executive committee of the East Pakistan Lawyers Association planned a special session for May 22 to consider the questions and prepare answers. Later the Dacca High Court Bar Association and the Mymensingh Bar Association each held a special meeting and formed a subcommittee to report on the questionnaire.[1]

Even before the Commission opened its first interviewing session in East Pakistan, the Bar Association of Dacca in a general meeting recommended a federal form of government with a cabinet responsible to a parliament elected by general adult franchise.[2] It was surprising that this recommendation was published for, with the exception of the

speeches of chief justices on the independence of the judiciary and the rule of law, very little of a political or critical nature dealing with Pakistan had appeared in *Dawn* or the *Pakistan Observer* since the military regime had come to power. Even more amazing was the reporting of several interviews before the Commission itself, as well as news stories on actions taken by certain organizations. Between June 5 and July 2, 1960, opinions on the future constitution were aired in the *Pakistan Observer* by eleven individuals and thirteen organizations, all from East Pakistan. The secrecy of their replies, which was to have been inviolable, was not necessarily desired by East Pakistanis. The response of Chaudhri Mohamad Ali, a former prime minister, is discussed at the end of this chapter.

Although the questionnaire contained forty questions, those of prime importance concerned (1) the causes of failure of parliamentary democracy and how to avoid them in the future; (2) the presidential vs. the parliamentary system of government; (3) the federal vs. the unitary form; (4) the electoral college vs. universal adult franchise for elections of the president and the members of the legislature; (5) joint vs. separate electorates; and (6) bicameral vs. unicameral legislatures.

On the first two days of hearings in Dacca, five newspaper editors were interviewed and their statements published as factual stories without comment. The editors of the *Pakistan Observer* and *Ittefaq*, a leading Bengali daily, were interviewed on June 9, while the editors of *Azad, Sangbad* and *Pasban*, the first two Bengali papers and the last Urdu, made their statements on June 10.

All five editors said that parliamentary democracy had not failed in Pakistan—it simply had never been tried. The failure of successive governments—seven prime ministers in eleven years—to frame a constitution and hold elections produced chain reactions leading to political instability. One editor blamed the breakdown on the center's interference with the provincial governments. Another said that the members elected to the Constituent Assembly of 1947 formed a conspiracy to keep themselves in power. Political instability was the result both of the economic disparity between the east and west wings and of the politicians' habit of "crossing the floor" (changing parties). The attempt by a powerful section of the bureaucracy to monopolize all powers had resulted in the dissolution of ministries through undemocratic procedures and delay in the framing of a constitution. Politics was never allowed to become an "open air" affair.

Suggestions made by the editors to correct past parliamentary abuses included: frequent free elections; political parties with clear-cut programs; prohibition against crossing the floor; and constitutional provi-

sions so written that there would be no opportunity for misinterpretation and misuse.

Two editors favored a unicameral legislature and one approved of a bicameral system for the center and unicameral for the provinces. Two men preferred adult suffrage for elections to the legislature and one man believed the president should be elected by a joint vote of the central and provincial legislatures—the electoral method set up in the 1956 Constitution. No respondent specified that the president should be elected by direct adult franchise. All five favored the parliamentary form of government and the federal system of organization. Two editors stated that, in view of the geographical and administrative difficulties, there was no satisfactory alternative to federation. In general, they felt that defense, foreign affairs and currency were the responsibility of the central government and all else should be reserved for the provinces.[3]

Two days later two more depositions made before the Constitution Commission were published.[4] The first was by Syed Qamrul Ahsan, a former member of the provincial assembly who, unlike the five editors, favored a presidential form of government under a federal structure. He believed democracy had failed because of the politicians' lack of understanding of the "game of parliamentary government," the death of Liaquat Ali Khan and the method employed by Ghulam Mohammad, a former governor-general, in dismissing his prime minister, Khwaja Nazimuddin. His sole suggestion for avoiding future failure was that no civil servant or member of the armed forces should be eligible for election to any legislature within five years of his retirement. The other statement was that of Abul Qasem, a former joint secretary of the Provincial Muslim League. He favored a parliamentary form of government with a unitary structure. Qasem believed that only one political party for Muslims should be recognized and—what one correspondent called "the more extraordinary portion of his proposal"[5] —that every Muslim elected should follow the dictates of the single party or forfeit his seat.

Nurul Amin, chief minister of East Pakistan from October 1951 to 1954, made a deposition before the Constitution Commission on June 25. He said that the late Constitution had not been given a fair trial and he named Governor-General Ghulam Mohammad and his successors, more than anyone else, as having "caused damage to the parliamentary system." Nurul Amin was in favor of the parliamentary form of government with "two if not more" federating units, and a unicameral legislature elected by unrestricted adult franchise. He suggested that "healthy opinion" and regularly held elections were neces-

sary for a stable government. He also suggested that party members should be brought under strict discipline and that crossing the floor should be met by the threat of expulsion from parliament. In most of his answers Amin followed the provisions of the 1956 Constitution. When asked by the Commission whether a president should be elected by the local councils under the Basic Democracies, he said he objected to this method because it was impractical for presidential candidates to acquaint 80,000 electors scattered throughout the country with their respective policies. He preferred that the central legislature and the two provincial legislatures form the electoral college.[6]

The published reply of Ataur Rahman, another former chief minister of East Pakistan (September 1956 to October 1958), pointed out, as had the witnesses before him, that parliamentary democracy had not failed, for it had never really been tried. He was "firmly in favor of the cabinet system of the parliamentary form of government" as well as of the federal form. The federating units should be East Pakistan and the four provinces of West Pakistan. The legislature should be unicameral and elected on the basis of universal adult suffrage and by joint electorate. The president, as titular head in a federation, should be elected by the legislatures of the units and of the center.

Ataur Rahman's answers are distinguished from those previously discussed by the historical detail he included. To prove that democracy had not failed he declared that certain persons, "whose views on the nature of the system are utterly superficial," did not point out any defect in the system "until the system was demolished and a system of their own ruthless pattern was established." He then used examples of the past decade to show that "the bogey of the parliamentary pattern was an inspired one not borne out by facts and circumstances."

Rahman said that the ills following partition were due to the fact that power had not been vested in the people at that time. He discussed the Constituent Assembly, an "improvisation" which, instead of enacting a constitution as India did in 1949, was converted into a legislature. Then ensued "a veritable scramble for power," "palace intrigues and other foul games." Within two months of the 1954 East Pakistan elections, the Muslim League, although "completely routed," was able to suspend the government and legislature and jail a large number of political workers. The bureaucracy, "a legacy of the British Raj," which had never respected the representatives of the people, played its part to the great detriment of the people. As a result, there were "constant rivalries and suspicions . . . leading to a series of upheavals."

The former chief minister continued, "Many Pakistanis feel that

there is a powerful clique in the bureaucracy which did not want democracy to function." He presented some instances to prove his point: Liaquat Ali Khan was murdered just as he was ready with a constitution; Khwaja Nazimuddin had a bill for a constitution drawn up when he was unceremoniously deposed; Mohammad Ali of Bogra, meant to be a puppet, was thrown out when he had a draft constitution prepared; Chaudhri Mohamad Ali, supposedly the leader of the bureaucracy, brought out a constitution and was promptly deposed; H. S. Suhrawardy, who had contested some of the provisions of the constitution, was removed as prime minister when he kept to his oath and set a date for the elections and ordered the electoral rolls prepared; I. I. Chundrigar tried delaying tactics, lost the confidence of the assembly and had to leave office despite the bureaucracy; Feroze Khan Noon, the seventh and last prime minister, did not play the game: he also set a date for elections, February 1959. Iskander Mirza, "the first and last president under the Constitution," seeing no chance of remaining president, became desperate, established martial law and abrogated the Constitution. What steps would have to be taken to prevent a recurrence of this situation? Rahman said it would be difficult to make recommendations, but that somehow it should be made impossible for anyone to assume government powers by abrogating the constitution.

In answer to the last question, which dealt with further suggestions, Rahman listed ten possible measures "to ensure security, peace and goodwill:"

1. Martial Law should be lifted immediately and a popularly elected Constituent Assembly should be set up which would frame a constitution within three months and hold general elections within six months.

2. If that were not possible, to restore the 1956 Constitution for the purpose of holding general elections.

3. The present Commission should recommend a constitution on the basis of popular views and in consideration of the geographical, linguistic and economic background of the country.

4. Political parties should be allowed to organize freely and function with definite plans and programs.

5. Economic disparity between the two wings of Pakistan should be immediately removed.

6. Parity in [government] service should be immediately established in all grades, if necessary by ad hoc appointments.

7. Industrialization should be encouraged in East Pakistan.

8. Bengali and Urdu should be made compulsory in the higher secondary grades in West and East Pakistan respectively.

9. A full-fledged Military Academy should be set up in East Pakistan.

10. Attempts should be made to allay the sense of insecurity, suspicion, distrust and injustice between different parts of the country.[7]

A written reply to the questionnaire from S. M. A. Majid, an East Pakistani member of the Provincial Development Advisory Council (the highest tier of Basic Democracies) and secretary of the Khulna Bar Association, was also published. Majid recommended a parliamentary pattern and federal form of government with bicameral legislatures and universal adult franchise. It was his opinion also that democracy had not received a fair trial. Politics had become a filthy game and government was run for the benefit of private interests. Wrangling between the two wings over the division of the spoils and intrigues between the head of state and the central cabinet had brought about the downfall of successive governments. Majid recommended that since democracy in Pakistan could not wait until an "ideal electorate" existed the country must proceed with the present "material." There must be no property or educational requirements for voting. Elections must be held at reasonable intervals and there should be "two and not more than two political parties." A member deserting his party should be forced to resign and seek re-election.[8]

Khan Bahadur Naziuddin Ahmed in his presidential address before the fifth annual session of the East Pakistan Lawyers Association, reviewed the country's political history as a background for making his recommendations. First he analyzed the questionnaire and the terms of reference of the Commission. He especially stressed the wording of the first term of reference, "to examine the progressive failure of the parliamentary pattern of democratic government," which he said was an assumption unacceptable to many Pakistanis. Khan Bahadur Naziuddin Ahmed described how the British type of democracy was "abruptly transplanted in the emotional Indian soil" under the Government of India Act of 1935. The Quaid-e-Azam did not live long enough following partition to establish a constitutional system and after his death Khwaja Nazimuddin as governor-general and Liaquat Ali Khan continuing as prime minister brought cabinet government into being for the first time. With the assassination of Liaquat Ali Khan in October, 1951, "the cause of parliamentary democracy received a severe setback." Then Governor-General Ghulam Mohammad began to "break and make" cabinets. His successor, Iskander Mirza, followed this pattern using political intrigue to continue in power. Khan Bahadur Naziuddin Ahmed concluded that the parliamentary system "never got a fair or adequate trial." It was in force for four years followed by "seven long years of naked despotism." His speech ended with his

recommendation of the parliamentary and federal form of government and adult suffrage.[9]

The thirteen organizations replying to the Constitution Commission's questionnaire, as reported in the *Pakistan Observer* between June 5 and July 2, were:

Bar Association of Dacca
Mymensingh Bar Association
Executive Council of the East Pakistan Mukhtears (attorneys) Association
Dacca High Court Bar Association
Executive Committee of Pakistan Medical Association (East Zone)
Chittagong District Bar Association
Faridpur Mukhtear Bar Association
East Pakistan Lawyers Association
Manikganj Bar Association
Tangail Pleaders Bar
Rangpur Bar Association
East Pakistan Income Tax Bar Association
Kushtia Bar Association

All thirteen spoke strongly in favor of the parliamentary form of government. Only ten expressed a choice between a federal and a unitary system and these unanimously favored a federal plan. Seven who gave their opinions on voting wanted adult suffrage for the general elections to the legislatures, and four of the seven preferred that the president be elected by the combined legislatures of the center and the provinces. Seven associations said that the Constitution had not failed but had never been tried because general elections were never held. The breakdown of parliamentary democracy was due to no fault of the system nor to any inherent defect in the 1956 Constitution. Five of the seven also named names: they said that the Constitution had not worked because of the "vagaries of particular persons at the helm of affairs," because of the "flagrant violation of the provisions of the Constitution by those who should have upheld it" and because of the "arbitrary exercise of the powers vested in the head of state." In short, parliamentary democracy "was shattered" by Ghulam Mohammad, "a despot," and Iskander Mirza, "who was even more dictatorial," both of whom "indulged in party politics with the ulterior motive of perpetuating their authority." Two organizations pinpointed crossing the floor together with the struggle for power among the parties as causes of the breakdown of parliamentary democracy. Six groups suggested that a member deserting his party should either resign or automatically lose his seat and a new election must take place. Two of the six stressed the need for sound national political parties and the value

of an opposition party. Two advocated that the president be detached from party politics, even if this required that the constitution specify that he must remain impartial. Two suggestions were given that elections should be held at regular intervals. One group urged strict adherence to democratic and parliamentary principles, and one stipulated that the services (the Civil Service of Pakistan or CSP, Provincial Civil Service or PCS, Finance Service, Police Service of Pakistan or PSP and others) should be kept out of politics.

Many *ulema* also answered the Commission's questionnaire but their answers were not published in the *Pakistan Observer* or *Dawn*. The replies of a group of nineteen *ulema* and other religious leaders who met in Lahore May 5 and 6 and who as leaders of different Muslim movements and associations represented a variety of religious points of view and were published in the monthly *Pakistan Review*.[10] Contending that sovereignty was never transferred to the people but rather to the services when Prime Minister Khwaja Nazimuddin was dismissed in 1953, the *ulema* concluded that the parliamentary form of government had never been established and therefore there was no question of its success or failure. To prevent a breakdown of democracy, the religious leaders recommended that the political leaders and the services should first of all fear God and recognize that the British government "actually abdicated in favour of the people of Pakistan." General elections should be held and sovereign power passed to the elected representatives who would then draft a constitution. The *ulema* declared:

> If instead of adopting this right course a Constitution is framed by a Commission and approved by a Council of Ministers in a state of Martial Law, it is feared that the New Constitution may not be able to command even that much respect which has been paid to the constitution framed by a representative Assembly in an atmosphere of free and unfettered discussion.

The final recommendation was that "all the servants of the State should be called upon severally to take an oath of allegiance to the Constitution." This group closely followed the provisions of the 1956 Constitution in preferring the parliamentary system and federal form of government, distribution of powers between the center and the provinces, and adult suffrage. They believed the method of indirect elections and electoral colleges to be "the worst possible under the conditions prevailing in our country."

Question thirty-four asked whether any special provision should be included in the constitution "to assist the Muslims in the study of the basic values of Islam and of their application to the changing conditions of life." This question seemed to enrage the religious leaders, for

it did not present "a happy picture" of the type of thinking "which made this problem the subject matter of the Commission's attention." The *ulema* first pointed out to "the learned Commission and to . . . the higher authorities who exercise the final power of giving a verdict on the Commission's report" that it was "by virtue of the sacrifices of the common Muslims" that Pakistan came into being. Their second point could not have been more forcefully expressed:

> . . . the general Muslim populace desire to make and see this country flourish as an Islamic State whose laws should be Islamic, whose system of government should be Islamic, whose educational system should be Islamic, and whose culture and civilization should be Islamic. It is for this object that the Muslims sacrificed their lives, property and honour to establish Pakistan. . . .
> . . . the Commission should decide whose satisfaction is more important in the matter of Constitution-making. If they attach any importance to the 86 per cent of the Muslim population of this country they must realise that the Muslims do not merely expect this State to assist them in the study of the basic values of Islam; they have been studying these values even before the establishment of Pakistan. . . . What they desire is to make Pakistan a full-fledged Islamic State and for this purpose the minimum that can satisfy them is that [the Islamic provisions of the 1956 Constitution] should be kept intact. . . . It need not be mentioned that from the Islamic standpoint even these clauses are defective and inadequate and a good deal more is necessary. Anyhow, there should be no question of going back on what has been accepted already.

The *ulema* sent the Constitution Commission a copy of the Basic Principles of an Islamic State which had been drawn up in January 1951 "to show what exactly justice, equality and tolerance mean in Islam and how best they can be established."[11]

Only one more reply to the Commission's questionnaire is to be considered, that of Chaudhri Mohamad Ali. A statement of his point of view was first reported from Rawalpindi on June 12[12] although the complete text of his reply was not printed until June 17 in *Dawn* and June 19-21 in the *Pakistan Observer*. But for several reasons his statement may be considered the most important to be made public. First, he was a former prime minister (August 1955 to September 1956). Second, he was not one of the corrupt politicians being investigated under the Elective Bodies Disqualification Order (EBDO), but currently held a high position as chairman of the Pakistan Industrial Credit and Investment Corporation (PICIC) and, according to rumors, had been expected to be a member of the constitution commission. Third, despite the confidence placed in him by the military regime, he did not limit his criticism to the period prior to the revolution but

even attacked the martial law government. Finally, the publication of his reply had rather widespread repercussions.

In answer to the first question, on "the nature and causes of the progressive failure of the parliamentary pattern of democratic government in Pakistan," Chaudhri Mohamad Ali replied that between March 23, 1956, when the Constitution came into force and October 7, 1958, when it was abrogated only the transitional provisions were in force and no general elections were ever held. Therefore "it is misleading to talk of the failure of the parliamentary pattern of government." He said the Constitution was abrogated by President Iskander Mirza "mainly because he found that however much he might juggle with various political elements he had little chance of being re-elected President." To claim that Mirza set out deliberately to destroy parliamentary democracy might be "too harsh a view," but he did contribute "more than anyone else to the creation of those conditions of political confusion" which led to the abrogation of the constitution.

The former prime minister said that all the blame did not devolve on President Iskander Mirza; he was singled out merely because he illustrated "more clearly than anyone else the corruption of mind and morals which the desire to hold power indefinitely produces." Chaudhri Mohamad Ali continued, "The fact that he was not a politician[13] might serve as a corrective to the view so assiduously propagated of late that lust for power is a peculiar failing of politicians only." He concluded that the failure was not of the Constitution "but of those entrusted with its running."

Nine suggestions were offered in response to the second question regarding steps "for preventing a recurrence" of the breakdown of constitutional government: (1) recognition "that only representatives of the people elected by . . . and accountable to the people are entitled to be in charge of national affairs"; (2) "fair and free elections"; (3) "fundamental rights . . . guaranteed"; (4) control by civilian power of the military; (5) rule of law and independence of the judiciary; (6) "political parties (preferably two) . . . sufficiently self-disciplined"; (7) "enlightened public opinion and a responsible press"; (8) equality of opportunity; and (9) loyalty to the state above "sectional, tribal and regional loyalties." Chaudhri Mohamad Ali pointed out that all of these conditions "in their fullness" are not found even in the most advanced countries. He stated:

> It takes time and practice to learn the right balance between freedom and order, and it takes steadfast faith in democratic values to persist in the process despite partial failure. The school in which this experience is gained is free elections and the instrument for imparting

this education is open public debate between political parties. . . .

This, however, is in many ways a new experience for our people. . . . Parliamentary democracy is said to have failed. Politicians are run down and politics itself is regarded as a reprehensible activity instead of being among the highest duties of a citizen. It is said 'our people are not fit for democracy . . . give them the system of government they understand.' The system our people have known through the centuries is despotism or personal dictatorship, or, to call it by its latest name, 'controlled democracy.' They know it and understand it, respect it and fear it, but it has kept them backward for centuries. . . .

Even when we are most disillusioned with the democratic process and most disgusted with the evils of political parties and politicians, we should never turn our minds in the direction of a personal dictatorship, however alluringly paternalistic it might appear. Nor should we cut the constitutional cloth to the measure of any one man, for constitutions are meant to last longer than individuals; or be misled by the fact that there have been good dictators in history, for they have been few and far between. . . .

In modern times it is usual to pay lip-service to democracy; and this type of government [dictatorship] is camouflaged under the forms of democracy but the substance of power, executive and legislative, is concentrated in the hands of one person. An impotent parliament and an obsequious press pay homage to the virtues of the president-dictator who appears to work all the apparatus of 'controlled democracy' effortlessly. Sometimes great projects are undertaken and they are of benefit to the public; but behind this facade of progress and stability, the spirit of the people is crushed.

Chaudhri Mohamad Ali then turned from generalizations about democracy and dictatorship to specific instances:

There are some people in this country who profess faith in Basic Democracies which, according to them, is a new form of government more suited to conditions in Pakistan than parliamentary democracy. . . . This view is based partly on confused thinking and partly on ignorance of constitutional history in this sub-continent. Basic democracies are a form of local self-government and have little that is new except their name. Local self-government in the form of panchayats has been known to our people for centuries. The basic constituent of Basic Democracies, namely, the Union Councils, is practically identical in its structure and functions with the Union Boards which have been in existence in East Pakistan for nearly 40 years. Local self-government in the form of Municipal Committees and District Boards dates back to the last quarter of the 19th century. These and subsequent reforms were introduced to train our people in the art of self-government and to make them fit for parliamentary democracy. If they succeeded in this object, the current diagnosis about the failure of our people to work parliamentary democracy must be wrong. If they failed, we can have little hope of the same remedy under a different label. . . .

It is said that the common man, particularly the villager, cannot

understand parliamentary democracy and cannot elect representatives
to it. But will the elected members of the village Union Councils . . .
be in a better position to elect those fit to rule . . . ? In fact, the position will be worse. . . . Our problem today is to spread the ferment of
democratic ideals among the masses of our people so that they come
to learn that their weal or woe is bound up with the quality and
conduct of their representatives in charge of national affairs. This
program of adult education which will teach our people that they are
masters of their political destiny can best be carried out by political
parties and will never bear fruit under official tutelage by whatever
high-sounding name it might be known.

Chaudhri Mohamad Ali concluded his answer to question two by
giving ten specific ways to achieve a workable parliamentary democracy. These detailed proposals[14] were designed to reach three objectives: placing the president above the political arena, ensuring free
and fair elections, and purifying political life.

In his answer to the third question of his preference for parliamentary or presidential and federal or unitary systems of government,
Chaudhri Mohamad Ali spoke strongly for the parliamentary form.
He took this opportunity to explain the circumstances in the United
States which had allowed democracy to develop. But Pakistan should
be more properly compared to the countries of South America and to
South Korea which, he said, illustrated "the ease with which a strong
executive [could] be converted into a tyranny." The former prime
minister's recommendation of the federal system was based on the
"unalterable fact of geography" that the two wings were divided by
more than a thousand miles of Indian territory. He declared that even
if there were a unitary system there would have to be separate provincial administrations, separate budgets, separate taxation policies and
separate development programs.

Chaudhri Mohamad Ali's first three answers covered most of the
remaining questions. Where they did not, he usually indicated that
on those points he preferred they be left as in the 1956 Constitution.
On the distribution of powers between the central legislature and
federating units, his suggestion was that the center must "exercise
effective power over the process of economic development as well as
over the maintenance of law and order"; but the provinces must be
allowed "sufficient freedom of action to carry out" their schemes. He
emphasized that the center "must have power to ensure that its direc-
tives are carried out; and the Civil Service of Pakistan and the Pakistan Police Service should be centrally controlled." On election to the
legislature, Chaudhri Mohamad Ali not only strongly favored universal
adult suffrage but also said that to deprive the people of Pakistan of

this right would be a retrogressive step. An electoral college would be a misfortune, especially if it consisted of the elected members of union councils, for, being a relatively small number, they would be easy to corrupt. In response to the last question concerning suggestions for establishing "a democracy adaptable to changing circumstances and based on the Islamic principles of justice, equality and tolerance," Chaudhri Mohamad Ali stated that the way to achieve this ideal was "to remove Martial Law, to restore the 1956 Constitution, to hold fair and free elections under it, and to recommend to the new Parliament to carry out the amendments suggested in reply to earlier questions."

## NOTES

1. *Pakistan Observer* (Dacca), May 20, 1960, p. 3.
2. *Ibid.*, June 5, 1960, p. 1.
3. *Ibid.*, June 10, p. 1; June 12, 1960, p. 3.
4. *Ibid.*, June 12, 1960, p. 3.
5. *Statesman* (Calcutta), June 19, 1960, p. 9.
6. *Pakistan Observer*, June 27, 1960, p. 1.
7. *Ibid.*, June 30, 1960, p. 5.
8. *Ibid.*, June 25, 1960, p. 6.
9. *Ibid.*, June 26, 1960, p. 1.
10. Abdullah Anwar Beg, "The Ulema on Future Constitution," *Pakistan Review*, VIII (July 1960), 29-33.
11. For background information on this subject see Leonard Binder, *Religion and Politics in Pakistan* (Berkeley: University of California Press, 1961), pp. 216-217, 227-232, 271-272.
12. *Pakistan Observer*, June 15, 1960, p. 1.
13. Iskander Mirza was "an army officer turned civil servant." Keith Callard, *Pakistan: A Political Study* (London: Allen and Unwin, 1957), p. 24.
14. The ten suggestions included: the president should be elected for a single five-year term after which he must retire with an adequate pension from public life and private employment; he must not be identified with any political party; he must act on the advice of the cabinet headed by the prime minister; the president should be fully empowered to hold fair and free elections, even having the power to impose president's rule for the three months preceding the elections; it should be the president's responsibility to control the conduct of elected representatives; every party must keep a detailed record of its funds and transactions; and the president may select his colleagues from inside or outside the legislature but not from among the civil services or armed forces, for they must be kept out of politics. *Pakistan Observer*, June 19, 1960, p. 5.

# CHAPTER VII

# THE GOVERNMENT'S REACTION
## (June—August 1960)

CHAUDHRI MOHAMAD ALI's public blast against the military regime undoubtedly shocked the government. One wonders how even the initial statement of the Bar Association of Dacca achieved publication. And why were subsequent replies permitted to be published? Why was at least a warning not issued to the press? It is usually inconceivable that such critical remarks can be published with impunity under a military regime. Why did the government take no action?

The motives can only be guessed at. President Ayub Khan liked to point out the contrast in freedom of the press not only between his regime and other military regimes but between his regime and the previous so-called democratic regimes in Pakistan.[1] In any event, from what happened, it appears that he determined to put up with the criticism until June 30, the deadline for receiving replies to the questionnaire.

But he did not bear it in silence. Just three days after the publication of Chaudhri Mohamad Ali's replies, the President was scheduled to address the opening session of a Basic Democracies convention in Lahore. He took this occasion to answer the former prime minister.[2] The President said that some political pundits in the country had recently claimed that the parliamentary system had not failed but rather the people who ran the system. He expressed his disapproval of this opinion and said that the very persons who framed the constitution had had an opportunity to enforce it. President Ayub described the evils and malpractices of the former leaders. He wondered why people thought parliamentary democracy had not been tried: "Today when an old political hypocrite[3] professes with profound innocence" that the Constitution was all right but not given a fair trial, one hardly knew whether to laugh or cry. "When they were exactly the people who created that system . . . what was responsible for the corruption that became rampant?" Speaking of the elections

to Basic Democracies which were held on an individual and not a party basis, the President averred that this new system, instead of pleasing, annoyed "most of our friends." Their indignation was caused because opportunities for making "politics a profession and democracy a toy" no longer existed for them.

In this speech, President Ayub gave the historical background of the struggle for the independence of Pakistan which, once achieved, was followed by a type of politics characterized by "malpractices . . . , selfishness and disruptionism of many of our leaders" and "newfangled political parties," so that in a short time "the physical scramble for power became the national symbol of politics." President Ayub accused the former politicians of playing a "great joke" by labeling the 1956 Constitution "Islamic" yet never putting Islamic principles into practice. Believing that Islamic principles should be followed in order to bring about a true democracy, the President stated:

> So far as I am concerned, it is my belief that without centralization, unity and solidarity, no system can claim to be an Islamic system. In the circumstances as prevailing in our country, these three conditions can be fulfilled only under such a presidential form of government, wherein the functions of the judiciary, executive and legislature as performed are free and harmonious, and strong as well as coherent.
>
> To evolve such a system we need not copy any other country, rather we should assess our own situation and draw a lesson from the early period of Islam.

An Islamic constitution for Pakistan could be achieved, he believed, only if the country chose the presidential form of government. He described Western political parties as having the aim of either remaining in power or of regaining power and totalitarian one-party systems which do not tolerate opposition or criticism. Neither of these, he said, provided for an independent legislative member which is the essence of the Islamic system where "every member of the assembly or parliament should express his opinion on national problems as a free member and should not be influenced by any party or group." The President pointed out that the Basic Democracies elections had been held in the Islamic tradition—not influenced by any party but on the basis of each candidate's character.

To justify his making suggestions about the constitution, even while the Commission was at work, President Ayub listed three reasons: (1) The Constitution Commission was completely free to make its own recommendations and was to be governed only by conscience and patriotism; (2) as a citizen, he had a right to express his views; (3) as the president, his duty was to "introduce a system of government . . . consonant with the conditions obtaining in Pakistan." He said there

were two conditions which the future constitution must fulfill: the reforms introduced during his regime must "not take a backward course after the advent of the constitution but should rather go ahead," and whatever type of government was established "must be so strong and firm that it [could] face the pressure of all those important elements [for example, the large landholders] which have suffered through these reforms." The President declared unequivocally, "If the Commission makes recommendations which are different from my personal view but fulfill all the requirements of the country, I will not have the least hesitation in accepting them."

Even more pointed than the President's remarks were two speeches of Z. A. Bhutto, Minister for Fuel, Power and Natural Resources. His addresses were an answer to and a criticism of former Prime Minister Chaudhri Mohamad Ali's response to the Constitution Commission's questionnaire. The first speech was delivered before the Law Society in Lahore. Bhutto asserted that it was incorrect to say that the parliamentary system had not been tried; it had been at work in the subcontinent since the Government of India Act of 1935. The root of the trouble, however, was inherent in the system for it nourished rivalry between the head of state and the prime minister and created executive dependency on the legislature whose three hundred members were able to hinder the reforms proposed by officials. Had the former politicians lived up to the parliamentary ideals which they now professed, Bhutto said, the present regime would not have been necessary. The duty of this administration was to see that the mistakes of the past were not repeated.[4]

Two days later Bhutto spoke to the students and staff of Gordon College in Rawalpindi. He cautioned against prejudging the future constitution and asserted that the present regime had never said that a presidential system of government like that of the United States would be adopted *in toto* in Pakistan. The Commission was an autonomous body whose task was to evolve a system suited to the genius of the Pakistani people. Any public discussion of the future constitutional set-up would have no influence on the Constitution Commission but, since "a public controversy" had arisen as a result of the circulation of the questionnaire, he felt it his duty and his right, as a member of the regime which had transformed the country, to express his own opinion publicly. Referring specifically to Chaudhri Mohamad Ali's remarks, Bhutto said it was wrong to blame any one person or even a few persons for the failure of the 1956 Constitution. He restated his belief that the system itself was at fault "because the executive was made dependent on a legislature which was neither disciplined nor

patriotic." He again refuted the charge that democracy had not been tried and then discussed Chaudhri Mohamad Ali's remarks on personal dictatorship. He called the argument "merely theoretical" and of no relevance to the situation in Pakistan since the present regime showed no "tendency towards any kind of dictatorship." He called martial law an emergency measure until the President's promise of a democracy which the people could understand was achieved. "There has been no hint at any stage," he declared, "that the present government wishes to perpetuate itself." Basic Democracies, the minister continued, constituted "the pillars on which the edifice of the new order [was] to be built." To call Basic Democracies just a new name for local self-government was a failure to recognize the new outlook, powers and functions assigned to these bodies. Mr. Bhutto rejected comparisons with the systems of the United States and Latin American countries. If there was any intention, he said, of making Pakistan's constitution a carbon copy of any other country's, a commission would have been unnecessary.

The minister further objected to the former prime minister's arguments in favor of the federal form. Bhutto said that the unitary form in West Pakistan had proved a success and there was no reason to think a unitary central government could not do likewise. Islam was a potent force which could overrule the dictates of geography. He also disposed of Chaudhri Mohamad Ali's argument that budget difficulties would prevent the smooth working of a unitary government by remarking that the government and security of the country were more important than budgetary considerations. He concluded by coming out strongly in favor of the presidential and unitary forms of government.[5]

Adding to the criticism directed against Chaudhri Mohamad Ali's answers to the questionnaire, *Dawn* published on June 19 and 20 a long two-part editorial called "Not So Innocent." The writer began by wondering how Chaudhri Mohamad Ali had been able to publicize his replies so dramatically, not referring to the fact that *Dawn* itself had published his answers in full only two days earlier. The editorial pointed out that the Constitution Commission was not a constituent assembly but was like "any other commission appointed by the present regime." It was not supposed to conduct its task "in the limelight of public debate" nor would its recommendations be binding on the government. There seemed to be something wrong somewhere, the editor wrote, "which [enabled] designing persons to seize upon the existence and functioning of the Constitution Commission for the purposes of tendentious political propaganda aimed at

sabotaging the aims of the Revolution." The editorial found it strange that Chaudhri Mohamad Ali, who blamed the failure of parliamentary democracy not on the system but on those entrusted with its running and "who was in the very thick of things, should now speak as if he were away and above the evils all around him." Commenting on the remarks about personal dictatorship, the editorial asked, when "the first blow against democracy and constitutionalism was struck" by Governor-General Ghulam Mohammad, was it not true that Chaudhri Mohamad Ali, then prime minister, "was in league with Mr. Ghulam Mohammad and lent his support to his high-handed and despotic action?" The former prime minister, *Dawn* felt, should "share a great deal of the blame." The implication that introducing the presidential system would lead to a Latin American type of dictatorship was unfair, the editorial continued, because "the temperament and traditions of an Islamic people are quite different from those of Latin races." But Chaudhri Mohamad Ali's arguments against the unitary system, continued *Dawn,* were perhaps "the weakest and shallowest of all his answers." Coming out strongly for the unitary form, this editorial ended on a constructive note:

> Whatever the Constitution Commission may or may not recommend, we suggest that the use of the terms "East Pakistan" and "West Pakistan" should be immediately abandoned. Pakistan can never be truly united into a single national and territorial entity as long as these dividing institutions remain.

The *Pakistan Observer* took a more moderate view. An editorial on June 23 said:

> We do not expect that there will be unanimity of views about any one of the questions; but we regard it as a good thing that people should be free to give their views and that an intelligent and sober discussion about them should go on. Chaudhri Mohamad Ali's opinions, however, as those of any other gentleman, should be examined on their merits and in the light of our circumstances and past history, but not on the basis of Mohamad Ali's own personal history. . . . Chaudhri Mohamad Ali's own share in the debacle is not however relevant to the present question except in illustration of the general truth that even a very honest and well-meaning person can be an unconscious victim of a system he has helped to erect but failed to understand. . . . It now devolves upon him to suggest specific safeguards against the debacle he witnessed, and in some way he himself along with others before and with him, brought about.

There was further criticism during the last week of June both by officials and newspaper readers of Chaudhri Mohamad Ali's statements. The governor of West Pakistan, inaugurating the Provincial Advisory

Council, made an oblique reference to the former prime minister when he said that some people still thought that "license of thought and action" constituted the "essence of democracy," and they favored the British parliamentary type of government. "Such people forget the lessons of past and contemporary history," he declared, and cited the failure of the multiple-party system to achieve governmental stability in France.[6]

The secretary to President Ayub Khan, addressing college students in Quetta, said that those advocating a return to the old system were those who had "lost their chance of malpractices and universal abuse of power and opportunities." He warned that the pleas of these former politicians "to revive the bad old system" should open their eyes.[7]

A *Pakistan Observer* reader in Rawalpindi took issue with Chaudhri Mohamad Ali on the question of separate elections[8] and a Lahore correspondent called the former prime minister "a convenient tool" in the hands of Ghulam Mohammad.[9]

The Foreign Minister, Manzur Qadir, at a press conference in Rawalpindi answered questions dealing with the recent publicizing of the views of various organizations and individuals. Qadir was very critical of the Dacca Bar Association's arguments, which had been published in the *Pakistan Observer* on June 27, favoring a return to parliamentary government. He discussed each point at length. Such publicity, he said, was intended to enlist public support for certain views and was equivalent to attempting to form political parties, an activity banned under martial law. The Foreign Minister called attention to the fact that up to June 30, the last date for submission of replies, the government had refrained from taking steps against those responsible for making public the responses to the questionnaire because this was essentially the concern of the Constitution Commission itself. Persons and organizations were given the opportunity to place their views before the Commission, not the public, as the purpose of the questionnaire was to invite suggestions, not elicit public opinion. The Commission's task was to assess the views, not take a majority vote; and to create something suited to Pakistan, not to choose between the American and English forms. Qadir repeated that the Commission was not a constituent assembly but an advisory body and although its members were experts all their recommendations would not necessarily be accepted. The final decision lay with the President who alone had received the mandate from the people.[10]

The scarcely veiled warning in Qadir's remarks was made official on July 3, two days after the Commission announced that the dead-

line for receiving replies would now be extended to July 31. The martial law administration issued a formal statement:

> The Martial Law authorities have noticed that certain persons have been playing politics, using this questionnaire as an excuse for reviving political activity by holding meetings and also publicizing their views through the medium of the press and printed matter. These persons have even sought to convert members of the public to their point of view. In doing so they had laid themselves open to action under Martial Law Regulations. However, in deference to the position of the Constitution Commission, the Martial Law authorities have so far desisted from taking action against these persons. The adoption of such mischievous and devious methods to misuse a legitimate opportunity for expressing views on the future constitution can do nothing but harm to the country. The Martial Law authorities therefore warn all such people that objectionable activities of this nature will not be tolerated and the full force of Martial Law will be brought to bear against them.[11]

Thus the President not only had the right to express his views as a citizen but also the power to silence the divergent views of other citizens. His "warning" effectively stopped public debate on the subject of the future government of Pakistan.

*Dawn's* editorial, "The Warning" on July 4, first reviewed Manzur Qadir's recent speeches as a basis for endorsing the martial law warning. The blame was put on those who "invited the warning by their provocative activities." By their actions certain former politicians showed that they were only "biding their time to recapture power." Such behavior was particularly unfair because the "better political elements" did not air their views "out of deference to Martial Law," so their case went by default. In order to get perspective on the search for a new constitution *Dawn* reviewed the history of the military regime up to the appointment of the Constitution Commission. The President could have written the constitution himself but it was his liberal outlook that inclined him to appoint a commission.

> It was, therefore, most undesirable—indeed dangerous—that the Constitution Commission should have been sought to be influenced by a public campaign in favor of a particular set of views. . . . The recommendations of the Commission may not now have the same weight as they otherwise might have. . . . The prospect of a return to democratic ways and institutions and the restoration of civic liberties in full measure may well have been seriously retarded . . . by the type of activities which erupted in recent days and which the Martial Law authorities' warning seeks to restrain.

The *Pakistan Observer* did not comment on the warning editorially but an article by "A Political Student" which appeared on the edi-

torial page on July 5 may well have represented the editor's views. The article, entitled "The Objective View," reviewed the events leading to the "raging public controversy." According to the writer, some West Pakistani "upholders . . . of an Islamic policy" prepared answers to the questionnaire and instructed people to send them in as their own replies. Then arrangements were made in Lahore to hold a convention where ex-politicians would debate on the constitution. These activities plus the published replies of Chaudhri Mohamad Ali and certain bar associations helped to "rouse political passions." The "Political Student" pointed out that the very nature of the Commission's first question, which asked why the parliamentary system failed in Pakistan, roused "passion and controversy." Therefore there should have been no public airing of the views on this question. Now the authorities were concerned, he said, lest an atmosphere "not conducive to calm and correct thinking" be brought about. The writer believed that, in spite of the President's role as the "supreme lawmaking power," no one could fail to be impressed by Ayub Khan's "obvious sincerity and his desire to place the country on a legal and constitutional system." Ayub Khan had many times said that "his mind [was] not closed on this matter" and that he would adopt any Commission suggestions which provided satisfactorily for the difficulties ahead. The article concluded that the Commission's task was a very delicate one and that it should be permitted to carry on its work in an atmosphere of perfect objectivity.

During July and early August, despite the martial law warning, a flurry of resolutions on the nature of the new constitution came from several union councils in the west wing. The West Pakistan government, in distributing the questionnaires, had advised all chairmen of divisional, district and *tehsil* councils to elicit the freely expressed views of their members.[12] First the Jacobabad district council endorsed the views expressed by President Ayub as to the type of government to be provided for.[13] Three weeks later a resolution of the Rawalpindi divisional council resolution supported the unitary and presidential form of government with an indirect mode of election and incorporation of Basic Democracies. Similar answers came from the district councils of Sukkur, Khairpur, Bahawalpur and Sanghar; the Kurram agency council; the *tehsil* councils of Hyderabad and Haripur; and the Khairpur divisional council. Only the resolution from the Multan district council endorsed the federal form of government.[14]

A month after the martial law warning was announced, the Interior Minister, Zakir Husain, cautioned that publication of any views about preference for a certain type of constitution was a violation of the law

and stringent action would be taken. His press note specifically referred to certain union councils and some members of the defunct Jama'at-i-Islami.[15]

## NOTES

1. For example, the President asserted that no action had been taken against anyone for criticism of the revolutionary regime, yet the previous so-called democratic governments ruthlessly suppressed freedom of expression and speech. "I am proud that during the last year and a half," he said, "the record of my Government is free from such malpractices. You know that no kind of criticism can be made in a country where Martial Law is imposed. But here everything is done by taking the masses into confidence. So long as I live, I and my Government will fully protect the freedom of expression." He said the country and the whole world had seen that no action was taken against any criticism of the revolutionary government. *Pakistan Observer* (Dacca), June 18, 1960.

2. Khan, Mohammed Ayub, *Speeches and Statements* (Karachi: Pakistan Publications, 1960), II (July 1959-June 1960), 139-151.

3. The word "hypocrite" was printed in both *Dawn,* June 16, 1960, p. 1 and in *Pakistan Observer,* June 18, 1960, p. 5. The version in the *Speeches and Statements,* p. 42, uses "Hippocrates," which seems meaningless in this context.

4. *Dawn,* June 17, 1960, p. 1.

5. *Ibid.,* June 19, 1960, p. 1.

6. *Ibid.,* June 25, 1960, p. 1.

7. *Ibid.,* June 28, 1960, p. 10.

8. *Ibid.,* June 22, 1960, p. 4.

9. *Morning News* (Dacca), June 28, 1960, p. 4. The *Morning News* is published simultaneously in Dacca and Karachi, but all references to the *Morning News* in this study are to the Dacca edition.

10. *Pakistan Observer* and *Dawn,* July 2, 1960, p. 1.

11. *Pakistan Observer,* July 3, 1960, p. 1.

12. *Dawn,* June 28, 1960, p. 1.

13. *Ibid.,* July 9, 1960, p. 5.

14. See *ibid.,* July 30-August 8, 1960.

15. *Ibid.* and *Pakistan Observer,* August 9, 1960, p. 1. The Jama'at-i-Islami was organized in 1941 as "a Renaissance movement in Islam." See Khalid Bin Sayeed, "The Jama'at-i-Islami Movement in Pakistan," *Pacific Affairs,* 30 (1957), 59-68.

# THE CONSTITUTION COMMISSION II
## (June 1960—May 1961)

IN THE MIDST of all the accusations and counter-accusations the Constitution Commission was meeting in East Pakistan. By the end of June hearings had been held in Dacca and Chittagong, and a new term of reference for the Commission was added by the President:

> In the light of the social, economic, administrative and political reforms which are being carried out by the present regime, particularly the introduction of Basic Democracies, what would be the most appropriate time-table for the implementation of the proposals to be made by the Constitution Commission?[1]

The Commission members left East Pakistan at the end of August. They were to reassemble in Karachi September 1 for hearings in West Pakistan. The secretary of the Constitution Commission, A. Majid, in an interview on Radio Pakistan at the end of August summarized the work accomplished by the Commission. The Commission had obtained views of a representative cross-section of the east wing province, Majid said. Although the sittings had been held only at the divisional headquarters—Dacca, Chittagong, Rajshahi and Khulna[2] —the persons who had testified were drawn from all districts. Two hundred witnesses were examined including between thirty and forty members of minority groups of Hindus, Buddhists and Christians. The secretary made it clear that it was not the Commission's duty to submit a draft of the constitution but simply to give its views. While no deadline had been fixed for the submission of their report, the members wished to complete it in the shortest possible time. Already six thousand replies to the questionnaire had been received. Majid said that hearings would continue in Quetta from September 23 to October 11 and in Peshawar from October 17 to 29. November would be devoted to hearings in Lahore and the tour of the country would be completed by the end of the year. The Commission would then start writing its report. Stressing the delicate and complex nature of the report, he refused even to guess when it would be submitted.[3]

On his arrival in Karachi a few days later, the Commission's chairman, Justice Shahabuddin, made substantially the same remarks as had the secretary. He stated that the work of the Commission was proceeding according to schedule. There was no deadline for completion of the report, for it depended on the volume of work before the Commission. He reprimanded newsmen for their excessive curiosity. When asked specific questions about the work of the Commission, Justice Shahabuddin advised reporters not to indulge in sensationalism in reporting matters of constitution-making.[4]

During September the Commission meetings were duly reported with the names of witnesses usually listed but nothing of their testimony was published. Although hearings began September 1 as scheduled, it was nearly two weeks before all ten members in addition to the chairman and the honorary adviser were in attendance. Altogether, ninety-nine were interviewed in Karachi during the month of September. Among them were the editor of *Dawn,* the inspector-general of police, the editor of *Imroze,* the former mayor of Karachi, a Christian leader, the director-general of Radio Pakistan, the vice chancellor of Karachi University, a former defense minister, a former education minister, Chaudhri Mohamad Ali and two women, one the editor of *Mirror* and the other a prominent social worker.[5]

Moving on to Quetta, the Commission interviewed eighty-one persons in the Kalat and Quetta divisions, including tribal *sardars* (leaders) and at least two leaders of the defunct Muslim League. This brought to 382 the total number of persons so far interviewed by the commission. The commission returned to Karachi for a two-day session during which five people were interviewed and then moved to Peshawar for the last week of October.[6] Nothing about the Constitution Commission's work during October appeared in the *Pakistan Observer* and neither the Dacca paper nor *Dawn* printed any news of the Commission during November and December. At the end of the year the Commission dispersed for a brief vacation.[7]

President Ayub Khan's public statements and actions during the second year of the military regime, October 1959 to October 1960, show clearly that he had not wanted a running debate between government spokesmen and the people over the future constitution. In general his plan was: first, organize the Basic Democracies; second, educate the people regarding the kind of government Pakistan needed; third, appoint a commission to prepare a constitution along the lines indicated; and finally, hold elections to the legislature before political parties could be formed and thus put the constitution into effect without submitting it to a referendum and possibly even without public discussion.

The program had started out more or less according to schedule. The first step led to the promulgation of the Basic Democracies Order on the first anniversary of the revolution. Then government officials led a campaign to convince the people that a unitary form of government with a strong president offered their best hope for a truly Islamic state. The Bureau of National Reconstruction, established in January 1959, was to help bring this about. President Ayub's principles for the constitution were laid down chiefly in his meet-the-people tour of West Pakistan (December 14 to 21, 1959), in a major speech delivered December 25 on the day before the beginning of elections to Basic Democracies and finally in a meet-the-people tour of East Pakistan (January 23 to 30, 1960). The President's next step after receiving the vote of confidence in February 1960 was to appoint the Constitution Commission. Public discussion on the future constitution was obviously not expected—government officials were to make no speeches, the public was to divulge its views privately to the Commission, and the Commission was to write its report as quickly as possible and without publicity. In fact, during the first few months following the appointment of the Commission, President Ayub Khan made only one major speech on the future of Pakistan and that was delivered in London.[8]

The persistence of reporters in asking officials when the Commission would make its report, when the constitution would go into effect, when martial law would be lifted, and whether political parties would be permitted, kept these issues before the public. Speeches by judges and lawyers on civil liberties, published answers to the questionnaire, and the attack by Chaudhri Mohamad Ali on the military regime finally caused an explosion. Undoubtedly the president had planned quite a different speech for the Basic Democracies convention in Lahore in June 1960. Bhutto also must have made some rapid changes in the two speeches he delivered at about the same time. Aside from these speeches and a planned press conference with Manzur Qadir, as little as possible was offered by government officials on the subject of the constitution. Almost everything else on the future form of government published between the Commission's appointment (February 17) and the three speeches of June 15, 16 and 18 had been vague statements wrung from officials at catch-as-catch-can interviews.

Scarcely noticed in the excitement engendered by the government's rebuttal of Chaudhri Mohamad Ali's allegations was the renewed emphasis on the need for a unified budget under a unitary system. In two articles in *Dawn*, "Unitary Government, Its Economic Aspects" on June 23 and "Federal Government, Its Financial Drawbacks" on July 3, Anwar Iqbal Qureshi, the economic adviser to the Planning Commission, set out to show that the federal form had been tried

but had failed to develop the concept of Pakistan—indeed, it tended to perpetuate "provincial and regional tendencies." Yet, those most "vocal in favor of full provincial autonomy" were the leaders of East Pakistan, "the worst sufferer from this policy." Qureshi believed that one budget, a uniform policy of central control over monies available and execution of development plans would result in "quicker development of the country and better use of the scarce resources." A federal form did not eliminate the separatist and disruptionist tendencies. "The distinction between East and West should be abolished," concluded Qureshi. "There should be one government and one budget. Then and then alone will we be able to develop a true national spirit." On August 7 he expressed his belief that the broad historical trend of Pakistan's finances pointed to such implications as inevitable.

During the last week in July the President toured East Pakistan. While in Dacca he addressed the Provincial Development Advisory Council and reiterated his belief in a strong, stable government. Despite the failure of parliamentary government in Pakistan, he said, intellectuals still insisted on this form of government. The President felt that the Westminster system could work only where political parties were few, stable and could command majorities. "Do you foresee the emergence of any political party in Pakistan with an overwhelming majority. . . ?" he asked. Only coalition governments could be formed and coalition governments were weak governments. They were like "mosaics of sand," he said, "which could be dissipated by just a whiff." President Ayub referred to the problem of Communist infiltration: "Indian Communism is near and it has been making persistent endeavors to reach East Pakistan. We cannot ignore these important facts of life."[9]

In Chittagong when questioned about the recommendations of the commission, President Ayub promised, "I will not dictate. I will do what the people think." He also told the people of Chittagong that it was the Communists who were supporting a campaign in East Pakistan for a federal government, a parliamentary system and direct elections. They were trying to convince the people that their only salvation lay in having a weak central government. He contended that when people parroted arguments to weaken the government, they were following the line of Communists abroad. The so-called public opinion of the moment, he asserted, was the result of a whispering campaign begun in Calcutta.[10]

From the end of July until the end of September various government officials answered questions about the constitution.

Zakir Husain told the union councillors of the Chittagong district

that one budget would reflect the unitary character of the country and be an advance towards a unitary form of government.[11] Finance Minister Mohammed Shoaib, who was on tour with the President, said a sound financial policy was possible only under the unitary plan.[12] The director of the State Bank of Pakistan, Hatim A. Alavi, believed that the importance of a unitary form of government should be seen in larger than national terms. East Pakistan was a part of Southeast Asia and West Pakistan was a part of the Middle East, he stated, and the "strongest of that silken bond binding them together is Islam." A united Pakistan would pave the way for "unity of thought and action by the Muslim countries. If only that can be achieved," the director said, "the basis for a third force in the world would have been established."[13]

The Law Minister, Mohammed Ibrahim, told the Dacca District Bar Association that the rule of law and independence of the judiciary were primary concerns of the revolutionary regime and that the Ministry of Law was preparing a draft bill designed to separate the judiciary from the executive. The martial law regime had preserved the civil structure of the administration, Ibrahim pointed out, which amply proved the government's anxiety to preserve the rule of law.[14] There was general agreement that the constitution should be ready by early 1961.[15] The Education Minister was the first to disclose that it would be drafted by a foreign expert.[16]

At the end of September, two months after his last public remarks on the future government, President Khan held a conference at Rawalpindi with several newspaper editors. He told them that the constitution should be in force by the end of 1961 and that the land reforms already achieved would be embodied in it. Elections would be held shortly after the announcement of the constitution. He assured them that it was not feasible to lift martial law until present reforms could be made a part of the constitution.[17]

Shortly after this interview, the President was welcomed by Nazir Ahmad at a Karachi convention of two hundred lawyers. Ahmad, after complimenting the President on his accomplishments—land reforms, recovery of evaded taxes, stringent measures against smuggling and corruption and the building up of foreign exchange reserves— stated, "Unfortunately, some of the evils are raising their heads again, and will again require your attention." Voicing the hope that the Constitution Commission would complete its task promptly, Nazir Ahmad expressed the conviction that the constitution "should ensure to its citizens a right to freedom of speech, freedom of association, dignity of person and right to hold property." He said there was a general

feeling both at home and abroad that martial law had "outlived its utility" and should be replaced by the new constitution as soon as possible. In reply, President Khan argued that if martial law were lifted some similar authority would have to be substituted for it. Military courts, he pointed out, were already being reduced in number and scope and were now trying only cases of hoarding, black marketing and similar offenses. The President said that Nazir Ahmad spoke as if all the fundamental rights had "existed in the past, but [had] been taken away now." President Ayub doubted "if either premise [was] correct." He admitted that criticism of martial law was forbidden but that, while he recognized the importance of the right to criticize the government, "it [was] necessary to have the capacity to distinguish between responsible freedom and irresponsible license." He concluded in the manner of other government commentators, "I do not think it would be proper for me to anticipate the recommendations of the Commission."[18]

The second anniversary of the revolution on October 27 elicited editorials from *Dawn* and the *Pakistan Observer*. Both newspapers praised the regime for its accomplishments but in quite different ways. "The achievements to the credit of the regime are impressive," said the *Pakistan Observer*. "The promise it has made for constitutional progress and economic development holds out even brighter prospects for the future." *Dawn* observed, "No government functioning through the normal democratic and representative institutions could have achieved within this brief period what the present regime has been able to do." The *Pakistan Observer* expressed hope for a democratic future, whereas *Dawn* appealed for continued authoritarianism. The Dacca editor wrote:

> There can be no question that until a constitution is framed and brought into existence, the Martial Law as the canopy under which all legislative and administrative acts are performed now must continue to exist. Except for this fact, we have a civilian administration run mainly by and for the civilians. That we are not like some other countries which have recently experienced the breakdown of the parliamentary system, we have much to be thankful for.
> None of the newspaper editors who heard the President expound his ideas at Rawalpindi recently found himself in basic disagreement with his views. That the paramount need of the country today is unity, stability, economic development and constitutional process, cannot be questioned, and except for this last the achievements of the regime have been impressive and promise to be more impressive in the future. As regards the making of a constitution, there could be no doubt of the President's sincerity and eagerness. We have hopes that at this time next year the country will have definitely known the shape of things to come.

The editorial of the Karachi *Dawn* brought into the open the fact that the unitary system was meeting strong opposition:

There is need, therefore, even for the Revolution's leadership, to search their hearts in order to ensure that their resolve and their faith do not in any manner weaken, inclining them to accept compromises. . . . We raise this question frankly and pointedly because we have a feeling that influences are already at work to condition the thinking of the Revolution's key men in such a way that they may be at least partly deflected from their declared faith in the unitary form of government. Believing that to be the only system which can preserve the integrity of Pakistan and integrate the country's so-called two wings politically, economically, socially and culturally under the rule of a single and strong central authority, he [President Ayub Khan] repeatedly declared his faith in this underlying and all-pervading unity of the people of Pakistan. . . . Hundreds of thousands of people have heard him proclaim that only a unitary form of government can truly reflect as well as preserve this basic unity. . . . All those who believe in Pakistan believe with the President.

But there are those who do not believe in the Pakistan of the Quaid-e-Azam's conception. They exaggerate the so-called "fact of geography". . . . A few of them may really have convictions about it due to mistaken thinking, but the motive of most of them would not bear scrutiny. Thus it is that in certain quarters the idea of a "federation" is being revived, despite the fact that our past experiments with the federal and parliamentary systems have dismally failed. . . . It will indeed be most surprising if the bitter lessons of the past were so soon to be forgotten and even the Revolutionary leadership were found to incline towards dangerous compromises on such a vital issue.

But if federation is unsuitable . . . there is another poison even more deadly whose name is "confederation." How comes it then that such a sinister word is beginning to be whispered too? In the context of the conditions in Pakistan, this word, to our mind, is just another name for treason. . . . It is a thought that would please only the empire builders of Communism. . . . If the concept of a confederation is allowed to spread at all, the Revolution, alas! will have come in vain.

. . . The leaders of the Revolutionary regime . . . know these dangers as well as we do. . . . Let them . . . give [Pakistan] a constitution which *they* think will be best for it—no matter who counsels what in the name of so-called public sentiment, or political theories. The vast masses of the people—as distinct from loose-thinking intellectuals and malcontents . . . want a unitary system which will ensure a strong and stable government.

Thus, a point of view which could not have been published by those who favored it was made public by a newspaper which only intended to excoriate it.

The political correspondent of the *Statesman* early in October an-

alyzed the situation in "Two Years of Military Rule in Pakistan."[19] Comparing the "sorry state" into which West Pakistan and East Pakistan had fallen and the "frightful" level of corruption just prior to Martial Law with the situation two years later—"orderliness, a sense of decorum, some expectation of continued progress and ad hoc but efficiently executed solutions to the country's numerous problems"— the commentator reviewed the "miracles" that had brought about the improvement. Land reforms, rehabilitation of refugees, administrative reorganization and the clearing up of political corruption were briefly discussed. The military regime had "completed its initial tasks efficiently and expeditiously," observed the author, but he felt it was "also becoming apparent that the military regime too [was] not without its dilemmas." Basic Democracies, the vote of confidence in President Ayub Khan and the appointment of a Constitution Commission were summarized. On the problems of drafting Pakistan's constitution, he wrote:

> The regime has given sufficient indication that it is opposed to the parliamentary system and that it prefers the presidential. The Commission's report is expected by the end of the year and it is likely that a number of new tensions may emerge in consequence. The first may arise from the contents of the report, especially because the Chairman of the Commission, Mr. Justice Shahabuddin, is a man of strong convictions and temperamentally wedded to more classic forms of democracy.
>
> Secondly, the constitution favored by the regime is of the unitary type, with parity for the two wings and a unicameral legislature, and this according to available indications may be unacceptable to East Pakistan. . . .
>
> However, in the present context it is not easy to forecast what kind of institutions would be acceptable to the Army on the one hand and to the people on the other and also what kind and degree and transfer of power would eventually become possible.

After considering the internal power struggle among military personnel, the part played by the Bureau of National Reconstruction, rival groups in the cabinet, the role of students and the significance of the political disbarment of former politicians, the article concluded:

> As stated before, in President Ayub Khan Pakistan has a competent and well-intentioned leader, one who can also look into the future and is not at the same time anxious to overstay. His problems arise from the circumstances of his own situation and from the fact that an ad hoc regime, army or otherwise, must one day make way for one which is more institutional. In the transition from the one to the other lurk many hidden but obvious dangers. Ingenuity lies in surmounting them. Of this President Ayub Khan, if left to himself, has enough.

During November and December 1960 several news items carried headlines on the constitution, yet in practically all cases the article dealt with some other subject. For instance, in early November Zakir Husain, Minister of the Interior, and a little later, Hafizur Rahman, Commerce Minister, visited Chittagong which had experienced two destructive cyclones in the previous month. In press conferences primarily concerned with the extent of damage from the cyclones the brief replies to questions about the constitution report and elections made the headlines.[20]

President Ayub Khan, in a November address to the Sukkur union councils, was asked whether political parties would be revived after the new constitution went into effect. He replied that political parties had brought the country to the verge of collapse and he feared that they would do the same thing if revived. He felt all effort should be made to run the country without political parties, at least through the first elections. But if, after that parties were still desired, they should be allowed, even though his personal feeling was that this would be disastrous.[21] A short time later he said the new constitution would definitely be in force by the end of 1961.[22]

During November prepared speeches were delivered by two cabinet members. Law Minister Ibrahim's talk, "Some Aspects of Law-Making in Pakistan," which was broadcast from Radio Pakistan, Karachi, was a lucid, unemotional recital of Pakistan's political and constitutional life from 1947 to date. He attributed the failure of parliamentary democracy to the "opportunistic personal power politics and reckless pursuit of self-interest" of the politicians. He cited the "swift and sharp actions" of the revolutionary government as being responsible for abolishing feudalism and regaining economic stability. Then, Ibrahim continued, at the end of a year the government's attention turned to constitution-making. Basic Democracies went into effect and the Constitution Commission was appointed. Its report was "being eagerly awaited."[23] The speech of the Foreign Minister, Manzur Qadir, on the future of Pakistan was delivered before the Gordon College Staff Literary Association in Rawalpindi. He said that Basic Democracies would be fitted into the new constitution if the Commission so advised.[24]

President Ayub visited Southeast Asia in December. In Rangoon, on being asked when he would restore "normal political life," the President countered with, "Do you mean lawlessness?" He said the report of the Constitution Commission which was expected shortly would be followed by the appointment of a drafting committee. He hoped that the elections would be held shortly afterwards and a new constitution launched by the end of 1961.[25]

A front-page news story on the Constitution Commission appeared in *Dawn* on December 8 and revealed that the Commonwealth Relations Office of the United Kingdom had been approached for the temporary loan of an expert—probably a senior draftsman from the House of Commons—to help draft Pakistan's new constitution. The article stated that the cabinet, after receiving the Commission's report in February or March, would take until about May or June to examine the material. Drafting would take another three to four months. Present indications, according to the writer, were that the Basic Democrats might be called upon to elect members to parliament. He concluded: "It will be remembered that the President has said on more than one occasion that the new constitution will be in force by the end of the next year. The earliest it can be enforced is October, and the latest, if the present tentative schedule is not upset, December. . . ."

According to the Interior Minister, Zakir Husain, the question of reviving political parties was receiving the Commission's consideration. He told newsmen in Karachi that, although an expert draftsman would be sought after the cabinet had studied the Commission's report, no country had yet been approached regarding the services of such a person.[26]

Little appeared in the press during the first four months of 1961 about the Commission and its work. On January 2 *Dawn* published an article reviewing the history of the Commission from its date of appointment to the completion of interviewing. The correspondent speculated that the report might be submitted to the President on March 23, the twenty-first anniversary of the Lahore Resolution. In that event, he surmised that the cabinet might complete its drafting by June so that the new Constitution could be promulgated on the third anniversary of the revolution (October 27, 1961). The system of government it provided for, according to "knowledgeable sources," would probably be presidential and unitary. Ibrahim, Zakir Husain and an unidentified cabinet source all assured the public that the Commission report would be in the hands of the President by the end of March, perhaps on the 23rd.[27]

The President made few references to the constitution during this period. In a televised interview in Bonn in January he told German correspondents that it was a misfortune when any country's constitution failed. He said a developing nation must have a constitution which defined the spheres of the executive and the legislative branches in such a way that there could be no breakdown of administrative machinery. He expected the Commission to complete its work in a month or so and hoped the new constitution would be launched by

the end of the year.[28] A few weeks later in Dacca a reporter asked when Pakistan was going to have an interim constitution and hold elections. The President's rejoinder was, "Why do you speculate?" He denied that there was any proposal for an interim constitution and said that while the report of the Commission was being awaited he disapproved of prejudicing the issues.[29]

At the same time in Lahore, Zakir Husain, while no longer suggesting a date for the submission of the report, expressed doubts that general elections could be held by December, even though the government was anxious to hold them as early as possible. He repeated his opinion that the presidential form was the most suitable for Pakistan, but emphasized that this would be decided by the cabinet after it had considered the report of the Constitution Commission. He stated there was no possibility of lifting the ban on political parties before the general elections.[30]

The *Pakistan Observer* had been editorially silent for several months. But in mid-February 1961 two articles and an editorial on the constitution were published. "A Plea for Fundamental Rights" on February 17 was written by a lawyer who urged that specific rights be guaranteed to the citizens with provision for enforcing them.

> We do not [he wrote] suggest that freedom is altogether non-existent in Pakistan. As a matter of fact, except for the setting up of military tribunals and the temporary suspension of parliamentary government, no more restraint is apparent than under the so-called democratic governments which preceded the 1958 Revolution.

"Parliamentary Democracy on Trial" on February 18 was a news story from Montreal discussing two lectures by Arnold Toynbee. Dr. Toynbee cited India as one eastern country which had achieved political stability with parliamentary democracy. He attributed Pakistan's abandonment of democracy for a military regime to the different manner in which Indian Hindus and Indian Muslims reacted to the West. However, he believed President Ayub was sincere in his intention to introduce a new constitution "designed to make his own regime ultimately superfluous."

In the editorial "Change is Life" on February 18 the *Pakistan Observer* stated, "It is not to be expected that there would be unanimity in the country about the constitution. . . . Perhaps it is just as well," the editorial continued, that there were always "some non-conformists . . . to question, to demur." The constitution should be flexible "so that it [could] conform to the changing tempers of a people." Stability and freedom were indispensable. "The future constitution should be such as to serve the purpose of both these fundamental values."

The editorial concluded, "This will be facilitated if the Constitution be not so rigid as to make change impossible when change would be vital."

A statement revealing the constant behind-the-scenes work of the government to influence people's attitudes was made by the director-general of Radio Pakistan. He told a meeting of the advisory committee of the Lahore Radio Pakistan station that the main aim of radio programs during the last two years had been to re-orient the listener's outlook in conformity with the spirit of the revolution. He said that special stress on the best in culture and tradition was reflected through all program categories.[31]

Shortly after this, from a quite unexpected quarter came an opinion on the failure of parliamentary democracy. Justice Sharif was presiding over the trial of Mushtaq Ahmad Gurmani before the West Pakistan EBDO tribunal. On a complaint by the prosecution that Gurmani, governor of West Pakistan from 1955 to 1957, used unconstitutional means in keeping a certain chief minister in power, the Justice broke in:

> Anybody would die rather than leave a chair. Application or success of a constitution depends upon the people who work it. Our people are not as awakened as Britishers are. In fact the late constitution was not even given a trial. It was yet in the transitory stage. Everybody was out in competition to violate the constitution. That is why it is stated parliamentary system can succeed most with hereditary monarchy; otherwise there would always be a tussle between the President and the Prime Minister. Mr. Iskander Mirza also wanted to continue with his office as long as he could.[32]

As the Constitution Commission approached the end of its work fewer speculations and no hasty interviews were reported in the press. On March 1 the Commission notified the temporary staff that their services would be terminated beginning March 14. Those who had been on loan to the Commission from various central and provincial government agencies were to return to their departments. At this point, according to the correspondent from Lahore, the Commission had completed its recommendations on most of its terms of reference. After the cabinet's consideration of the report, a team of experts was to draw up the constitution. This work was expected to take about six weeks.[33] After a session in Karachi dealing with the submission of the report and dissolution of the Commission, the members were to return to Lahore on March 21 to complete the final report which would run to about two hundred and fifty pages. The Commission expected to present its recommendations to the President April 15.[34]

With the report of the Commission so near completion, it seemed expedient to the President that steps be taken to insure the achieving of his goal even if he were personally "unable to discharge his duties due to illness or any other cause." Accordingly he promulgated an amendment to the State Arrangements Order 1959, which had provided a means of filling the office of president through a succession council, consisting of the members of the central cabinet, the three defense service heads and the two governors. The amendment of 1961 provided that the acting president elected by the succession council was to govern with the advice of the cabinet, which was enjoined to consider the Commission's report "with all convenient speed." The acting president was expressly forbidden by this order to dismiss any minister.[35] However, circumstances rendered it unnecessary to put this order and its amendment into effect.

Strikes, riots and demonstrations by West Pakistani students during March and April, while not apparently caused by the internal situation nevertheless had political overtones. On February 4 communal rioting broke out in Jabalpur in central India and quickly spread to other parts of India.[36] At this time the Algerian situation was acute and Patrice Lumumba had recently been assassinated in the Congo. Possibly any one of these events would have been sufficient cause for a student demonstration and on February 23 Lahore students appealed to the district magistrate for permission to march in protest against the murder of Lumumba and the massacre of Indian Muslims in Jabalpur. Permission was granted and the police maintained order as thousands of students swarmed through the main thoroughfare of Lahore in the largest procession since the military takeover.[37]

Unlike this peaceful demonstration, shouting Karachi students attacked the Indian Chancery with stones. Two days later, the students went out in even larger numbers, tried to enter a Hindu temple, and the police were forced to use tear gas and lathis. All Karachi schools and colleges were ordered closed for one week and the martial law administrator warned that anyone who broke the ban on public meetings and activities of a political nature would be dealt with severely. The Interior Minister, Zakir Husain, also warned against repetition of such acts of rowdyism. In two days the police arrested more than one hundred and eighty persons under Martial Law Regulations Nos. 55 and 79 which prohibited organizing or attending any meeting or procession of a political nature. Two persons died and more than three hundred were injured.[38] Most of the students were soon released and on March 16 only ten students began trial before the summary military court. Eight persons were convicted

and sentenced to imprisonment of from six months to a year; two were found not guilty.[39]

A few days after these sentences were pronounced the Karachi students again walked out of their classrooms to strike for the release of their classmates. During a procession on April 7, the students threw stones at the police who made "a mild lathi charge" against the students. Following this incident, no meetings were permitted and pre-censorship was imposed by the administrator of Karachi on any news relating to student affairs.[40] It was June 1 before that censorship was withdrawn and on July 1 the eight convicted Karachi students were released.[41]

In March 1961 a controversial but extremely significant piece of social legislation was promulgated by President Ayub Khan. On the recommendation of the Commission on Marriage and Family Laws set up in August 1955, the Muslim Family Laws Ordinance 1961[42] was published on March 3. The ordinance sought to protect women against polygamy, too-easy divorce and insufficient maintenance. The Family Laws Ordinance was met with enthusiasm by women, especially the members of the All-Pakistan Women's Association (APWA), who had long urged the passage of such a law.[43] The reaction of the traditional Islamic leaders was one of shock. Powers which had been theirs, traditionally for ages and legally since 1876, were now to be turned over to the chairmen of the union councils. Maulana Ihteshamul Haq, the "traditionalist religious scholar" member of the marriage commission and the lone dissenter to its report,[44] appealed to the government to postpone enforcement of the Muslim Family Laws Ordinance until after consultation with the *ulema.* "All ulema have a unanimous opinion regarding the Islamic Shariat Law," he said in a statement to the press, "and all of them are united on matters relating to marriage. To give a final shape to the order on the recommendations of some legal experts and social workers will, in my opinion, be a premature step."[45]

Twelve Karachi *ulema* issued a joint statement in which they agreed "that if the President set up a Ministry of Religious Affairs and appointed Ulema-i-Ahle as Qazis (registrars) the problems and difficulties of jurisprudence and religion . . . [could] be overcome through mutual discussions."[46] Fourteen Lahore *ulema* attacked the Muslim Family Laws Ordinance but the press was forbidden to report unfavorable views, and some persons were arrested for distributing pamphlets expressing these opinions.[47] The government arrested Khan Abdul Ghaffar Khan, leader of the Pakhtunistan Movement, because of his opposition to the ordinance.[48]

Another conflict between the government and Muslim leaders re-

ceived public attention in March 1961. The month of Ramazan, during which orthodox Muslims fast from before sunrise until after sunset, corresponded roughly with the period from mid-February to mid-March of 1961. Traditionally the new moon—which signifies the end of Ramazan and the beginning of the feast day of Id-ul-Fitr—must be sighted by properly qualified witnesses. The date set by the meteorological department was not accepted by the *maulanas* and East Pakistan observed Id on a different day from that celebrated in parts of West Pakistan, and Karachi observed the occasion on two different days. The confusion that prevailed led the President to determine that hereafter the date of Id would be set by the meteorological department.[49] Thus the antagonism between the religious leaders and the government was intensified just as the Constitution Commission was getting ready to present its report to the President, and student riots did little to ease the situation.

In mid-March President Ayub attended the Commonwealth Conference in London where he told the Pakistan Society:

> If our system of Government in Pakistan succeeds, it may be something that will be useful to many new countries in Asia and Africa bedevilled with the problem of finding out what will work and what will not work in their country. . . .
> We have appointed a Constitution Commission which has finished its investigation. In a month's time they should be ready with their report. We will examine it and let us hope that we shall have the right kind of constitution which will suit us.
> A lot of good things are happening in Pakistan. It shows our people are sound. Give them the right system and leadership and they will respond.[50]

The chief theme of the Pakistan Day Supplement of the *Pakistan Observer* (March 23, 1961) was exemplified by articles entitled "Pakistan an Islamic State," "Origin of Muslim Political Movement" and "A Scientist Reflects on the Islamic Way of Life." The role of Islam in the evolution of Pakistan was underscored by the President in his Pakistan Day message. He made a special appeal to the *ulema* to recognize "the progressive nature" and "stress on knowledge and discovery" of the Islamic religion.[51] The other theme of the day was national unity. President Ayub announced to the men of the armed forces at their ceremonial parade in Dacca:

> You will be glad to learn that we have decided to raise two more battalions from East Pakistan. This is another proof of the progress and onward march of the people of East Pakistan. Please do not forget that despite geographical distances, East and West Pakistan are one country and one nation. Our unity is not dependent on any material values but it depends entirely on a common spiritual base.[52]

The *Pakistan Observer* on March 25 commented favorably on the President's remarks, and agreed that the "political, economic and social affinities should be the result of . . . spiritual affinity, and not the other way about." The editorial courageously suggested that

> . . . while in broad outlines, it should be possible to frame economic policies that should apply to the whole country, East Pakistan's special problems give its economy a special character of its own that may require special fiscal, economic and administrative policies to deal with them. The very fact that West Pakistan's capital is rather shy in coming to this province is an indication that it would be a mistake to treat the economies of both provinces as wholly one.

The *Pakistan Observer* used the incorporation of Karachi into West Pakistan, since the capital had shifted to Rawalpindi, as the point of departure for another emphatic appeal on March 28 to avoid uneven development:

> Geographically Karachi always was and remains a part of West Pakistan. Its prosperity reacted favorably on the economy of West Pakistan. But to the building up of the city, its facilities and its status, the whole country has contributed. . . .
>
> The decision also by implication is an admission that West Pakistan and East Pakistan are, for administrative purposes, two distinct entities which come together on the national level in the national government alone. It also underlines the necessity of making special efforts for the balanced development of this province to correct the lopsidedness introduced into our economy by huge Central expenditure on development and defence incurred regionally in West Pakistan. The building up of the new capital at Islamabad will give employment to men and resources in West Pakistan. Promises of developments in East Pakistan have been made to correspond to developments in the other wing. We trust these will be fulfilled vigorously.

These two editorials represented a breakthrough in the publication of public opinion in East Pakistan. Heretofore, economic discussion had been a government monologue. There had been no published reply to the government's emphasis on a unified budget for a unified nation. Boldly but cautiously, the *Pakistan Observer* made a dialogue of it.

A three-day governors' conference was held in Dacca the last week of March to consider the report of the Planning Commission, the proposed survey of the industries in the provinces and the administration of the two provincial Water and Power Development Authorities. During the conference certain cabinet ministers spoke in Dacca and faced some difficult questions from their audiences. A. K. Khan, Minister for Industries, addressing the Dacca University Economic Association, emphasized the government's decision to accelerate development in East Pakistan. After painting "a rosy picture about the possibilities of

industrial development of the Province," the Minister "faced a barrage of questions." Asked to comment on the spectacular rise in prices after the decontrol of textile goods, he said that free play of the economy was essential, and called control a strait jacket which hampered development. Another questioner asked why East Pakistan's Karnafuli Paper Mill products were sold in West Pakistan at the same price as in East Pakistan whereas West Pakistan's Zeal Pak cement was more expensive than imported cement in East Pakistan. A. K. Khan's somewhat irrelevant reply was that East Pakistan would be allowed to import cement from Japan. The Industries Minister promised that jute industrialists would be required to reinvest part of their earnings for further expansion, that East Pakistan would have a steel mill and an oil refinery, and that the number of looms and spindles would be substantially increased. All this, he declared, would create employment opportunities for East Pakistani people.[53]

Commerce Minister Hafizur Rahman was bombarded with similar questions at the Dacca University Commerce Association meeting. A professor in the Department of Commerce asked the minister to explain the price differentials in East Pakistan's paper and West Pakistan's cement. Rahman replied, "I did not expect such a question from a university teacher. The price is higher because cement . . . has to incur high transport costs while in the case of paper this cost is comparatively small." Not satisfied, the professor appealed to vice-chancellor Dr. Mahmud Hussain who gave a similar answer and furthermore added that the production cost of West Pakistan cement was higher than that of imported cement. Still unconvinced, the persistent professor wanted to know why transport charges were not added to the cost of paper. The vice-chancellor conceded that the professor was justified in his statement while the Commerce Minister made no reply. When asked if industrialists would be required to reinvest their profits, Hafizur Rahman burst out, "This is a wild and ill-conceived suggestion. Create inducements for investment. Economic development can't be achieved with restrictions."[54] Both of these ministers were natives and residents of East Pakistan, as was Home Affairs Minister Zakir Husain, who showed an equal lack of sympathy for local aspirations when he said, sometime later, that the clamor about disparity between East and West Pakistan should end.[55]

During April government officials continued to emphasize national integration and the efforts being made to improve the economy of East Pakistan. The chairman of the Pakistan Railway Board said that decentralization of the Pakistan Eastern Railway was under active consideration, as part of the present regime's policy.[56] At an economic conference arranged by the Bureau of National Reconstruction Presi-

dent Ayub stressed the importance of national integration and economic development but stated that political stability was a prerequisite to both. He also discussed allocation of resources and economic development.[57] Later at the eleventh session of the All-Pakistan Economic Conference at Hyderabad, ten delegates participated in a symposium on "A United Budget for Pakistan." The consensus was that the present budget system with modifications could be made workable. It was considered premature, however, to speculate about the feasibility of a united budget until the form of the future government was known.[58]

Mohammad Shoaib, the Finance Minister, explained to journalists that the government planned to make up through PIDC any differential between anticipated and actual private investment in the industrial sector in East Pakistan during the second five-year plan period. According to the news story he emphasized the "more active role" which PIDC had already been assigned "with regard to East Pakistan as compared to West Pakistan where it would more or less remain dormant during the plan period." How much "more" or "less" the amount would be, Shoaib did not disclose, although he said PIDC was to spend Rs. 525,000,000 in the east wing.[59]

Toward the end of April it was announced that the Constitution Commission had completed its year-long deliberations. A final reading of the draft report was under way in Lahore and the Commission was holding daily meetings to end its work by April 30. It was expected that Justice Shahabuddin would present the recommendations to President Ayub Khan the first week of May.[60] Finally at 7:00 p.m. on April 29, 1961, the report—two hundred and eighty pages divided into seventeen chapters—was signed by Justice Shahabuddin and the other Commission members.[61]

The next day Minister for Home Affairs Zakir Husain, in an interview published in a Lahore daily, announced that the report would be submitted to President Ayub within two days. After a month or so for consideration by a special committee of the cabinet, it would be voted on by the cabinet and then turned over to a drafting committee. He indicated that the governments of the United Kingdom and the United States had already been approached to suggest the names of constitutional experts. These experts would be assisted by a team of Pakistani jurists. Husain did not feel the drafting would take long, but he could not be specific as to the length of time required. However, the new constitution would be in effect before the end of the year so that the general elections could be held in February and the new parliament could convene on Pakistan Day, March 23, 1962. The Minister for Home Affairs concluded by stating that the Presi-

dent's decision on the recommendations of the Commission would be given as soon as possible, after which no further suggestions on the future form of government would be entertained.[62]

On May 3 came the announcement that the Constitution Commission's report would be presented to President Ayub Khan at a formal ceremony in the President's House on May 6. The report would then be referred to a cabinet subcommittee which "informed circles" indicated, Manzur Qadir, Minister for Foreign Affairs and an eminent lawyer, would probably head.[63] Experts on constitutional law from both wings might be associated with the work at the drafting stage. It was now suggested that a foreign expert's services would be utilized only at the time of the final reading of the draft.[64]

Justice Shahabuddin made the presentation of the two-volume report during the May 6 ceremony and President Ayub noted that a momentous period of Pakistan's history had begun, that all must act with wisdom and courage and rise above petty or parochial considerations. He promised to give the recommendations of the Commission the greatest consideration in discharging "the supreme obligation of giving people a constitution that [would] bring solidarity, peace and happiness." He appealed to the people not to indulge in controversy or speculation regarding the constitution and said he had promised the chairman that the Commission's report would be published as soon as the draft of the proposed constitution had been completed. At the same time he intended to publish his own and his cabinet's thinking "as a historical record so that future generations [could] know the reasons and philosophy behind the provisions of the Constitution."[65]

No Pakistani newspaper had offered any explanation for the delay in the completion of the Commission's report nor was any indication of the recommendations of the Commission mentioned until after the constitution was announced ten months later. Yet the *Statesman* on June 4 hinted at the reason for the delay in giving a résumé of the Commission's report:

> The indications are that Pakistan will have a federal system of Government under the new constitution, though much against the wishes of the President who has repeatedly pleaded for a unitary system. The unitary system has not been found practicable, mainly because of geographical factors, by the Constitution Commission. The five members from East Pakistan, it is said, threatened to refuse to sign the commission's report if a unitary system was recommended. They took a united stand and ultimately they succeeded. . . .
>
> The 280-page report has recommended the Presidential form of Government on a federal pattern. The Centre will have two Houses . . . and the Provinces will have legislatures. . . . The electoral college for the first general elections will be the Union Councils (Basic

Democracies) but the next elections should be held through a direct vote. . . .

The elections will be held on the basis of separate electorate. The President, who will be the head of state and the Chief Executive, will have extensive powers to run the administration. He will be empowered to declare an emergency and dissolve Parliament. He will nominate his Cabinet Ministers from among the elected members of Parliament but will have jurisdiction to include in his Cabinet people from outside Parliament. . . .

Both Houses will maintain parity between the two wings of the country. The provincial administration will be run through a Governor to be appointed by the President. . . .

As a member of the Cabinet sub-committee put it, "Not many changes will be made in the Constitution Commission's recommendations. Only here and there some minor amendments may be made; otherwise the Commission's recommendations are fair enough and will be accepted in toto.

On June 7 it was announced that the central government had dissolved the Constitution Commission effective May 31. Government officers assigned to the Commission had returned to their original departments. Only a skeleton staff was retained until mid-June to wind up the administrative work.[66]

## NOTES

1. *Pakistan Observer* (Dacca), June 28, 1960, p. 3.
2. On June 25, 1960, the government announced the decision to make Khulna East Pakistan's fourth division.
3. *Dawn* (Karachi), August 27, 1960.
4. *Pakistan Observer*, August 31, 1960, p. 4.
5. *Ibid.*, and *Dawn*, September 1-October 2, 1960.
6. *Dawn*, October 11, p. 12; October 23, 1960, p. 9.
7. *Ibid.*, January 2, 1961, p. 1.
8. While he was in London attending the Commonwealth conference in May, 1960, President Md. Ayub Khan's article, "Pakistan Perspective," appeared in *Foreign Affairs*, XXXVIII (July 1960), 547-556. *Dawn*'s reaction may be seen in its editorial of July 17, 1960, p. 7, which said that the article "enunciates the philosophy of the Revolution in the most impressive and convincing manner."
9. *Statesman* (Calcutta), July 25, 1960, p. 1.
10. *Dawn* and *Statesman*, July 26, 1960, p. 1.
11. *Pakistan Observer*, July 25, 1960, p. 1.
12. *Ibid.*, July 27, 1960, p. 1.
13. *Dawn*, July 31, 1960, p. 1.
14. *Ibid.*, September 19, 1960, p. 6.
15. *Pakistan Observer*, July 24, p. 1; July 26, p. 1; August 9, 1960, p. 1.
16. *Ibid.*, September 10, 1960, p. 1.

17. *Ibid.,* and *Dawn,* September 28, 1960, p. 1.

18. *Pakistan Observer,* October 1, 1960, p. 1; Khan, Md. Ayub, *Speeches and Statements* (Karachi: Pakistan Publications) III (July 1960-June 1961), 25-32.

19. By Mahesh Chandra, October 3, p. 6; October 4, 1960, p. 6.

20. *Pakistan Observer,* November 8, p. 8; November 15, 1960, p. 3.

21. *Ibid.,* November 17, 1960, p. 5.

22. *Dawn,* November 26, 1960, p. 1.

23. *Pakistan Observer,* November 16, 1960, pp. 1, 5.

24. *Ibid.,* November 17, 1960, p. 1.

25. *Ibid.,* December 5, 1960, p. 1.

26. *Dawn,* December 18, 1960, p. 12.

27. *Pakistan Observer,* January 6, p. 1; January 18, p. 1; February 16, 1961, p. 1.

28. *Ibid.,* January 25, 1961, p. 1.

29. *Dawn,* February 17, p. 1; February 18, 1961, p. 1.

30. *Pakistan Observer,* February 18, p. 1; February 19, 1961, p. 1.

31. *Dawn,* February 23, 1961, p. 8.

32. *Pakistan Observer,* March 13, 1961, p. 6.

33. *Ibid.,* March 3, 1961, p. 5.

34. *Ibid.,* March 12, p. 1; *Dawn,* March 12, 1961, p. 9.

35. *Pakistan Observer,* March 7, p. 1; March 8, 1961, p. 8.

36. *Ibid.,* February 6, 1961, p. 1; *Dawn,* February 20-25, 1961, p. 1.

37. *Pakistan Observer,* February 24, 1961, p. 8.

38. *Dawn,* February 26-28, March 1, p. 1; *Statesman,* February 27-28, p. 1; *Pakistan Observer,* March 1, 1961, p. 1.

39. *Dawn,* March 17, p. 9; March 21, p. 6; March 22, p. 9; March 23, p. 8; March 25, p. 6; March 31, 1961, p. 1.

40. *Ibid.,* April 4, p. 6; April 5, p. 9; April 6, pp. 1, 9; April 7, p. 1; April 8, 1961, p. 1.

41. *Ibid.,* June 1, p. 1; July 3, 1961, p. 1.

42. Text in *ibid.,* March 3, 1961, p. 9.

43. *Ibid.,* March 4, p. 6; March 5, 1961, pp. 6, 12.

44. Freeland Abbott, "Pakistan's New Marriage Law: A Reflection of Quranic Interpretation," *Asian Survey* I, No. 11 (January 1962), 26-32.

45. *Dawn,* March 5, 1961, p. 6.

46. *Ibid.,* March 8, 1961, p. 6.

47. Abbott, *op. cit.,* p. 30.

48. *Statesman,* April 13, 1961, p. 8.

49. *Dawn,* March 15, p. 6; March 18, p. 1; March 19, p. 1; March 21, pp. 1, 8; March 22, p. 6; April 13, 1961, p. 1.

50. *Pakistan Observer,* March 17, 1961, p. 1.

51. Khan, Md. Ayub, *op. cit.,* III, 106-109; *Dawn,* March 23, 1961, p. 6.

52. *Pakistan Observer,* March 24, 1961, p. 1; Khan, *op. cit.,* III, 110-111.

53. *Pakistan Observer,* March 28, 1961, p. 1.

54. *Ibid.*

55. *Ibid.,* May 23, 1961.

56. *Dawn,* April 4, 1961, p. 1.

57. *Ibid.,* April 6, 1961, p. 1.

58. *Pakistan Observer,* April 17, p. 1, and *Dawn,* April 18, 1961, p. 8.

59. *Pakistan Observer,* April 30, p. 1, and *Dawn,* April 30, 1961, p. 9.

60. *Pakistan Observer,* April 26, 1961, p. 1.
61. *Ibid.,* April 30, 1961.
62. *Ibid.,* May 1, 1961, p. 1.
63. *Ibid.,* May 3, p. 8 and May 4, 1961.
64. *Ibid.,* May 6, 1961, p. 1.
65. *Ibid.,* May 7, 1961, p. 1, and Khan, Md. Ayub, *op. cit.,* III, 127-128.
66. *Pakistan Observer,* June 8, 1961, p. 2.

# CHAPTER IX

# THE CABINET SUBCOMMITTEE

## (May—September 1961)

ON MAY 9, 1961, *Dawn* reported the selection of the five-man subcommittee whose job it was to evaluate the recommendations of the Commission's report. The members included: Manzur Qadir, Minister for Foreign Affairs, chairman; Mohammad Shoaib, Finance Minister; Zulfiqar Ali Bhutto, Minister for Fuel, Power and Natural Resources; Mohammad Ibrahim, Law Minister; Abul Kasem Khan, Industries Minister. Shortly thereafter, two other members were added by the President: Habibur Rahman, Minister of National Reconstruction and Information and Akhtar Hussain, Minister for Education and Scientific Research.[1] Sheikh Abdul Hamid, secretary of the Ministry of Law, was also made available to the subcommittee.[2]

The *Statesman* of June 4 pointed out that parity was achieved between the two wings in the membership of the subcommittee. Ibrahim, Abul Kasem Khan and Habibur Rahman represented East Pakistan. Qadir was from the Punjab and Bhutto from Sind in West Pakistan. Shoaib and Akhtar Hussain were residents of the west wing but actually were representative of the refugees. It was noted, however, that no one represented the Northwest Frontier Province or Baluchistan.

According to the *Pakistan Observer*'s Rawalpindi correspondent on May 11 the subcommittee was expected to meet "more or less in continuous session," with intervals to give attention to important ministerial work, and should complete its assignment within two to three months. If the cabinet reviewed the subcommittee's report in August the fundamentals of the future constitution might be announced by the President by mid-September. Then constitutional experts from both wings would help in the actual drafting. "Any foreign expert —preferably British or Australian," according to the article, "may be secured only at the last stages when the draft constitution would need final touch-up and pruning."

Because of Qadir's and then Shoaib's absence, the subcommittee's

105

first meeting, originally scheduled for May 17, was postponed until the third week of June.[3] Meanwhile reporters tried to elicit as much information as possible from government officials.

Ibrahim told journalists that the constitution would definitely be put into effect by July 1, 1962, and elections would probably be held by the following March. The subcommittee would start its formal work, Ibrahim said, towards the third week of June and, meeting continuously, would probably take from one to one-and-a-half months to compile the members' views. In that event, the President might announce the fundamentals of the constitution, as he had promised to do, by the middle of August.[4]

The Minister of Home Affairs, Zakir Husain, told newsmen that the constitution might be introduced even earlier than July of next year. The President would hear all points of view but the final decision would be his. He assured his hearers that, at any rate, the new constitution would not be a bundle of compromises as the 1956 Constitution had been. Husain told the union councillors of Jessore district that one of the vital aims of the present government was to give the people through the new constitution "some system" to achieve political stability. The Minister was firm in the opinion that "the previous experience of the parliamentary form of Government [had] proved a failure" and that the country needed a different system. Speaking to members of Basic Democracies in Chittagong, Husain condemned the bitterness in sections of East Pakistan against West Pakistan. He said that both wings should see that nothing jeopardized the unity of the country.[5]

In an address to the Hyderabad Bar Association Z. A. Bhutto said that the constitution would provide realistically the basic ingredients for national progress, stability and solidarity. The constitution would be introduced by the end of this year, and there was no possibility of the Commission report being put to public vote before its acceptance. A question as to whether the government was contemplating any change in the Family Laws Ordinance in view of the criticism expressed by fourteen leading *ulema* of the country elicited only an evasive response from the Minister.[6] Bhutto told the Hyderabad municipal committee that the new constitution would be based on both the parliamentary and presidential systems.[7]

Individual subcommittee members began studying the Commission's recommendations in early June. Manzur Qadir was to leave for Nathiagali on June 2, "and it is presumed," wrote a correspondent, "he would devote the next six weeks to work relating to the constitution in the calm, cool and relaxed atmosphere of the hills there."[8] The

subcommittee met to begin its deliberations on June 27. Sessions were to continue until the end of July or early August, except for the period of July 11-20 when Qadir and Shoaib were to accompany the President to the United States.[9] However, the subcommittee adjourned July 4 and reassembled July 24 for the second round of meetings with the intention of keeping at the job until it was finished.[10]

It had been anticipated that an early June governors' conference would consider the administrative steps necessary to the launching of the new constitution. It had also been hoped that the President would reveal to the conference participants a broad timetable for completion of the constitution. However, the governors' conference was devoted chiefly to the Basic Democracies.[11]

At a press conference in early July Shoaib pointed out that the budget presented to the country on July 1 contained specific items for the holding of elections and the inauguration of the constitution. This was evidence, he said, of the present regime's keen desire to restore a full-fledged democratic government as soon as possible.[12]

During the summer of 1961 President Ayub Khan addressed various groups throughout the nation. Now that the Constitution Commission report had been submitted, he stressed more general themes such as the Islamic basis of the constitution and the need for national unity rather than the form of government. He referred frequently to Basic Democracies as a necessary prelude to the constitution. The President's speeches also became more closely directed toward particular groups: East Pakistan, resentful of economic and political injustice; the *ulema*, with divergent views on how to ensure an Islamic constitution and hostility to the new Muslim Family Laws; the bar and the bench, fearful that a new judicial system would be substituted for the English patterns to which they were accustomed; women, with the educated few strongly united and vocal in favor of the Muslim Family Laws; and finally students, unpredictable, inconsistent and volatile.

After the emphasis on the unitary budget during the summer of 1960 as the ministers toured the east wing, not much appeared in the press on East Pakistani economic matters. Now as the cabinet subcommittee began its work in June, 1961, the economic implications of the future constitution dominated discussions in the Dacca press.

President Ayub Khan visited the east wing in May, partly to inspect cyclone-struck areas and partly to propound the issue of one economy. The importance given to the President's remarks during this visit is reflected in the headlines of the *Pakistan Observer*. On May 24 the lead article's four headlines proclaimed: "Equitable development of East wing," "Ayub explains foreign exchange issue," "Officers to be

stationed in respective wings," and "Fallacy of two economies routed." The next day the lead article dealt first with the Kashmir affair, then "Ayub dwells upon gold price issue," "Cross-section of people met," and "One economy prescribed."

President Ayub Khan promised during a press conference in Dacca that his regime would do all in its power for the development of East Pakistan. He discussed in detail the manning of the provincial administration, development expenditures, and the utilization of foreign exchange earnings in the east wing. He announced that no West Pakistani officer would be sent to East Pakistan in the future unless it was "absolutely necessary." This decision resulted from the long-standing complaint that East Pakistanis were discriminated against in civil service appointments and that West Pakistani officers antagonized the local people. When various East Pakistani officers assured the President that the feeling against West Pakistani officers was the result of political emotionalism, he admitted they might be correct. However, since this emotionalism did create a "certain type of climate," it was better to let East Pakistani officers take over all responsibilities.[13]

President Ayub conceded that in the past some of East Pakistan's foreign exchange earnings from jute had been utilized in West Pakistan, but the government would now do all it could to assist in East Pakistani economic development. He explained that the Pakistan Industrial Finance Corporation had been reorganized to give loans to medium- and small-sized industries, especially in the east wing, and both the Water and Power Development Authority (WAPDA) and the Agricultural Development Corporation were now able to offer greater employment opportunities to East Pakistanis. The President was convinced that the idea of two economies which had been suggested to him was disastrous and might well lead to the disintegration of the country. On this visit President Ayub was exposed to a representative cross-section of viewpoints in East Pakistan when he addressed such leadership groups as officials, students, economists and members of Basic Democracies, from whom he had invited frank expressions of opinion.

Shortly after the President's departure, the monthly symposium of the Islamic Academy of Dacca was devoted to a consideration of "How to build Pakistan into a well-knit nation." One of the papers by Rehman Sobhan, an economist of Dacca University, pointed out that East Pakistan's per capita income had been going down while that of West Pakistan rose. He advocated that each wing should have full control over its own resources. After the papers were read, "the proceedings turned into a hot and lively discussion."[14] The idea of eco-

nomic autonomy for each wing had not been published earlier but it was extensively discussed among Dacca intellectuals. The President during his visit the previous week had denounced this idea as "loose and irresponsible talk." Discussions about two economies nevertheless continued privately through the summer.

The East Pakistan Chambers of Commerce and Industry and certain trade associations prepared a statement concerning the industrialization of East Pakistan. The statement noted the rapid capital accumulation of West Pakistan immediately after partition and asserted that the increasing disparity in the standard of living between the two wings was the result of a "deliberate" government policy. Particularly stressed was the inadequacy of the parity formula for allocation of resources under which the government's development expenditure for the fifty-five per cent of the population in East Pakistan would be the same as that for the forty-five per cent in West Pakistan. Because the central government's first five-year plan had underemphasized East Pakistan's needs in regard to the communications system, power supply, and educational and technical facilities, the statement by the business groups urged an accelerated program for East Pakistan in the second five-year plan.[15] The *Pakistan Observer* commented editorially on June 22:

> Even without belittling the genuine attempts for the balanced development of this wing of the country, and the real efforts now being made, it is doubtful if the deficiencies of the past can be made up by the rate of progress that can be maintained now. And this rate is higher than in the past.

The development program for 1961-62, approved by the National Economic Council in mid-June, allocated East Pakistan Rs. 62 crores and West Pakistan Rs. 60 crores.[16] Finance Minister Shoaib stated at the end of the fiscal year that the present regime had no intention of following the policy of separate economies for East and West Pakistan.[17] East Pakistani reaction to the new budget was mixed. The *Pakistan Observer* on July 2 said that "the belated recognition that East Pakistan was among the most underdeveloped areas of the country" was one of the heartening features of the budget. However, the budget provision was "not an adequate palliative. Its only redeeming feature [was] that the powers that be [were] conscious of the disparity in the level of development between the two wings."

The secretary of the Finance Department delivered a major address over Radio Pakistan on economic progress and policy under the military regime. He concluded,

> It will be apparent that determined efforts are now being made by
> the Government to overcome the deficiencies in the economic life of
> [East Pakistan] and to pave the way for a balanced economic growth.[18]

As the subcommittee's work stretched out through the summer of
1961 more and more concessions for East Pakistan were—if not promised—at least considered. Ibrahim said preparations for establishing
the subsidiary capital in Dacca would be started this year.[19] The central government announced that it would continue construction of
the Mercantile Marine Academy in Chittagong—work which had in-
explicably stopped in February.[20] Industries Minister A. K. Khan said
that bifurcation of PIDC was being considered and that the East
Pakistan cement factory would be expanded to meet that wing's needs.
He talked about a steel mill for Chittagong "in three to four years."[21]
However, ten weeks later he admitted that the subject of the bifurcation of the PIDC had not yet come up for discussion in the cabinet
and the final report of the proposed steel mill for Chittagong had not
been submitted by the foreign experts.[22]

In August a committee was appointed to submit a report on the
distribution of sources of revenue between the center and provinces to
the Cabinet subcommittee on the constitution. Finance Minister
Mohammad Shoaib said that the new fiscal committee had been asked
to recommend what changes could be effected in the existing pattern.
A reporter asked, "Does the fact that the committee is to report on
the distribution of revenues between the Center and the provinces
imply that the future constitutional structure will be federal?" Shoaib
stated no such thing was implied; the government had just asked for
data on the subject.[23]

Minister of Commerce Hafizur Rahman, at the opening of a new
electrical equipment manufacturing plant in East Pakistan urged rapid
industrialization in the east wing. At the same time he warned that
East Pakistanis should change their attitude toward West Pakistan
and the central government:

> The Minister regretted that some people were still suffering from
> complexes which, he said, were the result of foreign domination.
> He said that feelings of distrust, jealousy and rivalry existing among
> the people even after independence were disappointing. He hoped
> that people of all walks of life and professions, including industrialists
> would realize its seriousness and make a serious attempt to shake
> off those feelings and complexes to join hands together for the devel-
> opment of the country.[24]

The government continued to emphasize Islamic principles as the
basis of the future constitution, at the same time seeking to modernize
the attitudes of orthodox Muslim leaders. Family planning and the

new Muslim Family Laws were difficult for many tradition-minded Muslims to accept. Some religious leaders, however, believed these reforms were in conformity with Quranic principles. At the end of May on the celebration of Id-ul-Azha, which commemorates the willingness of Ibrahim to sacrifice his son, President Ayub's message to the nation was a moving appeal to rediscover and apply the principles of Islam. Over the centuries religion had become "more dogmatic and academic and less dynamic and practical," he declared. And while it was customary "to recite and teach the Holy Quran as a matter of grace," the President felt that little effort was made to understand its implications. Principles were not meant to become static, but rather to be followed and practiced.

> One of the most dominating features of Islam [he said] is that its principles are timeless and eternal, and make it possible for every age to apply and implement them in the light of its requirements and environments. . . . They are a beacon-light for the faithful. . . .
> Dear countrymen: Beacon-lights are meant for guidance and not for stagnation. Stagnation is a manifestation of darkness and needs no light to grow and flourish. The secret of real progress is that we should comprehend the basic principles of Islam, hold fast to them and under the search light of the past, discover fresh avenues for their application in the present and the future.

President Ayub stated his conception of the crucial importance of Islam to Pakistan:

> There is also another matter to which I wish to draw your pointed attention. Please do remember that no other country or nation is in such dire need of depending on Islam as Pakistan. If, God forbid, other countries of the world choose to stray away from the path of Islam, then, whatever the consequences in the other world, in this world at least they can still afford to exist as nations and communities. The position of Pakistan is entirely different.
> Our country was founded in the name of Islam and it can subsist only on this name. There is no other basis for our national cohesion and solidarity except Islam. . . . We must translate our idealism into action for our sheer survival.[25]

The central government, in an effort to make constructive use of the Islamic religious leaders' abilities and in the hope of modernizing their thinking, directed the West Pakistan government to work out terms of service in its religious institutions for trained *ulema*.[26] By the middle of June new pay scales had been established for the *imams* and *khatibs* and in August a leading United Arab Republic scholar was engaged to advise the Pakistan government on setting up an academy for training religious leaders.[27] There was even talk of setting up a ministry of religious affairs at the center.

President Ayub Khan replied at length in June to a letter written

him by Mufti Mohammad Shafi, chairman of the managing committee of the Darul Uloom, on the Family Laws Ordinance. The President referred the detailed points raised in the letter to the ministry concerned; he wished to make only a few general observations. He referred first to polygamy: "I consider it a barbaric torture of the highest order. As the Head of State, I just cannot close my eyes to it." The President proffered what he believed "the only effective way of eradicating matrimonial malpractices"—namely, "to formulate such rules and regulations within the framework of divine injunctions as may control the practice of reckless and indiscriminate polygamy." He declared that the new Muslim Family Laws did not conflict with any injunction of the Quran and he clearly charged the religious leaders with their role in the development of Pakistan:

> . . . I would like to emphasize that a great burden of responsibility rests on the shoulders of those whom God has endowed with the knowledge and understanding of our faith. That responsibility is to liberate religion from the debris of wrong superstitions and prejudices and to make it keep pace with the march of time.[28]

But the President's convictions were far from being accepted unanimously. A paper given at a weekly seminar of the Islamic Academy in Dacca appealed for the restoration of Muslim law to "its original form." The writer believed in the primitive law that an adulteress should be stoned to death and an incorrigible thief's hand should be cut off. Other members of the seminar contended that Muslim law needed changing from time to time but "within the limitations of the Holy Quran and Sunnah [Islamic tradition]." Justice Sharif warned that anti-Pakistan *ulema* were not extinct and that those who believed the very idea of Pakistan was un-Islamic might resume their activities at any time.[29]

The Muslim Family Laws, originally to become effective in June, went into effect July 15. Shortly thereafter the arbitration councils provided for in the Ordinance were set up and the regulations regarding registration of marriage, the taking of a second wife and divorce were made known in detail.[30]

In July Habibur Rahman, the Minister for National Reconstruction and Information, told the *ulema* and *imams* of East Pakistan that Islam had inspired the people to fight for the achievement of Pakistan and Islamic ideology would be the basis of the new constitution. Rahman urged the *imams* and *ulema,* as the true leaders of the country, to educate the people in the Islamic way but to reorient their outlook and keep pace with the modern world.[31]

In August a conference of *ulema* representing various schools of thought was advised to cooperate to promote Islamic principles. The

Pir Sahib of Dewal Sharif said the conference was called because the "bickerings and differences among the religious leaders [had] puzzled the Muslim community." He urged the *ulema* to settle their disagreements which had "acquired the form of deep-seated prejudices."[32]

The President seized every opportunity to reiterate that Islam was the foundation of Pakistan and that the purpose of the new constitution was to enable Pakistanis to lead the life of good Muslims. This was the theme of his speeches on a meet-the-people tour from Karachi to Rawalpindi after his return from the United States at the end of July. He also promised to give the nation an easy-to-understand and practicable constitution.[33] On August 14, the fourteenth anniversary of Pakistan's independence, President Ayub told the nation:

> One of the major demands of independence is the elevation of national character, progress of the country and prosperity of the masses. ... The achievement of this objective requires a constitution under which we can keep the date with our ideological destiny.
>
> Ever since the inception of Pakistan, I have seen the country being run and misrun in diverse ways. My work during the last three years has also given me further light regarding the management of the affairs of our country. I hope and pray that all this accumulated experience will show us the right path.
>
> My constant endeavour is to find a pattern of constitution which conforms to the basic traits of our national character and environments, which is workable, understandable, simple and inexpensive and which cannot be easily misused by self-seekers for the furtherance of their unpatriotic and undesirable designs. Besides, it is also essential that we should give our Constitution a [content] which enables us to make the principles of Islam the basis of our thought and action. This is by no means an easy exercise; but I hope that, by the grace of God, our efforts will soon be crowned with success—In-shallah [God willing].[34]

The President reiterated these goals and the difficulty in obtaining them while speaking to a large religious gathering celebrating the birth of the Prophet (Milad-un-Nabi).[35]

A long editorial in *Dawn* on the fourteenth Independence Day summarized President Ayub Khan's achievements and then considered the obstacles to achievement of the revolution's goals:

> ... But we have still a long way to go. The stage has not been reached which could justify the hope that our struggle will not be long or that years of hard work do not lie ahead. Ominous dark shadows still criss-cross our revolution-lighted path. ... Certainly, the most painful experiences would be ours if we allowed ourselves to relax, for no substantial change is discernible in the thinking, behavior and conduct of our industrialists, businessmen and officials. Corroding influences are surreptitiously at work to weaken the administrative discipline and disrupt the order of our

array. These influences successfully check-mate all attempts to bring down the prices, to fix a ceiling for profits or to make impossible the creation of artificial shortages. The nation has yet to free itself of the suffocating grip of the textile magnates, jute interests, tea estate owners and other big businesses and industries. Then there is corruption and provincialism, the cancerous growths which we have not been able completely to eliminate even by major surgical operations. . . . Our system of Basic Democracies is being bled of its vitality by the indifference of the bureaucracy. . . . Lip service is paid to the form of Basic Democracies, but its substance is ignored. The implementation of education reforms is . . . painfully slow. . . .

In Dacca Zakir Husain, the Minister of Home Affairs, addressing the Provincial Advisory Council, deplored the controversy over constitutional matters and said that it was not the form of the government but the objectives of the administration that mattered. Pakistan's constitution would not be a copy of any other, and it would certainly be Islamic in character.[36] The Minister stated to Dacca University students that government stability could be achieved only through the presidential system. The situation did not permit Pakistan to indulge in political wrangling and for that reason he opposed holding parliamentary elections on a party basis. He felt that candidates should be elected on the basis of individual merit and their spirit of dedication.[37]

Husain's remarks inspired an editorial in the *Pakistan Observer* on August 19 called "Building to Last" which recognized that the demise of political parties as they existed before October 1958 was not to be lamented and granted that the President had good intentions about introducing a constitution and holding elections. Nevertheless, if Zakir Husain's remarks had "a purely theoretical interest," the editor felt he too would discuss political parties "in an academic spirit alone." The editorial continued:

If he [Husain] believes deeply in the absence of parties, there are others (to whom both intellectual honesty and patriotism should be conceded by Mr. Zakir Husain) who believe that no kind of representative government, direct or indirect, presidential or parliamentary, can function effectively without organized groups and parties wedded to specific platforms, programs and ideas. . . . Individuals, however good, however well-meaning, however inspired by noble ideas, can do nothing unless and until they have behind them an organized body of opinion so strong that both the legislature and the administrative machinery . . . as well as the country as a whole will submit willingly to such policies and give their unstinted co-operation. Even in such dictatorial regimes as those of Stalin and Mussolini, the party although monolithic was a party after all, and could not be done without. . . .

With the evolution of the modern nation-states, democracy could only take the form of a representative government; and . . . the modern party system has grown up in every country of the world. In the old Union Boards . . . political parties as such were not much in evidence. But this did not prevent them from being reduced in many instances to scenes of unedifying cockfights and squabbles. Political parties have to have at least the semblance of a platform, a body of principles and ideas. In these local bodies only personal ambitions, piques and jealousies reigned supreme. Should we in the future welcome such a state of affairs on our national plane?

Contradicting Husain's observation that it was not the form of government but the intention of the administrative officials that mattered, the editorial concluded:

Thoughtful students of political systems have seriously questioned De Gaulle's Fifth Republic solely on the ground that it does not ensure another De Gaulle after the present President is gone from the scene. The permanence and strength of a system depends on the basic soundness of its structure and not on the exiguous or fortuitous circumstances of the incumbents of offices.

The President's opening address to the West Pakistan divisional commissioners conference[38] in September dealt largely with the need for decentralization. He said that the government's decision to delegate more of the central powers to the commissioners and deputy commissioners was motivated by the desire to meet the people's needs as far as possible within their own districts. "My attempt has been to make the Central Government a policy-making body," he told the commissioners, "a supervisory body, a body that will collect resources . . . and to make the provincial administration as effective an instrument as possible . . . with as little interference as possible."[39]

The Bureau of National Reconstruction was established in January 1959 with one of its chief objectives "ensuring and maintaining the unity of Pakistan and her independence." The Bureau sponsored discussion meetings and exchanges of journalists, students and cultural groups between the two wings as a means of achieving this objective. One such seminar was held in Lahore from September 18 to 23 on "Greater National Integration." The Minister for National Reconstruction and Information, Habibur Rahman, took the theme, "Economic indivisibility as a prelude to political stability," for his opening remarks. The second day's discussion, "Regionalism as an unpatriotic attitude," expressed the view that since Islam was the basis of Pakistan's existence no other factors deserved recognition. One speaker ventured the opinion that regionalism was created by the intellectual and moral bankruptcy of the political parties. Several days were spent

discussing Islam as the unifying national force. One group of delegates considered Islam the only answer to all problems of life, while the other group felt other approaches were also possible. Rehman Sobhan, a Dacca University economist, again advanced the two-economy theory and stressed the fact that, with West Pakistan's lead, the disparity between the wings could only be accentuated by the second five-year plan and the allocation of foreign aid since ongoing projects must be continued.[40]

Legal and judicial groups were the first to express public concern at the overlong duration of martial law and the delay in the restoration of fundamental human rights. Nothing, possibly, had lessened their apprehensions during the military regime and certainly not the fact that the union councils were now to function as conciliation courts.[41] As the subcommittee's work neared its end in late August, a deputation of Lahore lawyers waited upon the President. The two issues which they brought up concerned the separation of the judiciary from the executive and the restoration of fundamental rights, especially freedom of speech and action. President Ayub assured the deputation that the government would respect the wishes of the people on these two points. He told the lawyers that, as a substantial and effective group among the educated people, they should help in determining the country's future political and social systems. While the common man was prepared to do his best for the country he added—perhaps bitterly—this spirit was lacking among the intellectuals.[42] President Ayub told a large Lahore public meeting in August that he was at a loss to understand who was being benefited by the present legal system—certainly not the poor man. Under the present arrangement, he declared it was necessary to tell lies to prove a case and this system was spoiling the character of the nation.[43]

Law Minister Ibrahim told the APP that a draft providing for separation of the judiciary from the executive was prepared long ago but had been deferred due to certain provisions under consideration by the Constitution Commission. He thought that an ordinance pertaining to this separation would either be issued by the President or announced simultaneously with the constitution. With the separation of the two branches all judicial powers would be taken from the deputy commissioners who now act as district magistrates also. The lower magistrates with judicial assignments would come under the control of the High Court.[44]

This pronouncement of the Law Minister was not confirmed, however, when President Ayub spoke to the Karachi Bar Association on September 25. The president of the organization, S. Nasiruddin, wel-

comed the President by praising his achievements in land reform, the elimination of the corrupt from public life, and especially the introduction of Basic Democracies which would provide "a strong and stable system of government based upon a sound political system suited to the genius of the people of Pakistan." Nasiruddin then said:

> Sir, permit me to say that the independence of the judiciary, rule of law and freedom of speech have been maintained through your energetic efforts. Our judiciary is independent and performs its duties according to the dictates of its own conscience without fear or favor. The well planned reforms that have been introduced in the various spheres of our national life have re-inforced our faith in the rule of law. The citizens of Pakistan enjoy all the fundamental freedoms and I have no doubt in my mind that under your able guidance fundamental rights will be incorporated in the instrument which will eventually govern the political and administrative arrangements of the country.
>
> Sir, separation of the judiciary from the executive is a matter of special concern to us. It is all the more necessary at the present juncture lest the services in their enthusiasm may undo the good done by this regime. The success of any democratic institution depends on wide distribution of effective power in the society. Giving both the executive and judicial power to the same person obviates the necessity of his obtaining approval of the people because there is none to check and judge the validity and correctness of his conduct except himself.

Nasiruddin's speech concluded with a strong plea that Karachi be the seat of the Supreme Court.

In reply to the speech of welcome, President Ayub told the audience —approximately 1,000 lawyers, the Chief Justice of Pakistan, the judges of the West Pakistan High Court, diplomats and high government officials—that what had been accomplished during the past three years was "only a humble beginning." He declared that the reconstruction of a nation was "too immense a task to be completed by one man or one government." Rather it was "a continuous process in which generation after generation [would] have to participate." He said of the forthcoming constitution:

> According to the official time-table already announced, I expect to be able to give you the broad features of the proposed constitution in the month of November after which drafting will begin. . . .
> My endeavor is to frame a constitution which is Islamic in spirit, practical in execution, workable without confusion and much expense; a constitution which promotes unity, stability, and security, and which provides an opportunity to the poorest and the humblest persons with talent to aspire for the highest positions of service in the country.

President Ayub Khan's remarks on the independence of the judiciary must have confirmed the judges' apprehensions regarding the revival of the former system.

> I agree with you, Mr. President [Nasiruddin], that the independence of the judiciary is quite essential. An inevitable consequence of this is that the judges should be as immune as possible against influences, temptations and personal whims and prejudices.
>
> But this is a plain rule of life, that no functionary in the State, howsoever high, can be beyond everyone's reach. They have thus to be within someone's reach if rules of conduct, behavior and discipline are to be maintained. That someone surely must be an organization within the Judiciary itself.
>
> Earnest thought is being given to this matter and the arrangements proposed will be announced as constitutional decisions. . . .
>
> As regards fundamental rights, I agree that their substance is of paramount importance. It must, therefore, be ensured that no laws are made which vitiate them.
>
> The question whether it should be left to the courts of law to decide whether any law of the legislature is right or wrong, or to devise a machinery which would ensure that the legislature itself looks after the fundamental rights properly is, however, another matter. Careful thought is being given to this subject in our constitutional proposals.
>
> The question of the separation of the judiciary from the executive is indeed an old theme and has assumed the complexion of almost a platitude. From the reasons advanced by you in your address, I have a feeling that the real nature of this problem is only loosely understood.
>
> As you know, the judiciary is entirely distinct from the executive from the District and Sessions Judges' level upwards. It is only below that level that the question arises. Even there, the problem is not that the same person exercises judicial and executive powers at the same time.
>
> The Civil Judges are purely judicial officers and never perform any tasks connected with general administration. It is only with reference to the Magistrates who take cognizance of criminal cases that the question arises.
>
> Even there, the real problem is whether they should be under the administrative control of the Chief Executive Officer or the Chief Judicial Officer of the district.

President Ayub felt the suggestion that Karachi become the seat of the Supreme Court had "many implications other than the convenience of the gentlemen of the Bar. We are, however," he said, "giving very careful thought to this question."[45] Obviously the President of Pakistan was not behaving like a politician—he neither flattered nor made placating promises to this association which must have been one of the most influential among Pakistani intellectuals. His coldness stem-

med from his belief that such intellectual groups had been responsible for the breakdown of Pakistan's government.

On the same day as his address to the Karachi Bar Association President Ayub Khan also spoke to the Karachi women union councillors, wives of foreign diplomats and women social workers. He told this group that reservation of seats for women was under consideration, although he felt no useful purpose would be served by it, but that women could be properly represented if they voted wisely. In thanking President Ayub Khan, the chairman said that, although Mr. Jinnah had addressed the women on several occasions, this was the first time in thirteen years the head of state had personally tried to give Pakistani women proper political guidance.[46]

Also on September 25 President Ayub told the officers of the Pakistan navy that "a modern, progressive, united and strong Pakistan under the banner of Islam" was the philosophy on which he based major policy decisions. He discussed as the core of this philosophy the spiritual and psychological cohesion of the nation, the physical security of Pakistan and the reformation and reconstruction of Pakistani society. The constitution, he said, was now in its final stage of development: "It has been worked out from the very beginning in an atmosphere which was free from heat and excitement."[47]

President Ayub paid a visit to Peshawar a few days later. In April Khan Abdul Ghaffar Khan, one of the leaders of the Pathans (tribesmen of the Northwest Frontier Province) and of the rebellious Red Shirts, had been imprisoned on charges of subversive activities and of actively opposing the Family Laws. After Ghaffar Khan's imprisonment his followers were arrested daily for reviving political activity, campaigning for his release, demanding the disintegration of one unit in West Pakistan, and inciting trouble in the tribal area.[48]

President Ayub, himself a Pathan, told the students of Peshawar University that he had come to speak man to man of the problems of Pakistan, for he was confident that a number of capable men would emerge from this part of the country to serve the nation. He urged a national rather than regional outlook and said the aim of his government's program was three-fold: territorial integrity, a strong Islamic society and a more progressive society. He underscored the need for national cohesion, a common ideology, and subordination of individual, family and tribal interests to the larger national purpose. He spoke scathingly of politicians who stood between the people and their government and assured the students that the new constitution would be tailored solely to Pakistan's needs. "I believe that any constitution which guarantees a representative form of government," he stated,

"puts us on the road to Islamic ideas which is our ultimate objective."[49]

President Ayub also spoke to the Peshawar union councillors and in answer to a complaint that no good quality rice was available retorted that this sacrifice would help the country's development, for the export of 180,000 tons of good quality rice this year had earned a sizable amount of foreign exchange. He again emphasized the importance of individual sacrifice in bringing about national reconstruction and unity.[50]

By September reports from Karachi indicated that the President would announce the general structure of the constitution by the end of October. The tentative schedule called for parliament to begin functioning the middle of June 1962 with the 80,000 elected members of Basic Democracies comprising the electoral college. The election commission, headed by Abdul Majid, was expected to complete the elections within six weeks of receiving the go-ahead signal.

It was said that the subcommittee would submit its findings to the President within the next few days. After consideration by the cabinet and Presidential approval, the general structure would be announced by the President (the date most speculated upon was October 27) and the drafting of the constitution would begin. According to one journalist, it appeared that the present trend of high-level thinking favored a federal type of government. "It is, however, still in the womb of the future," wrote the correspondent. "To say how federal the Federal Constitution would be is to attempt the impossible." Another rumor mentioned in this story was that the President had consulted on constitutional issues with certain prominent ex-politicians, especially some former members of the now defunct Muslim League.[51]

The subcommittee completed its study of the Commission's recommendations early in September. According to the Foreign Minister, Manzur Qadir, the committee would adjourn until the third week of the month when it would reconvene for two or three days to draft its recommendations. Martial law would be lifted with the enforcement of the new constitution. When he was asked whether the committee had reached unanimous conclusions, Qadir said there were several recommendations. Later he said the last session would begin September 25 and last for three or four days.[52]

From the middle until the end of September, some news item about the constitution appeared almost every day. It was reported that the constitution would define the status of Rawalpindi as the interim capital until the construction of the new capital at Islamabad was completed.[53] "Authentic reports" from Karachi predicted that President Ayub would present his constitutional proposals to the governors'

conference October 23. Thus it was quite certain, according to this report, that he would announce the outlines of the new constitution in his Revolution Day Broadcast.[54]

The first authoritative announcement made from Rawalpindi by a cabinet secretariat spokesman disclosed that President Ayub would make public his decisions on the future constitution in November. With the report of the subcommittee due shortly, the President would begin consulting senior administrators, probably by the first week of October. Final consultations were to take place at the governors' conference; the broad outlines would be announced in November after which the drafting would start and all indications pointed to a new constitution by March or April of 1962.[55]

On September 25 the subcommittee began its final round of meetings in Rawalpindi and on September 27 its recommendations were prepared for the printer.[56]

## NOTES

1. *Dawn* (Karachi), May 9, 1961, p. 1; *Pakistan Observer* (Dacca), May 12, 1961.
2. *Pakistan Observer*, May 21, 1961.
3. *Dawn*, May 12, p. 1; May 14, 1961.
4. *Pakistan Observer*, May 19, 1961, p. 1.
5. *Ibid.*, May 23, 25, 30, 1961.
6. *Dawn*, May 29, 1961, p. 1.
7. *Ibid.*, May 30, 1961, p. 3.
8. *Pakistan Observer*, June 2, 1961.
9. *Ibid.*, June 23, 27, 1961.
10. *Ibid.*, July 5, 22, 26, 1961.
11. *Ibid.*, June 2, 1961; *Dawn*, June 22, 1961, p. 1.
12. *Pakistan Observer*, July 4, 1961, p. 1.
13. *Ibid.*, May 25, 1961. A complete reshuffling of East Pakistani top-level officers took place in the middle of September. *Statesman* (Calcutta), September 16, 1961.
14. *Pakistan Observer*, May 29, 1961.
15. *Ibid.*, June 22, 1961, pp. 1, 8.
16. *Dawn*, June 18, 1961, p. 1.
17. *Pakistan Observer*, July 4, 1961, p. 1.
18. *Ibid.*, July 8, 1961.
19. *Ibid.*, July 11, 1961.
20. *Ibid.* See *Pakistan Observer*, February 25, 1961, for cessation of work on the Mercantile Marine Academy.
21. *Pakistan Observer*, July 19, 1961, p. 1.
22. *Ibid.*, September 30, 1961.
23. *Dawn*, August 13, 1961, p. 1. Apparently nothing further was ever heard about this committee. G. W. Choudhury, *Democracy in Pakistan* (Dacca: Green Book House, 1963), p. 238 reports that a committee had been set up

in May 1961 to study the apportionment of revenue between the central and provincial governments, but at the time of Choudhury's writing the report had not been published. A careful scrutiny of *Dawn* for May 1961 reveals no mention of this committee.

24. *Ibid.*, August 22, 1961, p. 5.

25. *Ibid.*, May 26, 1961, p. 5; Khan, Md. Ayub, *Speeches and Statements* (Karachi: Pakistan Publications), III (July 1960-June 1961), 132-135.

26. *Dawn*, April 11 and May 17, 1961, p. 9.

27. *Ibid.*, June 12, p. 6; June 14, p. 8; August 18, 1961, p. 12.

28. *Ibid.*, June 11, 1961, p. 9; Khan, Md. Ayub, *op. cit.*, III, 137-140.

29. *Dawn*, June 20, p. 5; June 21, 1961, p. 9.

30. *Ibid.*, August 1, 1961, p. 9.

31. *Ibid.*, July 7, 1961, p. 5.

32. *Ibid.*, August 17, 1961, p. 12.

33. *Ibid.*, July 29, p. 9; July 30, 1961, p. 12.

34. *Ibid.*, August 14, 1961, pp. 1, 10; Khan, Md. Ayub, *op. cit.*, IV (July 1961-June 1962), 74-78.

35. *Dawn*, August 25, 1961, p. 9.

36. *Pakistan Observer*, August 12, 1961, p. 8.

37. *Ibid.*, August 17, p. 1; August 18, 1961, p. 1.

38. There were ten divisions in West Pakistan, three in East Pakistan. When the administrative reorganization decided on in June 1960 was completed—the process was to have taken three years—there would be an additional division in each province. *Dawn*, June 24, 1960. A commissioner heads a division, while a deputy commissioner is the chief government officer in a district. At that time there were seventeen districts in East Pakistan and fifty districts in West Pakistan.

39. *Pakistan Observer*, September 19, 1961, p. 1.

40. *Ibid.*, September 24, 26, 1961; *Dawn*, September 19, p. 9; 20, p. 5; 21, p. 9; 22, p. 5; 23, 1961, p. 4.

41. Decision taken by the governors' conference, June 19, 1961. *Pakistan Observer*, June 20, 1961, p. 1.

42. *Ibid.*, August 31, 1961, p. 1.

43. *Dawn*, August 30, 1961, p. 9.

44. *Ibid.*, September 11, 1961, p. 9.

45. *Ibid.*, September 26, 1961, pp. 4, 9; Khan, Md. Ayub, *op. cit.*, IV, 110-114.

46. *Dawn*, September 26, 1961, pp. 1, 9.

47. *Ibid.*, p. 9.

48. *Ibid.*, July 17, 1961, p. 5.

49. *Ibid.*, September 30, pp. 1, 9; October 1, p. 9; October 2, 1961, p. 9.

50. *Ibid.*, September 29, 1961, p. 1.

51. *Pakistan Observer*, September 2, 1961.

52. *Ibid.*, September 8, 1961.

53. *Ibid.*, September 15, 1961. Rawalpindi officially became the interim capital in October 1959 but its status had never been legally defined and it still remained administratively a part of West Pakistan.

54. *Ibid.*, September 22, 1961.

55. *Ibid.*, September 23, 1961.

56. *Dawn*, September 28, 1961, p. 1.

# CHAPTER X

# THE TURNING POINT
(October 1961—January 1962)

As soon as the subcommittee had submitted its report to the President, a new committee was formed to consider the administrative problems of putting the constitution into effect. Its report on method of change-over, stages of enforcement and holding of elections was expected to be ready for the President by the first week of October.[1] N. A. Faruqi, cabinet secretary, was chairman. Other members included: Qazi Anwarul Haq, Chief Secretary, East Pakistan, and three members from West Pakistan, Muzaffar Ahmed, Additional Chief Secretary; Khan Ghulam Ishaq Khan, WAPDA chairman; and Aftab Qazi, Finance Secretary. By October 4 this committee had concluded its deliberations and planned to present its report to the governors' conference on October 23.[2]

The period between the end of September and the governors' conference saw intensive governmental efforts to prepare the people for the new constitution. Not only the President, but Z. A. Bhutto, Minister for Fuel, Power and Natural Resources; A. K. Khan, Industries Minister; and Akhtar Hussain, Minister for Education and Scientific Research, appeared before the people to try to influence them toward acceptance of the future government.

At an October 3 press conference the President answered questions on a variety of subjects ranging from Outer Mongolia to Berlin and from minorities to the European Common Market. He spoke only briefly of political parties, yet this topic accounted for the first three of four headlines of the Dacca newspaper accounts. President Ayub said he would prefer to have the new institutions operate without political parties but the question was still open and would be determined in the constitution. Should parties be necessary, he said, then it would be desirable to restrict their number to one or two. He also thought parliament should issue a license before a party could be formed. President Ayub disclosed that the question of whether funda-

mental rights should be justiciable in law courts or protected by Parliament was being examined. He said the constitution-making process was approaching the final stages, administrative aspects were now being considered and the constitutional proposals would be taken up at the governors' conference October 23. "I will require a fortnight before announcing the outline of the constitution sometime by the middle of November," he stated.[3]

Bhutto, speaking in Sukkur, said that the new constitution would start functioning January or February. He urged the people to use their votes wisely and warned that if they failed to elect people who put a high value on national service all benefits of the revolution might be jeopardized.[4] In Khairpur he assured his audience that the elections would be held in an impartial and free atmosphere. Sovereignty would then rest with the people, he said, to be exercised through their elected representatives.[5] At the government college in Nawabshah the Minister stated that the elections to be held early the following year would be the most exemplary held in the subcontinent so far. There would be no interference, no tampering and no pressure from any quarter.[6] In Hyderabad Bhutto, after warning former Sind politicians against the revival of political activity, predicted that the new parliament would meet by next March. He would not specify whether elections would be direct or not, but said that the President was anxious to restore normal democratic order in the country as soon as practicable.[7]

In Karachi Akhtar Hussain told members of the Institute of Islamic Research, which had been established under the 1956 Constitution, that he believed this organization would find a prominent place under the new constitution. The Institute was founded to coordinate the efforts of several affiliated organizations and enunciate Islamic ideals in a manner acceptable to both the modern Pakistani generation and the world at large.[8]

President Ayub Khan went to East Pakistan for a three-day visit in mid-October. According to the *Statesman* of October 18, one of the chief reasons for his visit was "to explain to leaders of public opinion some of the more important aspects of the constitution." The President participated in a rather lengthy press interview at Dacca's Tejgaon airport, reviewed the progress of East Pakistan development schemes at a high-level conference at the President's House, answered questions at a meeting of union councillors and high ranking officials in Chittagong, spoke at a Dacca Municipal Committee reception in his honor at the Shahbagh Hotel and addressed a rally of 50,000 at the Dacca stadium.

To the newsmen at the airport President Ayub said that not all former politicians were unscrupulous and that any who had not been debarred under the Elective Bodies Disqualification Order would be allowed to participate in the elections.[9] It would be up to the people to see that good men were chosen. He also pointed out that the press had some responsibility in the matter. He urged them to give up partisan stands and think in terms of national interests. The constitution was man-made and therefore subject to error, but the people would have the right to change it. He planned to visit East Pakistan again when the constitution had been framed to explain the philosophy and thinking behind it.[10]

President Ayub informed the Chittagong Basic Democrats that parliament would be "absolutely sovereign," and although power would be balanced between president and parliament, parliament would not have the power to interfere with the administration. He again suggested that should Basic Democracies form the electoral college, the members would be able to vote for men whom they knew through personal experience.[11]

In the Dacca civic reception address the President admitted that some of the constitution's features might not yet be found in textbooks; nevertheless it would provide what Pakistan most needed—a stable government and a sound administration. President Ayub urged his audience to consider the constitution objectively as a whole and not to rush into adverse judgment before careful study. He said there was nothing sacrosanct about the constitution. It would be suited to a dynamic age, he stated, and could be changed as conditions required. In conclusion, the President reiterated the present regime's intention to continue to do all that was possible to aid development in the east wing.[12]

President Ayub announced at the rally in the Dacca stadium that he intended to appoint an impartial commission to look into equitable allocation of revenues between East and West Pakistan. He said this step would be taken in order to answer East Pakistani complaints about the comparatively slower development of this province. President Ayub admitted that some criticism might be warranted but pointed out that his regime was anxious to see East and West Pakistan developed equitably. He warned against indulging in talk about the separation of the two wings. The news story in the *Pakistan Observer* of October 19 continued:

> The President placed emphasis on the need for greater unity and solidarity between the people of East and West Pakistan because

only in that way could the country, now on the path to progress, be stronger and more prosperous.

If on the other hand the two wings are separated both would be weaker and the lives of the people endangered. Pakistan, he pointed out, was surrounded by enemies, and a slight mistake would jeopardize the security of the country.

Assuring the people of East Pakistan equal rights with their West Pakistani brethren in the collective affairs of the country, he said East Pakistanis were the owners of half and deserved to get it and should get it. They should also share the responsibilities of running the administration.

In East Pakistan, he said, there was a feeling that the Central Government had its seat in West Pakistan, the army was also in West Pakistan and the pace of development in West Pakistan had been faster than in the East wing. He did not blame East Pakistanis for this, but he reminded them that the Central Government has to be located, as in other countries, in only one place. As regards redress of other complaints, he referred to his decision to set up the commission and to the government's policy to let East Pakistan people share in the Central administration.

This visit, with the assurance of redress of East Pakistan's grievances, marked a turning point in the relations between East Pakistan and the President. As the first public expression in East Pakistan by the government that this wing had some justification for its complaints and with the promises that action would be taken to bring East Pakistanis into the government, this address was immensely reassuring to those who felt as though they were treated as second-class citizens.[13]

During the week after the President's departure, three *Pakistan Observer* editorials expressed an unprecedented hopefulness that the future constitution would remove the inequalities between the provinces and allow every capable person to serve his country politically. Entitled "The President's Declaration," the editorial of October 20 said,

Nothing can be more harmful to our national solidarity than a creeping suspicion, genuine or otherwise, about the existence of a state of inequality between the two wings of the country. . . . It should therefore be the concern of every sensible person . . . to see that no vague feeling of doubt may turn into a firm conviction. The most effective way to do so is to bring to the fore the factors responsible for it and tackle them with prudence or show that they are wholly unreal.

This is the correct and realistic approach which President Ayub Khan made while dealing . . . with what he called a "complaint" about the comparatively slow development of this wing. Instead of brushing aside the "complaint" as false and motivated, or keeping quiet over it, he referred to it in a frank and forthright manner and then proceeded to declare the step he proposed to take for its remedy. . . . His announcement regarding the appointment of an impartial

commission to examine the question of equitable allocation of revenues of the country between the two wings for a balanced development of both is therefore a much more practical and effective means of clearing any confusion than a plethora of platitudinous dissertations. . . . The findings of the proposed commission . . . are expected to . . . enable the authorities to take proper action to remove the resulting confusion.

The second editorial on October 26 dealt chiefly with the unrealistic approach of those who appealed for a return to Islamic democracy, a point of view in agreement with that of the President. The first sentence seemed to reflect the new optimism of East Pakistanis:

The country has been waiting for a Constitution for much of the last fourteen years; it can very well afford to wait for a few months more.

On the third anniversary of the revolution on October 27 optimism again keynoted the editorial:

. . . Since October 27, 1958—a most significant addition to the important dates in the history of Pakistan—the country has proceeded from a state of confusion to political stability. By March next the shape of things to come will be known. The full text of a constitution, now on the anvil, will then be announced leading to the *restoration of parliamentary government in the country* [italics added]. . . .

The last three post-Revolution years have been remarkable for several evident achievements; there have been some disappointments, too. The tempo of development has quickened and the administration is certainly giving more attention to the development of this wing of the country. . . . The realization that a balanced development making for a happy, contented and prosperous Pakistan is essential in the interest of the whole country, rather than a part of it, is clearly in evidence. . . .

Today we are encouraged to hope that when the political institutions come into operation here every worker capable of contributing to the country's progress will get the opportunity of rendering his or her service to the nation. . . .

Some of the editorial writer's optimism was undoubtedly based on the false assumption that President Ayub had promised "the restoration of parliamentary government."

The *Pakistan Observer* included with this series of editorials a fourth publication of Dacca University economist Rehman Sobhan's opinions.[14] Some of the facts which he used as the basis for his conclusions came from a man/land ratio and per capita income comparison of East Pakistan and West Pakistan. While West Pakistan had a population of 140 per square mile and a per capita income of Rs. 305, East Pakistan had 930 persons per square mile and Rs. 213 per capita income. The author explained the "law of cumulative causation" ac-

cording to which "there are automatic forces in the economy of an under-developed country which tend to accentuate inequalities." Professor Sobhan showed how this applied to the Pakistani provinces under the provisions of the first and second five-year plans. His conclusion was that each wing should have economic autonomy.[15] President Ayub had declared in May that the government had no intention of allowing two economies. However, his public statement in East Pakistan that there was ample justification for dissatisfaction indicates he evidently was impressed by the facts on which the young Dacca University economist based his conclusion.

The governors' conference began its sessions as scheduled on October 23 in Rawalpindi with President Ayub Khan presiding and the governors, cabinet ministers and cabinet secretary in attendance. On the second day consideration of the Constitution Commission report, the cabinet subcommittee recommendations and the report of the special committee was begun. A press communiqué said that, instead of giving the "broad outlines" of the future government as had been promised for several months, the President would announce the new constitution in its entirety some time in March. The drafting which would begin after the close of the governors' conference was expected to take at least four months.[16]

At the close of the week-long conference a two-member committee, consisting of Manzur Qadir and Law Secretary Justice Abdul Hamid, was directed to undertake the immediate drafting of the constitution. The committee was empowered to enlist, if necessary, the services of experts both Pakistani and foreign. The announcement and induction of the constitution would be simultaneous. The news report further stated that the announcement of the appointment of the fiscal commission promised by the President was expected shortly. The commission's recommendations on allocation of finances between the center and provinces would probably form a part of the constitution.[17]

The third anniversary of the revolution provided an opportunity for newspapers and government officials to express themselves on various matters of national importance although the constitution was uppermost in everyone's mind. In accordance with the decision reached at the governors' conference two days earlier, however, President Ayub Khan did not forecast the constitution's framework in his anniversary eve broadcast. He said only that it was his endeavor to give the country a constitution which would not easily be subject to "political misguidance and exploitation," and which would be able to produce a strong and stable government. The President suggested that it would be well "to take a brief stock of some of the bold realities of life which

are likely to confront us." First, it should be remembered that, "except in the fundamentals of faith," there was "no inflexible quality in human affairs." Change was inevitable and therefore a pragmatic approach to everyday problems was essential. Second, he said, each person's attitude should be oriented toward the nation as a whole, a sense of "service above self." President Ayub's third point was the necessity to become "as sensitive to our responsibilities as we always are to our rights." The press, public servants, intellectuals and all educated men and women should take a leading part in "this crusade against national waywardism."[18]

In contrast to the enthusiasm of the *Pakistan Observer*'s editorials during the period of the governors' conference and the third anniversary of the revolution, *Dawn* seemed reluctant to have a constitution put into effect so soon. Its editorial of October 27 said:

> Many would have preferred—and we are among them—that President Ayub himself had written out and given a constitution to the country for at least the next ten years or so, embodying the ideas which he has often publicly expressed.

The Revolution Day supplement of 1961 of the *Pakistan Observer* contained only articles relating to democracy or the new constitution in contrast to former supplements in which articles on Mohammad Ali Jinnah, Pakistani poets, industrialization or other such subjects tended to dominate. "The Problem of Freedom," a historical survey of political theories, stressed the democratic principle as the ideal of providing "the good life" for the majority of the citizens by investing ultimate political power in the people. "On the Eve of the New Constitution" pointed out the need for two economies, equality between the wings in appointments to the civil services, as well as in parliament and the cabinet, maximum decentralization in the administration of central affairs, and for a second federal capital in Dacca. "Reflections on Our Time" considered democracy, dictators and civil rights. In "Federalism" the author defined the concept and pointed out that Pakistan was confronted with the problem of distributing power among various levels of authority. The author of "In Search of a Constitution" felt that, whatever the form of government might be under the new constitution, the most important thing to ensure its success and growth was "the spirit of the people working the Constitution" and "their political vision and fortitude in upholding the constitutional principles."

The mood in Dacca as Pakistan celebrated the anniversary of the revolution was perhaps best described by an Indian correspondent in

the *Statesman* on October 29. He pointed out that East Pakistan's celebration combined "mixed feelings of solemnity and gaiety." However, "the former sentiment was more dominant," apparently due to the imminence of the new constitution. The article was explicit regarding the efficacy of the influence of public opinion in East Pakistan:

> Ample food for thought was conveniently provided by the announcement two days ago from Rawalpindi that it had been decided to withhold publication of the broad outline of the new Constitution in November and instead to publish it in its entirety some time in March 1962. Coming so soon after President Ayub's recent visit to this wing when he is known to have sounded leaders of public opinion here and particularly in the light of certain 'concessions to local thinking' announced by him during his stay here, the postponement is being considered by some as an indication of last-minute revisions to accommodate local wishes.
>
> Whether this is true or not, there is no gainsaying the pressure that is being brought to bear (and has been for some months past) on the powers that be regarding East Pakistan's basic claims. The two-economy demand has been divested of its former strictly political approach and is now being pressed solely on the economic plane. It is understood that after careful thought a body of eminent economists from this wing have formulated such an economic approach to the demand and a memorandum incorporating it is understood to have been presented to the authorities some time ago. . . .
>
> The new approach finds ample representation in the voluminous Revolution Day supplements published by Dacca newspapers today. One of them has even editorially said that the root of Pakistan's internal problems of the past has been the failure of Pakistan's former leaders to implement the Lahore Resolution of 1940 which envisaged Pakistan as a federation of two fully autonomous units.

It is the judgment of the authors that the *Pakistan Observer* fairly represented the views of the educated East Pakistanis. The newspaper's attitude toward the military regime had evolved from initial coldness through grudging admiration to cautious optimism and finally, in October 1961, to outright acceptance when it said, almost complacently, Pakistan can afford to wait for a constitution for a few months more. Given that attitude in East Pakistan and President Ayub's obvious determination to remedy the causes of the east wing's grievances, it seemed that a turning point in the writing of the constitution had truly come.

In various speeches and interviews during the following weeks, President Ayub and certain cabinet ministers managed to mention the constitution without revealing much that was new. The President told members of the Commonwealth Press Union that all freedoms including that of the press would be restored.[19] He disclosed at a conference of

the All-Pakistan Women's Association (APWA) that a number of seats in assemblies and the parliament would be reserved for women.[20] This statement confirmed the rumor that there would be provincial assemblies in addition to the central legislature. The President cautioned the Aligarh Muslim University alumni against the divisive tendencies of tribalism, provincialism and parochialism, for Pakistan, besides being burdened with its inherent geographical handicaps, was surrounded by powerful nations. Any sign of weakness could prove fatal to its national integrity.[21]

Habibur Rahman, the Minister for National Reconstruction and Information, told newsmen that the future constitution could be amended by the elected representatives, that martial law would be lifted when the constitution went into effect and that there would be no government appointments to the union council level of Basic Democracies during the second election. When asked how information about the draft constitution would be taken to the doors of the common man, Rahman replied that he had invited suggestions from journalists on what means should be adopted, for the government was anxious that full details reach as many people as possible.[22] A. K. Khan, the Minister of Industries, told reporters that the question of the bifurcation of the PIDC into two autonomous bodies, one for each wing, was receiving serious consideration by the government.[23] Mohammad Ibrahim, the Minister of Law, thought the drafting might be completed by December and that foreign experts might be called in at a later stage.[24]

Z. A. Bhutto, the Minister of Fuel, Power and Natural Resources, in a stirring appeal to the East Pakistan Advisory Council said that those people who had made a fetish of geographical distance had "lost their faith in Pakistan's capacity for indestructible and imperishable unity." He exhorted them to "recapture the spirit of the freedom movement. . . . It must never be forgotten that Pakistan was the creation of a formidable will, the like of which history has not witnessed before."[25]

The Lahore Seminar on Greater National Integration held in September was followed early in November by a similar seminar in Dacca organized by the East Pakistan Bureau of National Reconstruction. The meetings were reported at length in both the Karachi and Dacca newspapers. Forty eminent scholars from both wings had been invited as delegates and the five-day seminar was well attended. Discussions centered on three topics—the basis of Pakistani nationhood, national character and cultural homogeneity. Opening the first session was Dr. Mahmud Hussain, vice-chancellor of Dacca University and chairman

of the organizing committee of the seminar. His theme was that the disparity in man/land ratio between the two wings meant that the same policies, institutions and implementing measures "would be unlikely to be best calculated to attain the goal of integrating the 93 million people into one individual society."

In discussing Pakistani nationhood Dacca High Court Justice S. M. Murshed stressed Islam as the power to bind the two wings into a nation. Dr. Mahmud Ahmed, professor of philosophy, University of Karachi, said unity of thought and uniformity of character were necessary steps in moving toward national integration. Two papers were read on the development of a national character pattern by Dr. Imdad Husain of Lahore and M. U. Ahmed, principal of Dacca College. Both felt that sound education emphasizing Islamic values would develop a proper national character pattern. "Cultural Homogeneity" somehow became entwined with economic disparity. Dr. Mohammad Shahidullah, an eminent East Pakistani scholar, said disproportionate development hurt the united image of a nation. Suggestions he made for attaining a strong cultural entity were: the teaching of Urdu and Bengali in both wings, adoption of the Roman script for both languages and interwing marriages. Dr. Sajjad Husain, head of the Department of English of Dacca University, also mentioned economic disparity and the complex cultural traditions of the linguistic groups as stumbling blocks to cultural homogeneity. But he believed it was "utterly unrealistic" to expect to achieve such integration and felt Pakistan must learn to live with its cultural complexity. He suggested that the uniting factor should be a common "national purpose, namely the creation of a nation in which men will be able to live in dignity and freedom." The Governor, Lieutenant General Azam Khan, addressing the closing session of the seminar, said any misunderstanding between the wings was due to the failure to follow in the early years of independence "the ideals for which Pakistan came into being."[26] The importance attached by the *Pakistan Observer* to the opinions expressed at this conference may be understood by the position of the news stories. On November 6, 7, 9 and 10, the news of the conference was the leading article on page one.

In an editorial on the seminar the *Pakistan Observer* on November 10 characterized it as showing an "objective academic spirit" rather than airing "political and sectional prejudices." It pointed out that "to know and understand" the problems that make the work of national integration "a task of unique difficulty" is to have advanced "halfway towards finding a solution." Another editorial on November

13 said that, while Islam was indeed the unifying force of the 1940's, the greatest motivating factor of the 1960's was economic.

A less optimistic view of the results of the two seminars on Pakistani nationhood was taken by Dacca University economics professor Dr. M. N. Huda, who saw the discussions as proceeding along two parallel lines with no meeting point. One line was the dependence on Islam as the binding force; the other was economic disparity as the divisive force. National integration could be brought about, he concluded, only by removing the disintegrative tendencies.[27]

National integration was discussed with apparent freedom in the *Pakistan Observer* and a few letters were published in reaction to the seminar papers. On November 16 a Dacca writer said that justice is the foremost Islamic principle in social life. Therefore, the economists showed more faith in Islamic injunction than the exponents of Islamic ideology. Another Dacca contributor on November 20 took issue with Dr. Sajjad Husain's idea that talking about Islam instead of doing something practical about national integration was a dangerous policy; he wrote that Islam "contains a practical solution of all the problems confronting mankind in the world today." The letter provoked readers from Dinajpur and Rajshahi to rise to Dr. Sajjad's defense on November 29.

The *Statesman* revealed that the reporting of the seminar had not been as full and free as had been thought. In referring to the third day's meeting the correspondent wrote on November 11:

> The inherent danger in the path of cultural integration of the people of Pakistan into one homogeneous unit presented by existing racial, linguistic and other differences and by such factors as political and economic inequalities, which had only been hinted at on previous days, was today squarely faced. . . .
>
> So frank indeed were today's discussions that they produced the somewhat strange spectacle of Mr. Jinnah being accused by a West Pakistani speaker, Mr. Shariful Mujahid, of a serious lapse in his insistence in 1948 that the future Pakistani nation must be based on rejection of the established idea that Hindus and Muslims were politically separate entities in Pakistan even though they might continue to be different from the religious viewpoint. It was left to a refugee from Bihar, Mr. Salahuddin Mohammed, to censure Mr. Mujahid for his summary dismissal of an important policy statement of Mr. Jinnah.
>
> Mr. Mohammed Shahidullah, the eminent East Pakistani litterateur and scholar, who by no stretch of imagination could be accused of chauvinism, said 'disproportion in matters of development between East and West Pakistan hurts the image of a united nationhood and feeds interregional resentment and rivalry.'

The Dacca correspondent of *Dawn* on November 17 concluded:

> The most remarkable feature of this seminar was the free, frank and unfettered nature of the discussion. There were occasional sharp cleavages on certain issues, particularly in respect of cultural integration, but they were a further evidence of the frank talking that the delegates did on the whole. . . .
>
> The two main points that emerged from the deliberations were: (1) Islam continued to be the basis of Pakistani nationhood and formed the uniting link between the two wings; and (2) that integration must be sought on the basis of unity in diversity and economic disparity eliminated.

The provincial seminar was followed by similar seminars in some of the districts. In Dinajpur, for example, a letter to the *Pakistan Observer* on November 15 expressed great indignation at the "scornful and ridiculous comments" of some members of the audience when a speaker was talking on behalf of an Islamic constitution. He complained that any economic or political matter given an Islamic basis "is often termed by the younger generations a 'bogey.'" At a Feni meeting Islam vs. interwing equality as the means of bringing about national integration was thoroughly discussed.[28]

"The Basis of Pakistani Nationhood," an article by Professor Abul Fazl in the *Pakistan Observer* on December 7, suggested that politics and economics, not religion, were the dominant factors in a modern state. He asserted that the "politically shrewd Quaid-e-Azam realized this truth. He never said that Islam was in danger. During the Pakistan movement the slogan was that Muslims of India were in danger, not as a religious community, but as a political and economic entity." The article elicited at least two letters, one on December 12 heartily agreeing with Professor Fazl's proposal for interwing marriages as a step towards cultural homogeneity; the other on December 16 disagreeing strongly that economic and practical considerations could outweigh Islam as a binding force between the two provinces. In a later article on December 19 Husain Khan agreed with Professor Fazl on the importance of economic equality and cultural integration, but he called the discussion about religion "confusing and contradictory."

An economist, Israrul Haque, in a long three-part article in the Dacca *Morning News* on December 12, 13 and 14 called "National Economy," took an objective look at Professor Sobhan's two-economy theory which, he said, could not be "dismissed as a mere academic exercise." Rather it represented "the culminating point of the longstanding controversy . . . over the allocation of resources." The President's decision to appoint a commission to look into this question demonstrated his "realistic view of the ever-present and deep-seated discontent" of the East Pakistanis. After explaining Professor Sobhan's theory and a West Paki-

stani's rebuttal of it, Haque went into its political and economic implications. He showed that it would be impossible to have one political unit composed of two economically autonomous provinces. This situation, he concluded, "could lead to more confusion than advantages."

Apparently the only action—so anxiously watched for by East Pakistan—taken in the month following the President's visit to the east wing was the appointment of a committee to report on the decentralization of central institutions which provided monetary assistance to industries, trade and individuals.[29] Some comfort may have been derived from the implications in Z. A. Bhutto's speech to a businessmen's seminar held in Lahore in which he said:

> It would be perhaps appropriate to call the present an age of equalization . . . which means equal opportunity for development and competition.
>
> Just as there is a demand of the underdeveloped countries to better their status . . . that quest is equally potent, if no more acute, in a limited and homogeneous community. In a society in which conditions are even more relatively similar, the underdeveloped parts of it feel the resentment and bite of relative poverty much more painfully and poignantly.
>
> Historical, geographical and other like conditions are invariably responsible for leaving certain regions behind others. Development obviously cannot take place in as harmonious a rhythm as would the best of music. It is, therefore, fallacious to expect a mechanical pace of uniform development. . . .
>
> In an underdeveloped country the limitations of resources, manpower, machinery, technology and natural wealth make it all the more difficult for the disparity to be bridged with the result that the gap between the more fortunate and the less fortunate increases instead of diminishing. . . . This is not a deliberate development, it is a natural one. It becomes all the more accentuated when Government permits the free play of market forces to operate without interference. . . .
>
> I have often wondered at the exact difference between economics and politics. Without political calm there can be no orderly economic growth, and without economic expansion political stability is illusory. . . .
>
> It is, therefore, essential for a national Government to address itself to the ever-rising demand for systematic national growth. It is vital for Government in its own sphere of activity to give weightage wherever it is due. . . . Government has to build the whole community and not only its industrial might. . . .
>
> Policy for national integration, including regional equalization, will be only a phase of cumulative social process of economic development, and this process has to be conceived of as a higher order since it embraces, in addition to the evolution of the market forces, a people's attitudes and aspirations.[30]

Bhutto repeated this idea when he told students in Larkana that the revolutionary government's prime concern was economic equality among the people of the two wings.[31]

Within six weeks after President Ayub's heartening talks in Dacca, however, doubts were being expressed in the province. An editorial in the *Pakistan Observer* on November 30 was quite specific about East Pakistan's expectations and sense of unease at their lack of fulfillment:

> We heard it some time back that autonomous and semi-autonomous public bodies concerned with economic development of East Pakistan will now have a status that should enable them independently and finally to deal with matters that fell within their purview. Progress in this direction has been slower than expected. Snags may have developed in carrying out the policy of which we are not aware, and Authority has been singularly uncommunicative in this regard recently. The first and obviously the most important organization that was mentioned was the PIDC. It was recognized that with West Pakistan already at what the economists would call the take-off stage and entrepreneurs available there in adequate numbers to take on where the PIDC left off, this body would now concentrate on East Pakistan and its headquarters be transferred to the scene of its main operations. Unfortunately, all does not seem well in the domestic affairs of PIDC and stories of cliques and wire-pullings have been rampant. Perhaps more discipline and efficiency could have been maintained with the top directional powers concentrated there.
>
> Other organizations in which public funds have been invested and in the working of which the public are vitally interested, such as the State Bank, the National Bank of Pakistan, House Building Finance Corporation, PICIC, the Agricultural Bank, etc., have all their local branches here headed often by an executive of sufficiently high status. But in practice, they are often found unable to make final decisions even on unimportant details. This has necessarily hampered progress.
>
> Even in a country such as Soviet Russia, the realization has already dawned on the leaders of the Communist Party that extreme concentration of economic powers at the apex makes for inefficiency and retarded progress. The emphasis is now all on decentralization. It should be obvious by now that one of the main causes of the backwardness of this province was bureaucratic inertia and the jealous guarding of their decision-making power by the Central authorities. The present regime has wisely recognized the necessity of arriving at some sort of final settlement of the question of allocation of financial powers between the provincial and the Central administrations. Even this innocuous and necessary measure now proposed is coming in for some sort of adverse criticism by some, it is reported, West Pakistani newspapers. It may have been an accident that the Finance Department of the Government has always been headed by a non-East Pakistani. Those who expected that the temporary absence of Mr. Shoaib would give the occasion for an East Pakistani member of the Cabinet to take acting charge of the portfolio did not see their hope fulfilled. We do not give much importance to the particular incumbent; but

probably unfamiliarity with conditions prevalent in this part of the country has rendered the financial decision-making machinery incapable of dealing with the urgent problems of a developing economy.

Two weeks later on December 14 another editorial pointedly remarked, "Probably, if the Muslim League regime had not delayed in introducing a constitution . . . much of the disruption, turmoil and uncertainty . . . during the first twelve years . . . could have been avoided." The writer observed that Syria and Turkey had both recognized the "dangers of not holding popular elections." The present regime in Pakistan was also aware of this, "and we trust a constitution and elections are really coming this time." The editorial concluded by saying that after much bitter controversy there were certain principles accepted by the country as a whole and that the President was wise to settle the allocation of financial resources before announcing the constitution.

President Ayub appointed a committee to search for a suitable building in Rawalpindi for the national assembly until the permanent capital was built in Islamabad. Bhutto said the first session would meet there in May 1962 and the winter session would probably meet in Dacca. By the third session in 1963 the State Bank building in Islamabad, with its modern auditorium, would be ready and in another year the regular parliament house would be completed. For parliament's first meeting the committee chose the G.H.Q. Study Center in Rawalpindi which until recently had been used as the general headquarters of the Pakistan Army. The interim parliament house, to be called Ayub Hall, would have such conventional requirements as a room for the members, a press room and galleries for the public, and also a separate room for women.[32]

The Dacca *Morning News* on December 10 previewed what could be expected in the political field in January 1962. The President was to arrive in Dacca by the middle of the month to inaugurate the All-Pakistan Convention of Basic Democracies. Following this a governors' conference, attended by the President, the two governors, the martial law administrators and the cabinet ministers, would convene in Dacca to hear the President's final views on the constitution. After this conference the President was to make a whirlwind tour of every East Pakistan district to explain the new constitution. According to the preview, a meeting of the East Pakistan Provincial Advisory Council was also expected to be held in January to make preliminary arrangements for the new government. A separate branch, Constitution and Election, had already been set up in the provincial secretariat to deal with these matters. Finally, after the constitution was announced, the

ministers would tender their resignations. The steps to be taken after the launching of the constitution were still "closely guarded secrets," but it was believed that the President himself would administer the country through the governors of the two wings. The news story also predicted—rightly—that 1962 would see "brisk political activity."

A few weeks later on January 3 the *Morning News* again looked into its crystal ball to foresee the nature of the constitution. It reported that a preamble would define the objectives of the state with a stress on moral and spiritual matters. Pakistan was to be an Islamic nation based on the fundamental principles of the Quran and the Sunnah. Equal rights would be guaranteed to all citizens regardless of religion. It was also safe to predict that the new constitution would provide for a joint electorate for all elective offices.

The *Pakistan Observer*'s mood was less prophetic and more hopeful. An editorial on January 11 said that while history does not repeat itself, yet "out of this past, the future is born. Our future, however, is not conditioned solely by history; it is shaped also by our will." Asserting that hope is born with man, the editorial attributed to this hope "our faith in freedom and the right of every individual to have a say in the shaping of his and his generation's future." Leaving the theoretical, the *Pakistan Observer* on January 25 stated bluntly,

> We do not know what the future is going to be. The President is expected shortly to announce the Constitution.
> But whatever be the form, one trusts that provincial administrators will not have to run to the other wing, the seat of central power, for every little issue.

In December President Ayub told a meet-the-people gathering in Campbellpur that the constitution was to be promulgated by the end of January and elections should be completed by May 1962. He advised the people to elect persons of high integrity and with a strong sense of responsibility. He assured them, "When we have the new constitution, political and administrative instability will disappear."[33] Speaking to a three-day Basic Democracies convention in Karachi, the President told the audience of over fourteen hundred that the constitution was likely to be made public in a month or so.[34] In Jacobabad he stated that the ban on political parties would not be lifted before the new constitution was put into effect.[35] The President's Quaid-e-Azam Day broadcast (December 25) expressed the belief that the new constitution would provide equal opportunities to all citizens to work and prosper according to their ability, for it would not be the "monopoly of a particular class, party or group." The President emphasized that the success of the constitution depended primarily on personal

character and national unity.[36] At a question-and-answer meeting in Bahawalpur he revealed that the constitution was almost ready and would be announced along with the report of the Constitution Commission at an early date. He said that it would be based on Islamic ideology and all legislation would be scrutinized to ensure that nothing was enacted against the tenets of Islam.[37]

*Dawn*'s editorial of December 25 dealt with national integration and economic justice. "The very fact that a planned campaign for national integration has been undertaken shows that there is an awareness of the risk of disintegration," this editorial contended. "If the lost ground is to be recovered . . . then the foremost plank in the campaign for national integration should be a determined crusade for the redress of economic inequalities." Although *Dawn* recognized that an attempt was being made to bring about "a better equilibrium in economic development between the different regions," it concluded that the pace was still "much too slow."

On December 12 the appointment of the Finance Commission was announced. The first meeting was scheduled for December 20 in Rawalpindi and the Commission was asked to submit its report by January 15, 1962.[38] Another announcement in the middle of December concerned the moving of PIDC headquarters to East Pakistan. Two proposals were under consideration: either the headquarters of the PIDC would be shifted to Dacca or PIDC would be bifurcated with headquarters in each province.[39]

Shoaib told a press conference two weeks later that there would be no bifurcation of central credit institutions such as the State Bank and the PICIC, only decentralization. He also said that a section of the Finance Commission report would form a part of the new constitution. When he was asked for the terms of reference for the new commission, Shoaib explained that its purpose was to suggest procedures for an equitable allocation of central revenues. The journalists wanted to know whether the commission would also make recommendations regarding the sharing of the central resources by the provinces but the Finance Minister declined to elaborate further.[40]

Meanwhile, one important step in the promised decentralization of administration had been carried out in West Pakistan. Certain provincial departments, such as public works, education, health and agriculture, were abolished and their powers handed over to regional or divisional officers. These changes had been approved by the Cabinet on December 26. The consideration of the reorganization of East Pakistan was nearing completion and the report was to be submitted to the President within a few weeks.[41] This reorganiza-

tion was considered to be a prelude to the announcement of the constitution, according to the *Pakistan Observer*'s Rawalpindi correspondent December 30. He said it was "considered certain" by many that there would be a federal system and that West Pakistan would remain an integrated unit. The constitution was to be announced in Dacca towards the end of January, probably just preceding the meeting of the governors' conference. The document itself was reported to be almost complete, although the chapters on financial provisions had not taken final shape. Meanwhile, the Finance Commission was at work considering allocation of the central revenues.

President Ayub disclosed early in January 1962 that the final draft was almost ready and would be announced with the report of the Constitution Commission very soon. He said that the constitution would be "simple, practicable and easily understandable. In its preparation," he said, "no efforts [had] been made to copy constitutions of other countries. Our own country is an open book," he continued, "and we have tried to find what it really needs."[42]

According to the Minister for Home Affairs, Zakir Husain, the constitution would be announced on the eve of Ramazan,[43] soon after the conclusion of the governors' conference. He said it would go to press around January 15 after the final check by the President and the Cabinet.[44]

Some obstacle, perhaps the Finance Commission, again appeared to prevent the government from keeping to its planned schedule of presenting the constitution. The *Morning News* reported on January 12 a new possibility:

> The new Constitution will be announced early in February in Rawalpindi, it was reliably learned here today. It was further known that the salient features of the Constitution might not be announced at the Governors' Conference at Dacca as was thought by some.
>
> Final touches will be given in another eight days' time and as such the Constitution will be ready in its final form when the Governors' Conference meets in Dacca. . . .
>
> The complete Constitution may not be promulgated in the beginning and to begin with, the President may promulgate those sections of the Constitution necessary for the convening of Parliament and the creation of machinery for its functioning. The President will, however, acquaint the people with the details of different provisions relating to finance. . . .

The Minister for National Reconstruction and Information, Habibur Rahman, told Basic Democracies members in Dacca that there would be no provision for any nominating system in the new constitution. He assured them that the country would be adminis-

tered by the elected representatives of the people.[45] In Sibi the President said the constitution would be presented some time in February. At present, he said, it was in the printing stage. He declared that women would be the only class enjoying reservations in the legislature; all others had to fight their own battles.[46] Zakir Husain asserted that the miltary regime was not trying to give the country an "orthodox" constitution, but rather "something that would meet [the people's] requirements."[47]

The *Morning News* on January 17 explained the "massive publicity campaign," estimated as costing a million rupees, planned for the constitution and speculated on the extent to which public opinion could find expression:

> To what extent the people in general and the organs of public opinion will be allowed to debate and discuss the new Constitution is still uncertain. The orders which banned a public discussion of the Constitution are still in force. . . .
>
> The public was reminded last Saturday that the Martial Law regulations banning public meetings, political parties, etc. had still not been withdrawn. The penalties were also spelled out. . . .
>
> About 5,000 copies of the new Constitution are now being printed in the English language. Copies will also be printed in Urdu and Bengali to be put on sale. An equal number of copies of the Constitution Commission's report are being simultaneously printed for distribution.
>
> There will be a set of pamphlets explaining the new Constitution and these will be distributed on a massive scale. According to information trickling in from Rawalpindi, about a million copies of these pamphlets will be in the hands of the people shortly after the official announcement is made.
>
> The full version of the President's speech, a brochure aimed at the intelligentsia, another brochure aimed at the less educated, and a Press summary will comprise this set of pamphlets. A film dealing with the framing and announcement of the new Constitution will also be released.
>
> It is interesting to note that the chief target of the publicity drive will be the intelligentsia. Is it because the intelligentsia is supposed to be relatively more recalcitrant?

Lieutenant General Burki, the Minister for Health, Labor, and Social Welfare, told the East Pakistan Union of Journalists: "As the biggest medium of news and views here it will devolve on you to give a lead which is *right*, sensible and patriotic [italics added]."[48]

The President, inaugurating the West Pakistan Basic Democracies convention in Lahore, said explicitly for the first time that Basic Democracies members would form an electoral college. They would elect not only the new assemblies but also the President. He cautioned

the union councillors against the evils of political parties and political maneuverings and suggested they concentrate on developmental activities for the country's reconstruction. He assured them that the new constitution would prevent legislators from interfering in the day-to-day administration. In reply to a suggestion that the various tiers of Basic Democracies should have elected chairmen, President Ayub said the history of the district boards and municipal bodies showed that elected chairmen were not successful. The appointed chairmen were only there to help the elected representatives.[49]

In the latter part of January the economic committee of the cabinet redeemed A. K. Khan's promise of the previous July and approved a plan for a steel mill in Chittagong. The mill, which was to cost Rs. 13.32 crores, would be completed in three years.[50]

Two important government activities during December and January concerned preparations for the elections and the proceedings of the Finance Commission. By the middle of December the Election Commission, at that time a permanent body but lacking a full staff, was keeping the electoral rolls up to date and collecting revenue maps for the delimitation of constituencies. In January the President named as chief election commissioner Akhtar Hussain, the Minister for Education and Scientific Research, Kashmir Affairs and Minority Affairs. The appointment was to become effective as soon as the constitution was promulgated. It was considered likely that Hussain would also head the Delimitation Commission which would be set up after the announcement of the constitution and start its work as soon as the date for parliamentary elections was fixed. Meanwhile, the Election Commission was expanded by the addition of two regional election commissioners and two assistant regional election commissioners. Hussain planned to start talks with the regional commissioners early in February.[51]

The President, as Chief Martial Law Administrator, announced an amendment to Martial Law Regulation No. 94 (prohibiting political meetings and processions) which permitted public meetings and processions for purposes of the forthcoming elections. The only restriction was that such meetings and processions must be held within the candidate's constituency.[52] Meanwhile, the contractor for Ayub Hall in Rawalpindi, said work was proceeding round-the-clock and the building would be turned over to the government March 31.[53]

In preparation for the first meeting of the new parliament, members of the former national assembly secretariat who were retired after the revolution were being re-employed. Those who were nearing the age of sixty would serve for periods of from six months to two years. If the

new parliament secretariat was not to have its own secretary at once, the law secretary would also act as the parliament secretary. The staff of the former national assembly which was not retired had "been working in a separate wing of the Law Ministry," said a *Dawn* special representative on February 4, "known as the Former National Assembly Wing."[54]

The *Pakistan Observer*, ever mindful of lapses from democratic procedure, commented on December 22 that the members of Basic Democracies had no mandate from the people to act as their electors except in the original yes or no vote for President Ayub Khan February 14, 1960, and that in other countries draft constitutions were usually placed before the people in referendums. More philosophically, the editor recognized it was necessary at that time "to avoid if possible the excitement, controversy and bitterness unavoidable in open and public discussions of constitutional provisions." Still he believed that it was necessary to demonstrate to the world that Pakistan's constitution was one "to which the great majority of Pakistanis [had] given their unquestioned allegiance."

The Finance Commission appointed by President Ayub Khan on December 12 was chaired by H. A. Majid, the secretary to the Finance Ministry (Economic Affairs Division). Three members were from the central government, two each from the provincial governments, one representative each from the Industrial Development Bank and the State Bank and an economist from Dacca University; altogether five members from each wing. The commission had been asked to submit its report by January 15, 1962.[55] At its first meeting in Rawalpindi on December 20, the commission discussed issues and procedures. Necessary data and comprehensive working papers would be prepared for the next meeting on January 2, 1962 from which time the commission would remain continuously in session until January 15.[56]

The terms of reference of the finance commission were made public December 23 in *Dawn*. The three main issues, in essence, concerned: the allocation of revenue sources between the center and the provinces; the apportionment between the two provinces of their respective shares of the sources of revenue; and the principle which should govern the allocation to the provinces of the resources at the disposal of the center. The issues considered at the January 2 session were (1) the specific taxes and duties which should be collected and administered by the center and by the provinces, and (2) which taxes and duties administered by the center should be divided between the center and the provinces. Other problems to be studied in subsequent meetings were the distribution between center and provinces of taxes and duties raised

by the center and the apportionment between the provinces of such proceeds; any modification in the terms of repayment of debt liability of the provinces to the center and of the center to the State Bank; and the borrowing powers, internal and external, of the provinces under the constitution. The news story in *Dawn* on January 3 concluded:

> Underlying the spirit behind the appointment of the commission is the Government's desire to ensure harmonious development of both the wings through equitable allocation of Central Government resources between East and West Pakistan.
> . . . The main object of the Commission will be an objective and detached study of the question.
> A report from the Commission, which includes financial experts from both wings, is expected to go a long way in allaying any misgivings which some people might have about the disparity.

The *Morning News* published on January 12 a brief item recapitulating the appointment of the members and the terms of reference of the Finance Commission. An "informed source" said the Commission was "working hard to prepare an objective report." The *Pakistan Observer* the next day complained that although the Commission was dealing with a matter "of vital interest," the public was informed neither of the proceedings nor of the subjects they discussed. Possibly it was proper for the Commission to be undisturbed, the editorial noted, but they could not "ignore the basic political and national purposes of the allocations." It was not just the *procedure* of allocation that was important, but "the exact division of physical assets and finances."

The explanation for the secrecy soon came out—the Commission was badly split and could not agree on its recommendations. The report was not submitted on January 15 nor was a new target date fixed for its completion. The chairman, H. A. Majid, said he did not know whether or not part of the recommendations would be included in the constitution. The Commission resumed meetings in Dacca on January 16,[57] and within a few days was reported to have completed its discussions. Neither of the Dacca English-language papers had any official confirmation of this but on January 20 both papers cited two Dacca Bengali-language newspapers which said the division between the East and West Pakistan members had resulted in the submission of two reports. The chairman neither confirmed nor denied this rumor nor one that followed soon to the effect that three reports were presented to President Ayub—one by the chairman and two by the provincial delegations. According to the *Morning News* of January 24, it was not known whether the chairman had been able to persuade the members

to accept his views. A few days later Shoaib said that the report of the Finance Commission had been submitted and was now being considered by the Cabinet but he would not comment on the rumors regarding the number of reports.[58]

The situation was rather thoroughly analyzed by the *Statesman's* Dacca correspondent on January 29:

> . . . the crux of the deadlock is the adamant attitude of the East Pakistani team that their province has had a raw deal from past regimes in the matter of economic development and as such very special measures are called for to help her make up leeway. The West Pakistani members while sympathizing with the Eastern wing's plight do not agree that she merits any more special attention than is now being afforded her by the country's present rulers. . . .
>
> The only way out now would seem to be a final decision by the President with or without Cabinet advice on the basis of the separate reports of the commission, but considering the wide divergence of views on fundamentals in these reports any such unilateral action might only increase the risk of aggravating, on one side or the other, the already existing antagonism to the proposed Constitution. As it is, the somewhat belated appointment of the commission and the decision to incorporate its findings in the new Constitution have been interpreted here as probable insurance against too great an opposition from this wing [East Pakistan] to the far more controversial political aspects of the country's proposed fundamental law.
>
> The deadlock was not altogether unexpected. It had been hinted at shortly after the sittings of the commission in West Pakistan had ended. The chairman parried references to it when questioned on his arrival at Dacca for the sittings in East Pakistan earlier this month. But scepticism had manifested itself even earlier when the President first promised the commission in November last year, after having acknowledged publicly in the presence of foreign diplomats the justice of East Pakistan's complaint about exploitation. . . .
>
> However, it is significant that even in failure the commission's efforts are being viewed by East Pakistanis in general as being not altogether without fruit. If nothing else, they seem pleased that viewpoints which were once dubbed 'subversive' have now been given the respectability of an economic base and have apparently at long last been further sanctified by full endorsement by local officialdom. Four of the five East Pakistani members on the Finance Commission were top level administrators who could never be accused of playing politics or of sentimentalism.

Thus, October 1961 proved not to have been a "turning point" after all. Convinced of the merits of East Pakistan's arguments, President Ayub had attempted to begin to remove interwing economic disparities. Instead, his efforts met with a solid wall of resistance from West Pakistan which had no intention of relinquishing its privileged position.

Within a week of receiving the Commission's report, the Cabinet

made a decision on the allocation of revenues between the two wings. Md. Shoaib, the Finance Minister, in making the announcement from Rawalpindi on January 28, said that "the committee of the Cabinet [had] reached agreed decisions on all the issues referred to the Commission." Shoaib enumerated the major decisions on allocation of the income tax, sales tax, excise duties, and export duties on jute and cotton. As a concession to the provincial governments their debt liability to the center (with the exception of foreign loans) was to be reduced by 50%. To implement the government's policy of accelerating the country's development and reducing the "gap between the less developed regions and the more developed regions," it was decided that "in the formulation of development plans . . . and their implementation, it will be ensured that every possible effort is made to reduce and remove disparities in per capita incomes between provinces."[59]

Two tables best permit comparison between the allocation formula known as the Raisman Award which had been in effect for the preceding decade and the proposed allocation formula announced by the Finance Minister.[60]

TABLE I.  ALLOCATION OF REVENUE BETWEEN THE CENTER
AND THE PROVINCES

| *Source of Revenue According to:* | Share Allocated to: | |
|---|---|---|
| (a) The Raisman Award Formula of 1951 | *The Center* | *The Provinces* |
| Income tax, not including corporation tax, taxes on federal emoluments, or taxes collected in Karachi | 50% | 50% |
| Sales tax | 50% | 50% |
| Excise taxes on tea, betel nuts and tobacco | 50% | 50% |
| Export duty on jute | 37½% | 62½%* |
| (b) The Cabinet Formula of 1962 | | |
| Income and corporation taxes, not including taxes on federal emoluments, or taxes collected in Karachi | 50% | 50% |
| Sales tax | 40% | 60% |
| Excise taxes on tea, betel nuts and tobacco | 40% | 60% |
| Export duty on jute and cotton | 0% | 100% |

* For East Pakistan exclusively. Neither province received any of the cotton export duties.

Source: Tables I and II are based on text of Shoaib's speech as published in *Dawn,* January 29, 1962, p. 8.

TABLE II.  ALLOCATION OF THE DIVISIBLE POOL BETWEEN EAST
PAKISTAN AND WEST PAKISTAN

| Source of Revenue According to: | Share Allocated to: | |
|---|---|---|
| | East Pakistan | West Pakistan |
| (a) The Raisman Award Formula of 1951 | | |
| Income tax | 45% | 55% |
| Sales tax | On the basis of collection | |
| Excise duties | 45% | 55% |
| Jute export duties | 100% | 0% |
| (b) The Cabinet Formula of 1962 | | |
| Income and corporation taxes | On the basis of population | |
| Sales tax | 70% on basis of population | |
| | 30% on basis of collection | |
| Excise duties | On the basis of population | |
| Jute and cotton export duties | On the basis of population | |

Source: Same as Table I.

Table I shows that the center proposed to increase the total amount
of the divisible pool. But the crux of the problem was whether the
*relative* amount for East Pakistan was to be raised. Shoaib omitted too
many pertinent facts from his statement to permit a clear picture to be
drawn. It is true that according to the new population allocation
(Table II) East Pakistan should get 54% of the income tax, excise
duties and export duties on jute and cotton and the amount of the sales
tax may have been increased by the new formula. Offsetting any pro-
portional gains by East Pakistan under this plan, however, were the
gains of West Pakistan through getting 46% of the jute and cotton export duties, when previously that province had not received any
revenue from this source. Not mentioned in Shoaib's statement[61] was
a special concession to West Pakistan, namely, the suspension during
the remaining three years of the second five-year plan of the recover-
able interest charges on its debt to the center, amounting to Rs. 4
crores.[62] At the press conference, Shoaib was asked, "Are there any
dissenting notes?" The Finance Minister replied, "I told you of the
agreed decision of the Committee of the Cabinet [which was] approved by the Cabinet. . . . I know of very few reports in which there
have not been people [holding different views]. . . . The Cabinet
Committee . . . really spent hours and hours discussing it and ultimately
we were able to reach completely agreed conclusions." Shoaib explained that one of the prime considerations in allocating resources
was to remove the disparity in per capita income between the provinces

and among the regions within each province, for this was "very important from the point of view of harmonious relationships."[63]

The *Pakistan Observer* of January 29 had printed only a brief story of Shoaib's statement, while both *Dawn* and the *Morning News* gave complete coverage. Whereas *Dawn* pointed out on February 3 that the reduction of West Pakistan's "share in the Central revenue from taxes and duties [would] be substantially offset by the suspension" of the interest charges, the *Pakistan Observer* of January 31 glumly remarked that now West Pakistan would get all the revenue from Karachi too, as that city was no longer the capital and had merged with the province of West Pakistan. This newspaper's treatment of the story on the allocation of resources suggests a depth of despondency in sharp contrast to the high hopes of the previous October. It was not surprising therefore that the *Statesman* headed its article of January 31 on the revenue pool, "Dacca confused by announcement":

> Our Dacca correspondent says the announcement evoked little reaction there today.
>
> Published details are considered too meager and confusing and a full official announcement is awaited.
>
> Initial confusion results from the reference to only one report of the Finance Commission having been considered by the Cabinet before it reached unanimous agreement on the new formula. Doubts about the accuracy of the published announcement are also raised by the fact that it covers only the fiscal aspect of the problem posed by the economic disparity between the two wings with no mention about the adjustments that will have to be made in other allied fronts which were known to have been discussed in the Finance Commission settings.
>
> Finally the suddenness of the announcement and the speed with which the Cabinet apparently reached agreement despite the known wide divergence of views in the Finance Commission is considered puzzling. Some of the new proposals appear to be a gain more for West Pakistan than East Pakistan. For instance, there is the principle which gives West Pakistan a share proportionate to its population of the export duty on cotton and jute when under existing arrangements she receives no share of the cotton duty while East Pakistan receives $62\frac{1}{2}\%$ of the duty on jute.

The *Morning News* appeared quite pleased with the results of Shoaib's announcement saying that East Pakistan's increased share of Rs. 11 crores next year would "go a long way towards reducing its proverbial deficits" and since the basis of dividing the pool would be population rather than parity "the interest of East Pakistan [would] get a due recognition in the future." With the scaling down of debt liabilities, the editorial concluded, "the ground has thus been prepared

for the two provinces to start their new career on an even financial keel."[64]

The editorial in *Dawn* on February 3 used one and a half columns to explain the old and the new formulas and the task of the finance committee. It concluded that the new formula represented a "marked improvement upon the Raisman Award." After recognizing the advantages to West Pakistan in having its interest charges suspended for the balance of the second five-year plan period, *Dawn* stated, "But East Pakistan, which is denied this concession, will have much larger resources accruing from the export duty on jute, excise duties and sales tax. . . ." Actually, East Pakistan's share of jute export duty was reduced from the $62\frac{1}{2}\%$ of the Raisman Award to the $54\%$ of a formula based on population.

*Ittefaq,* a Bengali daily published in Dacca, stated that revenue allocation was only a part of the economic problem which faced the two wings; it was also necessary for the government to consider fair allocation of development expenditure, inter-regional trade, foreign aid, etc. The newspaper recommended that all the country's resources should be so allocated that the disparity would be eliminated within a definite period of time. *Ittefaq* further urged that equal representation in political and administrative affairs be given due consideration.[65]

The suspense and tension of the long waiting period were building up to an explosion which the government itself touched off.

## NOTES

1. *Pakistan Observer* (Dacca), September 28, 1961.
2. *Ibid.,* October 5, 1961.
3. *Ibid.,* and *Dawn* (Karachi), October 4, 1961, p. 1.
4. *Pakistan Observer,* October 6, 1961.
5. *Ibid.,* October 10, 1961.
6. *Dawn,* October 11, 1961, p. 1.
7. *Pakistan Observer,* October 16, 1961.
8. *Ibid.,* October 10, 1961.
9. Between ninety and ninety-five persons were disqualified by the three tribunals, although over three thousand in East Pakistan were automatically disqualified under Article 5 of the Elective Bodies Disqualificaton Order from contesting elections until December 31, 1966. *Pakistan Observer,* January 17, 1960.
10. *Ibid.,* October 16, 1961, p. 1.
11. *Ibid.,* October 18, 1961, p. 1.
12. *Ibid.*
13. The Calcutta *Statesman,* October 20, 1961, gave added light on the reaction of the public to the President's speech: "This fresh approach to

East Pakistan's long standing grievances from one at the head of Pakistan's affairs was extremely well received by many among East Pakistan's intelligentsia. The reaction at the public meeting, however, was not as spontaneous as one might have expected but this undoubtedly was accounted for by the fact that the President spoke in Urdu." The *Statesman* also revealed that the President's admission of East Pakistan's justification for its complaints was made not only at the huge rally but also the day before to the "intelligentsia" at the civic reception.

14. Originally expressed in a paper, "The Indivisibility of the National Economy," read at the Lahore seminar of the Bureau of National Reconstruction in September 1961. Previous publications were a short résumé on May 29; about 2½ columns on the first page of the Sunday magazine section on June 4, and another and slightly longer résumé on September 24. Rehman Sobhan's ideas in a more objective form were presented in "The Problem of Regional Imbalance in the Economic Development of Pakistan," *Asian Survey*, II, 5 (July 1962), 31-37.

15. *Pakistan Observer,* October 23, 25, 1961.

16. *Ibid.,* October 25, 26, 1961.

17. *Dawn,* October 29, 1961, p. 1.

18. *Ibid.,* October 27, 1961, p. 4; Khan, Md. Ayub, *Speeches and Statements* (Karachi: Pakistan Publications), IV (July 1961-June 1962), 123-126.

19. Khan, Md. Ayub, *op. cit.,* IV, 127-130.

20. *Pakistan Observer,* November 4, 1961.

21. *Ibid.,* November 8, 1961.

22. *Dawn,* November 6, 1961, p. 4.

23. *Pakistan Observer,* November 3, 1961.

24. *Ibid.,* November 10, 1961.

25. *Ibid.,* November 11, 1961.

26. *Ibid.,* November 6, p. 1; November 7, p. 1; November 8, p. 8; November 9, p. 1; November 10, 1961, p. 1.

27. *Ibid.,* November 13, 1961, p. 4.

28. *Ibid.,* December 15, 1961.

29. *Dawn,* November 14, 1961, p. 1.

30. *Ibid.,* November 25, 1961, p. 4.

31. *Ibid.,* November 26, 1961, p. 1.

32. *Pakistan Observer,* November 23, p. 1; December 7, p. 3; *Morning News* (Dacca), December 9, 1961, p. 1.

33. *Dawn,* December 9, 1961, p. 1.

34. *Morning News,* December 15, 1961, p. 1.

35. *Pakistan Observer,* December 18, 1961, p. 1.

36. Khan, Md. Ayub, *op. cit.,* IV, 145-146.

37. *Pakistan Observer* and *Morning News,* January 4, 1962.

38. *Dawn* and *Morning News,* December 14, 1961.

39. *Pakistan Observer,* December 14, 1961.

40. *Ibid.,* December 29, 1961.

41. *Ibid.,* December 29, 1961, p. 1.

42. *Dawn,* January 4, 1962, p. 1.

43. Because the Muslim year is based on the lunar calendar, any given date of the Muslim year comes eleven days earlier each year than the year before in the Gregorian calendar. In 1962 Ramazan began February 7.

44. *Pakistan Observer,* January 9, 1962, p. 1.

45. *Dawn,* January 16, 1962, p. 1.

46. *Morning News,* January 17, 1962.

47. *Dawn,* January 24, 1962.

48. *Statesman,* January 18, 1962.

49. *Pakistan Observer,* January 30, 1962, p. 1. Only the lowest tier of Basic Democracies, the union councils, had elected chairmen.

50. *Ibid.,* January 25, 1962, p. 1.

51. *Ibid.,* January 20, 22 and *Morning News,* January 29, 1962.

52. *Dawn,* January 21, 1962, pp. 1, 9.

53. *Ibid.,* January 25, 1962, p. 1.

54. One cannot help wondering what they had been doing for the past three years.

55. *Morning News,* December 13, 1961, p. 1.

56. *Pakistan Observer,* December 21, 1961, p. 1.

57. *Ibid.,* January 15, 1962, p. 8.

58. *Ibid.,* January 28, 1962. According to one rumor, there were five reports.

59. *Dawn,* January 29, 1962, pp. 1, 8.

60. G. W. Choudhury in *Constitutional Development in Pakistan* (Lahore: Longmans, Green, 1959), p. 192, explains that Pakistan's original distribution of financial resources in 1947 was based on the provisions of the Government of India Act 1935, which leaned heavily toward the center. "By 1952, Sir Jeremy Raisman, who was appointed to examine the allocations of revenues . . . recommended that the original distribution of financial resources should be resumed. The provinces, particularly East Pakistan, however, continued to press for greater and greater shares. . . . East Pakistan legitimately complained about the inadequacy of funds. . . ."

61. The text of which appeared ostensibly in its complete form in *Dawn,* January 29, 1962, p. 8, and whose source was the APP.

62. As revealed in an editorial in *ibid.,* February 3, 1962.

63. *Ibid.,* January 30, 1962, p. 9.

64. February 3, 1962.

65. Summarized in *Morning News,* February 11, 1962, "Gleanings from the Bengali Press."

# CHAPTER XI

# ACTION AND REACTION

(February 1962)

"Suhrawardy Arrested" was the stunning headline of January 31. In order to prevent H. S. Suhrawardy from acting in a manner "prejudicial to the security and defence of Pakistan," the government of Pakistan had found it necessary to arrest and detain him in the Karachi Central Jail under the Security of Pakistan Act.[1]

H. S. Suhrawardy was one of the few outstanding "ex-politicians" of East Pakistan. He had been active in politics in pre-partition India and was the last chief minister of undivided Bengal. Some months after independence he moved to Pakistan, entered politics and by 1952 had organized the Awami League as an opposition party to the Muslim League. At one time he was Law Minister and served as Prime Minister from September 1956 to October 1957.[2] Suhrawardy was one of the nineteen politicians who received notices to appear before the Central Elective Bodies Disqualification Tribunal on charges of corruption and maladministration. He contested all the charges but was found guilty on four of seven counts and on July 15, 1960, was declared disqualified as a member of any elective body until the end of December 1966.[3]

The press note issued by the government to explain the surprise arrest said in part: "It is already well known that Mr. Suhrawardy ever since the inception of Pakistan had been . . . indulging in activities which were of a highly prejudicial nature and . . . he with several others, was responsible for the predicament in which Pakistan found itself in the latter half of 1958." The military regime had stemmed the rot, according to the press note, and even those politicians whose conduct had been scrutinized by the EBDO tribunals had been treated generously. "But Mr. Suhrawardy, misunderstanding this generosity," resumed the press note, "continued to indulge in activities prejudicial to the integrity and safety of Pakistan. . . . [He] has taken it upon himself to play a destructive role even after the revolution. Mr. Suhrawardy

has openly associated with anti-Pakistan elements both within and outside the country." His recent activities were "fraught with such danger
to the security and safety of Pakistan that one could fairly describe
them as being treasonable."[4]

It is hardly necessary to note that there were no editorial comments
in Pakistani papers on Suhrawardy's arrest. An Indian correspondent
in the *Statesman,* however, described the effect of the announcement in
Dacca:

> The report of the arrest took Dacca completely by surprise this
> morning and for many a moment those who heard the news from
> friends and acquaintances could scarcely believe their ears. With the
> passing of the initial shock, surprise gave place to concern, not so
> much for Mr. Suhrawardy personally but more because of the timing
> of the arrest. Many interpreted it as indicative of more such possible
> arrests, particularly in East Pakistan, and of perhaps further delay
> in the promulgation of the new Constitution and in the promised
> return of power, in however truncated a form, to the people.
> It was only later, when the Press Note was issued advancing much
> more serious charges against Mr. Suhrawardy, including possible
> treason, that people began to take a much more serious view and
> initial comments on the arrest completely dried up. A few seemed
> particularly taken aback by the allegations of Mr. Suhrawardy's
> anti-Pakistani associations and tended to recall the days shortly after
> the 1958 take-over when, during a spate of political arrests, Mr.
> Suhrawardy was deemed almost untouchable because of the influence
> of some of his known close friends in the new regime. The present
> allegations are thus being interpreted here as possible confirmation
> of the belief that there has recently been a modification in Pakistan's
> international relations.[5]

Suhrawardy was arrested on January 30. The next day President
Ayub and other government officials went to East Pakistan for a week-
long visit. The first questions asked by reporters at the airport dealt,
of course, with Suhrawardy. They wanted to know why the government delayed action when, according to the press note, the former
Prime Minister had been indulging in anti-state activities since the
beginning of the new regime. President Ayub said that they had
hoped Suhrawardy would mend his ways, but now that the new
constitution was about to be launched, he wanted the people to benefit
by it and "get it to work." The President said that although Suhrawardy
was a very good and intelligent man, he did not think that he had
"much love for Pakistan." He also stated that the government had
"direct proof" to show that Suhrawardy's activities were aimed first
at the disruption of East Pakistan and eventually all of Pakistan.[6]

During this interview President Ayub Khan also answered questions

relating to the constitution. It would be announced the third week of February, he said, and explained that the delay was not deliberate but due to the time-consuming, meticulous process of drafting. He was still determined not to lift the ban on political parties before elections but if it became inevitable there would be legislative curbs on them. The governors' conference, he said, would discuss not only the issue of the bifurcation of PIDC but also the future location of all aid-giving organizations. He personally favored decentralization to expedite the work.[7]

President Ayub had a full schedule planned for his East Pakistan visit. Of greatest significance perhaps was the governors' conference. Other important events included the third anniversary of the Writers' Guild, the first All-Pakistan Basic Democracies Convention held in Dacca, the annual observance of East Pakistan Week and the meeting of the Provincial Advisory Council. He also took part in ceremonies opening the PIDC fertilizer factory at Fenchuganj in Sylhet district. He made several important speeches and a major address which was broadcast over Radio Pakistan on the night of February 6. He left for Karachi the following afternoon.

Until the February 7 editions, no news story reported anything about the outburst of demonstrations and riots begun February 1 by Dacca University students. It is doubtful, however, if many people in the province failed to recognize the significance of a small item in the *Morning News* on February 6: "Dacca University Declares Vacation during Ramazan." Ramazan had traditionally been a holiday period for students but as a result of the Education Commission's recommendations the school-year schedule had been changed. The University's decision now to observe Ramazan as a vacation period entailed changes in the whole year's program. The first demonstration occurred February 1, the day after the announcement of Suhrawardy's arrest. Two days later, when Manzur Qadir was scheduled to address the students, another demonstration took place. The Foreign Minister, it was said, had to be escorted to safety by faculty members. On February 6 and 7 large numbers of students took part in processions that ended in riots. Against this troubled background, not publicly acknowledged but known throughout East Pakistan, the activities of President Ayub and the various government officials were reported by the press.

To the Pakistan Writers' Guild, President Ayub admitted that he had been skeptical of writers as people who lived in a world which "did not exist, at least not in Pakistan." He told them a new country was emerging from the old feudalistic society. If the writers wished to contribute to the country's development they could help solve certain

practical and psychological problems by their realistic and objective thinking. He said they should abandon their emphasis on an international outlook and concentrate on national problems.[8]

The governors' conference which opened its session on February 1 had a heavy agenda of twenty-three items. Among the more important subjects considered were those relating to agriculture and education. A major decision of the conference was to create two separate PIDC's on the basis of the recommendations of the committee on decentralization of institutions.[9]

President Ayub's speech to the 240 participants of the Basic Democracies convention contained the usual exhortations to select good representatives and a reminder of the great responsibility that devolved on them. He said new criteria for leadership were emerging—determination, character and the will to serve the people—as opposed to the disruption and deception of the people as in East Pakistan, or cries of regionalism, provincialism and tribalism as in West Pakistan. The President expressly urged the union councillors not to put too much emphasis on politics. Nefarious propaganda against the constitution might be circulated, he warned, and it was the obligation of the councillors to "checkmate and counter" this.[10]

He pointed out in his speech at the opening of the giant Fenchuganj fertilizer plant in Sylhet how much industrialization in East Pakistan had accelerated in the last two and a half years. "A lot has been given to East Pakistan and a lot more will be given," promised the President. Addressing a public meeting at the district town of Sylhet, he declared that the constitution would be workable and would help in maintaining a strong and stable government. He classified the people of East Pakistan as being, for the most part, pious and Islamic-minded, and cautioned them against antisocial and subversive elements.[11]

His talk with the members of the Provincial Advisory Council was very practical. Among other topics he spoke on WAPDA, the bifurcation of the PIDC, the Karnafuly Dam project and the Agricultural Development Corporation. He said he was trying to provide a constitution which would enable the people to run the administration on democratic lines. He hoped the advisory council members would approve of the constitution and use their influence to see that people were not misled. Peace and stability were the prerequisites for development. While he was not worried about outside hostility, he said he wondered at the stupidity of people who would harm the country to serve their own ends. President Ayub also referred to the government's policy for improving and equalizing the people's standard of living as quickly as possible. In this connection he cited the govern-

ment's decision that the total amount of duty on jute should go to East Pakistan[12] as well as a larger share of other taxes. Without referring to the two-economy theory, the President said Pakistan could not order any country to give money to this wing or that.[13] Foreign aid could be used to finance only projects demonstrated to be sound and feasible.[14]

The broadcast speech of February 6 dealt entirely with the facts and figures of economic development of East Pakistan and the military regime's improvements in this situation. He expressed the belief that neither wing could survive economically or politically unless there was a healthy growth in both wings and in the nation as a whole. The President concluded,

> We are now on the eve of our new Constitution. Its aims amongst others will be to give us stable Governments and sound and vigorous administrations. . . . So our future is bound up intimately with the way we work that Constitution. Therefore, if you remember this and work with sincerity and zeal, God willing we shall achieve our objectives of progress and strength.[15]

President Ayub's parting words at the airport were that the present administration had "with great difficulty" brought about a base for development and built up a good and sound administration. He warned the people not to lose this asset by irresponsible action or utterance, for if they did so, they would suffer. This was the first published remark by the President that clearly related to the students' demonstrations. On his arrival in Karachi he told the waiting newsmen that no date had yet been set for the announcement of the constitution.[16]

During this eventful week several cabinet ministers also visited various districts in East Pakistan. Zakir Husain, the Home Affairs Minister, visited Chittagong, his home city. At a press interview he stated that the constitution was expected to be announced by the President over Radio Pakistan on March 1. He made it clear that the constitution as announced would be final and decisive and no change would take place until after the parliament had met. Husain reminded the reporters that the constitution was based on the Commission's report, that it represented an agreed decision, and he hoped it would meet the requirements of the country. On the question of fund allocations for East Pakistan the Minister reported that during the next financial year, because of consortium aid, fund allocations for East Pakistan would be much larger than before.[17]

Hafizur Rahman, the Commerce Minister, told Comilla union councillors that the constitution had been framed with a keen eye to the development of the country and that since amendment by parliament

was provided for, it would be flexible.[18] Habibur Rahman, the Minister for National Reconstruction and Information, urged the delegates to the Basic Democracies convention to remember that economic development was their prime concern. He stated that Islam was the basis of Pakistani ideology and to try "any other ideology . . . would be a great disservice to the country."[19]

The hoisting of the flag at the Comilla cantonment on February 4 marked the raising of the Third Battalion of the East Bengal Regiment; recruitment for the fourth battalion had already started as a result of the President's 1961 promise to raise two more battalions from East Pakistan. Another event of importance to both wings of Pakistan was the February 6 inauguration of twice-weekly Pakistan International Airways jet service between Dacca and Karachi.[20]

The clashes between Dacca University students and the city police already referred to followed on the heels of other student demonstrations during the preceding week. On January 18 when a group of twenty-five East Pakistani tourists, mostly students, were returning from West Pakistan by train through India, ugly incidents occurred in two railroad stations in West Bengal, Sealdah and Belghoria. As the Pakistani group with their luggage more than filled their train compartment, they refused to admit more passengers. A scuffle ensued and stones were thrown into the compartment. Four Pakistanis were injured and the next day two persons were admitted to the Dacca Medical College Hospital with serious chest and head injuries. Dacca students were incensed and officials expressed great concern. January 24 the entire student community of Dacca went on strike and demonstrated against "Indian hooliganism." Students throughout the province held protest meetings and the East Pakistani government lodged a strong protest with the government of West Bengal.[21]

Keyed up by these events, the students reacted quickly to the news of Suhrawardy's arrest. The only news published in the English-language press about the student riots was issued by the government to the press associations in the form of press notes. A press note is generally printed verbatim in its entirety. While these accounts were not necessarily false, they did not always tell the whole truth. It is likely that more damage and violence was involved in the student riots than the press notes reported.

The first demonstration on February 1 had supposedly been in protest against Suhrawardy's arrest but it appeared probable that the true purpose was to demonstrate against the government and the President.[22] The next riot—on the occasion of Manzur Qadir's speech on February 3—left no doubt of that. The riot of February 6 brought forth

the first press note on the student demonstrations.[23] It described how the students had again left their classes and the university premises shouting "slogans"—the nature of which was not disclosed. Near the entrance to the High Court the students, when the police tried to restrain them, started throwing brickbats. The police then made "a mild lathi charge." Some students and policemen were injured in the mêlée. Later the students marched through the main business section of the city, forcing shops to close down and setting fire to a truck. The press note said ten persons were arrested and concluded:

> The members of the public are requested not to listen to mischievous rumors which appear to have been deliberately set afloat to confuse and mislead the people.[24]

As a reminder to the people, this press note was followed by the text of Martial Law Regulations Nos. 24 and 51 prohibiting any writing or actions that attempted "to promote feelings of enmity" against the armed forces, the police or the government.

In "midnight-to-dawn" raids on February 6 the government arrested seventeen persons in Dacca under the East Pakistan Public Safety Ordinance, among them some former members of the Awami League and five known Communists.[25] "These people have once again resorted to their old nefarious activities of exploiting the students for their selfish coterie interests and for subversive purposes," concluded the press note on the arrests in the *Pakistan Observer* of February 8.

Despite the vacation that was scheduled to begin on February 7 (the beginning of Ramazan) and despite the anxiety of the university and the government to have the students leave Dacca, the students staged their most violent riot on that day. They started assembling early in the morning and at eleven o'clock began a march which led to a brickbat attack on the police pickets. The procession continued downtown, causing serious damage to shops and manhandling of people as students tried to stop traffic. The police dispersed the mob with tear gas and arrested several students. Another procession coming from Tejgaon, at the northern edge of the city, set fire to a ceremonial gate. Near the Holy Family Hospital they were asked to disperse. Instead the marchers became rowdy and a large number of persons (reported to be 101) were arrested and the remainder dispersed. Later "goonda elements" (hoodlums) were seen inside the university compound, throwing brickbats at the police.[26]

Although the President had left Dacca by this time, the infection was spreading rapidly throughout the province. The press notes' headlines for the succeeding days read: "Situation in Dacca quiet; 32

arrested in Barisal and Kushtia"; "101 arrested in Dacca yesterday"; "Processions in Barisal, Perojpur, Narsingdi"; "Dacca situation normal; processions in Sylhet, Khulna"; "Dacca remains quiet; Chittagong Medical Students observe strike"; "Dacca remains peaceful; train in Noakhali stoned"; "Processions in mofussil [hinterland] areas"; "Procession at Daulatganj"; "Students rally at Comilla"; and "Procession near Laksham."[27]

The Indian correspondent of the *Statesman* apparently reported these disturbances too candidly. East Pakistan subscribers received only five issues of this newspaper during February 1962 and the journalist was served a government expulsion order requiring him to cross the border by midnight of February 12.[28] Copies of the *Statesman* were banned first in Dacca and later in Chittagong beginning with the February 3 issue which carried news of the student strikes. The only issues to be delivered during the month were those of February 1, 2, 4, 12 and 13.[29] All others were impounded by the Dacca District Intelligence Branch in order to prevent the distribution of news "which [might] lead to the disturbance of public tranquillity."[30]

News items covered by the banned *Statesman* which did not appear in the local papers included: the first day of the student strike and the display of posters demanding release of Suhrawardy (February 2); the story of the meeting at which Manzur Qadir spoke and which had to be abandoned because of the students' "boisterous behavior" (February 5); violence on the Dacca University campus when a man "who repeatedly declared himself as a member of the intelligence branch of an armed police unit" was "savagely beaten up," and the postponement of President Ayub Khan's visit to Rajshahi University to receive the honorary degree of Doctor of Laws (February 6); and the student threat to attack newspaper offices on the following day if the demonstrations were not reported in the press (February 7). Material printed in the *Statesman* on the arrest of Suhrawardy's lieutenants and the student riots that was not mentioned in the government press notes included: burning, tearing and trampling upon pictures of the President (February 7); use of the army to supplement armed local police squads, "a truly formidable sight" (February 8); strict censorship of the local press by inspection of news items before publication (February 4, 7 and 8); and double censorship (before and after printing) even including advertisements of the Bengali *Ittefaq* whose editor, Taffazzal Husain, was arrested in the recent night raids (February 9).

The *Statesman*, commenting editorially on February 9 on the arrest of Suhrawardy and the student riots, felt there may or may not have been a connection between the two events:

. . . it may be taken for granted that the main cause of his confine-
ment was that he had regained some of his former influence in East
Pakistan. Possibly the demonstrations which have followed his arrest
would not have taken place without it. Possibly demonstrations were
planned to take place some time later, perhaps in the third week of
the month, especially if the new constitution were promulgated then
and so coincided with the anniversary of the language riots of 1952.
It is interesting to see that medical students began the demonstrations
this time as they did ten years ago.

The thousand miles separating the two wings of Pakistan, which
appeared so formidable a barrier to national integration, proved no
obstacle to the spread of student-fever. Punjab University students in
Lahore expressed their sympathy with the Dacca students and appealed
to the government to release those who were arrested.[31] A spate of
strikes, non-political in nature and allegedly resulting from conditions
in the colleges, erupted in King Edward Medical College and the
College of Animal Husbandry, both in Lahore, the Agriculture College
in Lyallpur, a Bahawalpur college and Emerson College in Multan.[32]
According to one correspondent, the wave of strikes in West Pakistan
involved several thousand students and, although the issues were local
in character, what had really happened was that a "chain reaction" had
been set off so that in some instances "issues" were invented to justify
participation in the strike wave.[33]

Student-fever also leaped the distance to England. At a meeting of
the Pakistan Students Federation where recent events in East Pakistan
were being discussed the deputy high commissioner urged the students
to refrain from activities that might further distort the "poor image" of
Pakistan which the British seemed to have. The students heeded the
advice and "recoiled from the brink of political activity" on that occasion. The following night, however, left-wing Pakistani elements convened a meeting of "The Committee for the Restoration of Democracy
in Pakistan" which was extremely disorderly. When the East Pakistani
President of the group declared that Tagore was as great a "national
poet" of Pakistan as Allama Iqbal, the high commissioner reminded the
students that such provincialism could only harm the interests of Pakistan.[34] Presumably he was also concerned over the sentiments expressed on placards—"Down with Military Dictatorship," "Reopen
Dacca University," "Release Political Prisoners in Pakistan"—but this
news was not included in the *Dawn* story.[35]

When the strikes and riots of the students in East Pakistan continued instead of abating, a new worry assailed the authorities. Shaheed
Day, February 21, 1962, was the tenth anniversary of Martyrs' Day in
memory of those who lost their lives in the 1952 demonstrations for

recognition of Bengali as a national language along with Urdu.[36] For several years black flags had been hoisted on this day and all East Pakistani government offices, educational institutions and places of business had closed.[37] In more recent years it had been the students who had taken charge of the program for the day and it was hoped that dispersing the students for Ramazan would minimize the "massive student demonstrations" which were expected.[38] The government also tried to placate the students by announcing that it would undertake the construction of a suitable memorial for the students who lost their lives in the language movement. A half-finished monument, actually an eyesore, had stood in Dacca for several years and on previous observances of Shaheed Day one of the students' demands had been that the memorial be finished. The implementation committee set up for completing this monument was to meet before February 21 and the Government hoped to start construction by May 1.[39]

Representatives of the Dacca University Students Union announced that the Martyrs' Day program was to include visits to the martyrs' graves and the Shaheed Minar (the half-finished monument), prayers in mosques, temples and churches, a symposium on the Bengali language and cultural evening activities.[40] Despite the government's anxiety, the day was apparently observed in a solemn and peaceful manner in Dacca and the *mofussil* towns. Again the *Statesman* gave a little more information than the local papers. According to the Press Trust of India, a resolution was passed at the symposium urging the government to introduce a democratic and parliamentary system of government and to provide for complete provincial autonomy for East Pakistan.[41]

The trial of eleven persons, the majority students, charged under Martial Law Regulations Nos. 24, 51 and 79 "for allegedly damaging Government property (the ceremonial gate), shouting anti-state slogans and attending a procession" on February 7 began in Dacca February 18 at a special military court. A week was devoted to hearing nine prosecution witnesses and the students who had pleaded not guilty and the trial ended with the court reserving its judgment.[42]

Officials of the central and provincial governments and university and college administrators had a great deal to say about the student unrest. A Lahore English daily (unnamed in the report from Associated Press of Pakistan) asserted that "an important Western Power" had fomented the student troubles in East Pakistan and among Pakistani students abroad. Asked to comment on this, the Home Affairs Minister, Zakir Husain, said he would look into the press reports.[43] The vice-chancellors of Dacca University and Rajshahi University viewed the "recent unfortunate happenings" with "sorrow and dismay" and said

that the saddest aspect was that the name of the President had been dragged into the controversies.[44] East Pakistan's governor, Lieutenant General Mohammad Azam Khan, wrote to the guardians of all students in the province urging them to impress upon their wards "the vital importance of the maintenance of peace and order."[45] West Pakistan's governor, Malik Amir Mohammad Khan, after assuring the students that he would look into their grievances, advised them to devote their time to their studies and not to agitate through strikes.[46] The *Pakistan Observer* of February 25 began an editorial by saying, "Unrest among students, like television and nuclear weapons, is a marked peculiarity of our age." But the *Morning News* two days later wrote, "Restlessness among students is neither peculiar to this age nor confined to any country."

President Ayub Khan told newsmen the disturbances in East Pakistan were "a sad occasion" and said the students were being exploited by professional anti-state agitators in both wings.[47]

Meanwhile, on February 5 the hearing on a *habeas corpus* petition filed in the West Pakistan High Court, challenging the detention of H. S. Suhrawardy, was postponed until February 12 to allow the petitioner, Hamid Safaraz, a friend, to brief Suhrawardy's counsel, Khan Abdul Qayyum Khan.[48] On February 12 the hearing was again postponed until February 28 because the government had allowed neither the petitioner nor the counsel to interview the *détenu*. Khan Abdul Qayyum Khan told the court the allegations against Suhrawardy were serious and outside the ambit of the Security of Pakistan Act. They were intended to frighten the former Prime Minister's followers, he said, to keep them from taking part in the forthcoming elections. The judge asked the counsel to show that the court had jurisdiction in this case in spite of Martial Law Regulation No. 27.[49]

Several bar associations passed resolutions urging the government to try Suhrawardy in a court of law. The West Pakistan High Court Bar Association pointed out that the accused was "an eminent and senior member" of that body and, since he had been arrested under the Security of Pakistan Act and the government allegedly had "clear and definite proof of treasonable activities," the association "which firmly believe[d] in the rule of law" urged the government "in the interests of the country, justice and equity to try Mr. Suhrawardy in a court of law."[50] Similar resolutions were framed by the district bar associations of Lahore, Khulna, Lyallpur, Rajshahi, Dacca, Rangpur and the Pabna Pleaders' Bar Association.[51]

On February 9 President Ayub Khan promulgated an ordinance amending the code of criminal procedure so that a person detained

under the 1952 Security of Pakistan Act would be debarred from filing a *habeas corpus* petition against his arrest. The ordinance was to take effect at once.[52] Hence on February 28 the West Pakistan Chief Justice dismissed the *habeas corpus* petition challenging the detention of Suhrawardy. The counsel, Khan Abdul Qayyum Khan, fumed that the recent amendment was not civilized but a law of the jungle. He suggested that the court recommend that the President repeal it.[53]

Meantime the government was proceeding with programs designed to improve East Pakistan's economic situation. The committee appointed to implement the bifurcation of the PIDC held its first meeting in Rawalpindi on February 17 and was expected to complete its work in two to three months.[54] Abdul Qadir was named Finance Minister, since Mohammed Shoaib, temporarily Minister of Economic Coordination, was soon to devote his full time as a director of the World Bank in Washington.[55] Qadir, in his first news conference, outlined his financial policy, although he said he could not yet spell out the measures which could be taken to reduce disparities in income. He mentioned the development work that had been carried on in Dacca, Chittagong, Narayanganj and Bogra during the last three years and cited as two of his ten objectives: "Economic and fiscal policies will be so framed as to make distribution of wealth more equitable . . . [and] the pace of development in East Pakistan must be further stimulated."[56]

The *Pakistan Observer*'s staff correspondent analyzed on February 11 the development program of the Pakistan Eastern Railway (PER) during the second five-year plan as approved by the economic committee of the Cabinet. It was pointed out that: "The Pakistan Eastern Railway's development program . . . will cost in total Rs. 42.40 crore with a foreign exchange component of Rs. 25.87 crore, compared to Pakistan Western Railway's development program during the same period of Rs. 97.60 crore with a foreign exchange component of Rs. 64.10 crore." Two days later the second five-year plan for the public sector program of the center (including transport and communications, housing and settlements, agriculture and education) was examined by the *Pakistan Observer*. The last sentence revealed the disillusionment felt: "The total share of East Pakistan in the Central Government's Public Sector Program of Rs. 382.9 crore during the Second Plan appears to total between Rs. 75 and 80 crore."

It was announced on February 13 that the government had appointed a committee, headed by the Economic Coordination Minister, Mohammad Shoaib, to submit proposals for improvement in the administration of the railways.[57] The committee met in Rawalpindi on the 15th and 16th and its meetings were attended by both governors.

Lieutenant General Azam Khan of East Pakistan told the newsmen that the railways would function better if they were bifurcated and handed over to the provinces[58] and Governor Malik Amir Mohammad Khan said that West Pakistan would not oppose the provincialization of the railways. Newspapers conceded that the issue was practically settled and that only the committee's recommendation as to how the decision could best be effected was to be left for the Committee to work out.[59] The committee unanimously recommended that the railways be provincialized from the next financial year, beginning July 1, 1962, and on February 22 the Cabinet formally agreed to decentralize the Pakistan railways and entrust administration to the respective provincial governments. This decision was expected to become part of the new constitution and end over one hundred years of central control over railway administration.[60]

By the middle of February the only facts known about the new constitution were that the elected members of union councils would form the electorate and that the government would be federal. The governor of West Pakistan told reporters that no major change in the administrative structure of the west wing was anticipated and that there was no possibility of integrating the various divisions into zones with lieutenant governors as their heads. He felt such a merger would be the undoing of West Pakistan unification which the government was determined to maintain in the larger national interest.[61]

Hafizur Rahman, the Commerce Minister, told union councillors in Comilla district that the aim of the present regime was to improve national life by pooling all available resources under stable administration without political parties.[62] In the west wing, Z. A. Bhutto, Minister for Fuel, Power and Natural Resources, said that Pakistan was surrounded by enemies and therefore national unity was imperative. He said the new constitution would be announced this month by the President and that it would be acceptable to the people. He told another group that President Ayub's promise of the restoration of complete democracy which was made at the time of the revolution would be fulfilled with the announcement of the new constitution. Bhutto said that the introduction of Basic Democracies had provided the common people their first opportunity to participate equally in the administration of their affairs.[63]

In Rawalpindi the East Pakistan governor, Azam Khan, said that the urge of the East Pakistani people to develop their province should not be misunderstood. He asserted that East Pakistanis were one hundred per cent patriotic and had no ill will against the people of West Pakistan. Lieutenant General Azam Khan said there were no

separatist tendencies in East Pakistan, that only Pakistan's enemies raised this cry, and that equal development of each wing was necessary. He characterized the people of East Pakistan as staunch Muslims.[64]

The Minister for National Reconstruction and Information, Habibur Rahman, told members of the Administrative Staff College in Lahore that national integration was vital, that the elimination of economic disparity was essential, and that public servants were destined to play a pivotal role in strengthening the bonds between the different regions.[65] The Industries Minister, Abul Kasem Khan, speaking in Khairpur said a presidential form of government was the only one suitable for Pakistan. He said the new constitution contained a blueprint for a welfare state and the future government must make it complete.[66]

The February 15 cabinet meeting in Rawalpindi, attended by both governors, discussed the launching of the constitution, but "no clue was yet available about the precise stages of the gradual changeover to a constitutional setup." The correspondent of the *Pakistan Observer* on February 16 continued, "It has been generally believed here that the Constitution would be announced . . . probably on February 24 but so far no authoritative statement has yet been made." Two days later he wrote that February 28 would be the day. Elections to parliament and provincial legislatures had been tentatively fixed for the end of April, and the preparation of electoral rolls was under way. The delimitation of constituencies was already complete at district and divisional levels.

The government of East Pakistan took an unprecedented step during this period by employing front page space in the *Pakistan Observer* and *Morning News* to assure direct communication with the English-reading public. Each day from February 18 to 25 a box of about four by five inches contained some of the President's February 6 radio speech on "Economic Development of East Pakistan." The first quotation began, "Let me tell you that it is my conviction that the strength of Pakistan lies in the greater strength of each of the two wings. . . ." Others dealt with the amount of money utilized by East Pakistan during the first five-year plan, the balancing of the provincial revenue budget, increase of foreign allocation to East Pakistan, the distribution of central revenue and the increase in imports. Only the first two inserts contained the words, "Issued by the Information Department, Government of East Pakistan."

The official announcement of the constitution promulgation date was finally made public. A February 22 press communiqué issued by

the cabinet division of the President's secretariat said that President Field Marshal Mohammad Ayub Khan would address the nation on Radio Pakistan at 7:15 p.m. on March 1 by which time the printing of the new constitution was expected to be completed. The Associated Press of Pakistan (APP), observed that although some provisions, such as those relating to the creation of election machinery, would become effective immediately, this did not imply that Martial Law would be lifted at once, as the main provisions of the constitution would not become operative until the induction of Parliament some time in May or June.[67]

On February 24 the Rawalpindi correspondent of the *Pakistan Observer* speculated on whether the present cabinet would become a caretaker government during the transitional period. He also ventured to predict "with some amount of certainty" that the constitution would have these main features:

(1) It will give federal structure to the State; the list of the Central subjects may be smaller than that of the last Constitution.
(2) The form of government will be Presidential.
(3) At least the first election under the new Constitution will be on non-party basis though political parties may be allowed later on.
(4) There will be one House at Center with membership somewhere between 150 and 200. Women may have 10 seats reserved for them.
(5) The present one-unit structure in West Pakistan will remain undisturbed.
(6) Provinces will have their own legislatures although it is yet to be seen what their exact relationship with the executive will be.

The article concluded that it would be particularly interesting to see whether fundamental rights will be justiciable or not. As the end of the month approached the country was filled with a "feeling of expectation," according to the *Morning News* of March 1, and Pakistanis throughout the world were "all agog to know the new Constitution," according to the *Pakistan Observer* of February 28.

Plans called for the President to hold a special briefing session on the evening of February 28 in Karachi with fifty-two editors of Pakistani news agencies and newspapers and present them with copies of the constitution. On the morning of March 1 they were to meet the President for a question-and-answer session. The Presidential address that evening would be made in English over Radio Pakistan. It would be broadcast simultaneously an hour later in Urdu in West Pakistan and in Bengali in East Pakistan. Radio Pakistan Karachi would also broadcast the Bengali version.[68] According to *Dawn* of February 28, the speech had already been recorded when the President visited Karachi in the third week of February. In East Pakistan alone 900,000

copies of the synopsis were to be distributed and around 100 public relations officers were in Dacca receiving instructions on how to play their roles most effectively. Steps had been taken at all levels—provincial, divisional, district and *thana* or *tehsil*—to inform the people without delay of the principal features of the constitution.[69]

"During the present regime," wrote the *Statesman* on March 1, "seldom have the people of Pakistan awaited an official pronouncement with such unconcealed interest as the publication on Thursday of Pakistan's new Constitution." Pointing out that public discussion on the constitution had been prohibited since the publication of Chaudhri Mohamad Ali's views in June 1960 the article said that men everywhere had been debating its character among themselves:

> The important question being asked is 'to what extent will the executive share its authority with the legislature and what protections will the constitution offer to a citizen against any arbitrary executive action'. . . .
>
> Unless some last minute changes have been made in response to the recent development in East Pakistan the new constitution should provide for a federal system with wide powers for the President.
>
> Indications are that under the new Constitution there will be separate legislatures for East and West Pakistan besides the Parliament. The legislatures will be elected by the country's 80,000 'basic democrats' elected some time ago. It is unlikely that Parliament will be invested with power to question the authority or decisions of the President. The executive head will also be assured of substantial security against challenge from the judiciary.

"New Constitution Today—Fulfillment of yet another Promise—Eager Expectation in Country" headlined the *Morning News* on March 1. "Constitution to be Launched this Evening—Ayub to Address Nation over Radio—Election Commissioner to Take Oath of Office," announced *Dawn*. In contrast, the *Pakistan Observer*, reflecting a mood of disillusionment, announced the forthcoming constitution in a short three-paragraph story on the bottom of page one. The headline, only one column in width, said laconically, "Country Poised for New Constitution."

### NOTES

1. *Pakistan Observer* (Dacca), January 31, 1962, p. 1.
2. Keith Callard, *Pakistan: A Political Study* (London: George Allen and Unwin, 1957), pp. 68-69.
3. *Pakistan Observer*, July 16, 1960, p. 1.
4. *Ibid.*, January 31, 1962, p. 1.

5. *Statesman* (Calcutta), January 31, 1962, p. 1. According to a well-informed visitor to Pakistan, the delay in producing the constitution led to disappointment and impatience. "The leaders of the Calcutta-inspired Communist campaign . . . exploited this impatience with their customary skill. Certain malcontents of the former political parties, disgruntled by their exclusion from place and power under the Revolutionary Government, started an agitation; some Hindu money seems to have been involved. The Government thought it wise to place Mr. H. S. Suhrawardy under house arrest." L. F. Rushbrook Williams, *The State of Pakistan* (London: Faber and Faber, 1962), p. 234. Suhrawardy was placed, not under house arrest, as Williams states, but in the Karachi Central Jail.

6. *Pakistan Observer* and *Morning News* (Dacca), February 1, 1962.

7. *Pakistan Observer*, February 1, 1962, p. 1; *Statesman*, February 2, 1962.

8. *Pakistan Observer* and *Morning News*, February 1, 1962, p. 1.

9. *Dawn* (Karachi), February 1-3, 1962, p. 1.

10. *Morning News*, February 3, 1962, p. 1.

11. *Dawn* and *Pakistan Observer*, February 5, 1962, p. 1.

12. Instead of 62½% as had been the practice for several years. This also differed from Shoaib's statement.

13. Sobhan had asked that each wing be allowed to deal directly with foreign governments in the matter of aid.

14. *Morning News*, February 7, 1962, p. 1.

15. *Dawn*, February 7, 1962, contains the full text of the broadcast; see also Khan, Md. Ayub, *Speeches and Statements* (Karachi: Pakistan Publications), IV (July, 1961-June, 1962), 163-167.

16. *Morning News*, February 8, 1962, p. 1.

17. *Pakistan Observer*, February 6, 1962, p. 1; *Dawn*, February 8, 1962, p. 1.

18. *Morning News*, February 8, 1962, p. 1.

19. *Dawn*, February 4, 1962.

20. *Ibid.*, February 5, 7, 1962.

21. *Statesman*, January 19, 21; *Dawn* and *Pakistan Observer*, January 20-30, 1962.

22. *New York Times*, International Edition, February 14, 1962.

23. No mention was made in the press notes of the students burning pictures of the President. *Newsweek*, February 19, 1962, p. 36.

24. *Pakistan Observer*, February 7, 1962, p. 1.

25. *New York Times*, International Edition, February 8, 1962.

26. *Pakistan Observer*, February 8, 1962, p. 1.

27. As printed in *ibid.*, *Morning News* and *Dawn*, February 9-14, 1962. A résumé of the situation appeared in *Dawn*, February 14, 1962.

28. *Statesman*, February 11, 1962, p. 9.

29. As the *Statesman* had a dual dating system, these same issues might be dated January 31, February 1, 3, 11 and 12, 1962.

30. *Ibid.*, February 3, 1962, p. 7.

31. *Dawn*, February 7, 1962.

32. *Morning News*, February 19, 20, 22, 1962.

33. *Pakistan Observer*, February 24, 1962.

34. *Dawn*, February 18, 20, 1962.

35. *Statesman*, February 18, p. 5; February 20, 1962, p. 7.

36. Callard, *op. cit.*, p. 183. The 1956 Constitution recognized both Urdu

and Bengali as national languages.

37. See Richard D. Lambert, "Factors in Bengali Regionalism in Pakistan," *Far Eastern Survey,* 28 (April, 1959), 55-56.

38. *Statesman,* February 9, 1962, pp. 1, 7.

39. *Pakistan Observer,* February 13, 1962, p. 1.

40. *Morning News,* February 17, 1962.

41. *Ibid.,* and *Pakistan Observer,* February 22; *Statesman,* February 22, 1962, p. 7.

42. *Pakistan Observer,* February 18-28, March 1, 4, 1962. The defense pleaded that the accused were "bona fide pedestrians" who "accidentally found themselves in the midst of the crowd."

43. *Ibid.,* February 23, 1962.

44. *Morning News,* February 24, 25, 1962.

45. *Pakistan Observer,* February 25, 1962.

46. *Morning News,* February 24, 1962.

47. *Pakistan Observer,* February 26, 1962.

48. *Ibid.,* February 6, 1962, p. 1.

49. *Ibid.,* February 13, 1962, p. 1.

50. *Ibid.,* February 9, 1962.

51. *Ibid.,* February 9, 12, 15, 21, 27, 1962.

52. *Dawn,* February 16, 1962.

53. *Pakistan Observer,* March 2, 1962.

54. *Morning News,* February 9; *Dawn,* February 18, 1962.

55. *Statesman,* February 1, 1962.

56. *Pakistan Observer,* February 10, 1962, p. 1.

57. *Dawn,* February 14, 1962.

58. *Morning News,* February 14, 1962.

59. *Pakistan Observer,* February 15, 16, 1962.

60. *Dawn,* February 23, 1962, p. 1.

61. *Morning News,* February 15, 1962.

62. *Pakistan Observer,* February 9, 1962.

63. *Dawn,* February 10, 11, 1962, p. 1.

64. *Pakistan Observer,* February 15, 1962, p. 1.

65. *Morning News,* February 16, 1962.

66. *Dawn,* February 25, 1962.

67. *Pakistan Observer,* February 23, 1962, p. 1.

68. *Ibid.,* February 28, p. 1; *Morning News* and *Dawn,* March 1, 1962, p. 1.

69. *Morning News* and *Dawn,* March 1, 1962, p. 1.

# THE ANNOUNCEMENT OF THE CONSTITUTION AND THE REPORT OF THE CONSTITUTION COMMISSION

(March 1, 1962)


AT 6:50 p.m. on March 1, 1962, President Field Marshal Mohammad Ayub Khan "affixed his signature to the green leather-bound master copy of the new constitution." The signing took place in the Presidential House in Karachi. Mr. Justice A. R. Cornelius, the Chief Justice of the Pakistan Supreme Court, signed as witness. All cabinet members were present except the Law Minister, who was reported ill, certain secretaries and Mr. Quayle, an Australian constitutional expert. After the signing the President asked all those present to join him in silent prayer. Shortly afterward the President was asked how he felt. "I am feeling greatly relieved," he replied. "I hope this will give the country a nice start. I have great faith in it. My heart and soul have gone into it."[1]

At seven o'clock that evening over Radio Pakistan[2] President Ayub explained the philosophy behind the Constitution which he said comprised a "blending of democracy with discipline."[3]

In fulfillment of the President's promise to the chairman of the Constitution Commission "that the Commission would be unfettered in due discharge of its functions and that its report would be published whether it was accepted or not,"[4] the Commission's 177-page report was now released to the public.[5] Finished ten months earlier, the Report had received practically no attention from the press since April 29, 1961, when it was signed by Mr. Justice Shahabuddin.[6] From the inconsistent statements of President Ayub and government officials during the three and a half year period of the military regime, it is clear that for a long time no one was quite certain of the role to be played by the Commission. Was it to draft a constitution or was it just to make recommendations? Were its recommendations to be mandatory or

merely suggestive? Was the proposed constitution to be submitted to the people in a referendum? Other plans that proved subject to change were the pre-announcement of the general outlines of the constitution and the use of foreign experts in drafting the final document.

In his first press conference as Chief Martial Law Administrator in October 1958, General Ayub had promised that the best qualified people would be consulted on the drafting of a constitution which would then be presented to the people in a referendum. The two ideas, that a commission would draft a constitution and that the constitution would be put before the people for approval, were expressed several times during the first year of Martial Law. But by the end of 1959 the President was quite emphatic in stating that the Constitution Commission would not be a constituent assembly. At the beginning of 1960 and before the Commission was announced, President Ayub said that the Commission, after tabulating and collating questionnaire replies, would draft the constitution. However, he no longer felt that the draft constitution should be circulated before adoption because a popular referendum would only cause confusion. It is possible that the President used the phrase, "draft the constitution," from habit. Within a few days Manzur Qadir discreetly but firmly corrected the President by declaring that the commission's job was to study and make recommendations; it would be up to the cabinet to make the final decision. This statement pretty well settled the questions of the nature of the Commission's task and the holding of a referendum.

The matter of full acceptance of the Commission's recommendations first arose in December 1959, when President Ayub said that, even if the Commission advocated direct elections, he would never accept any unsound recommendations. Qadir said that while the President had his own ideas, if the Commission made better suggestions they would surely be accepted. On the day before the swearing-in of the Commission, the President affirmed that the Commission would have a free hand in making recommendations, but the Cabinet would give final approval. Several times during 1960 this point of view was expressed but always with the provision that the Commission's recommendations should be better than those of the President.

In the middle of 1960 Bhutto said the Commission was an autonomous body whose recommendations would be respected by the government. Qadir stated that the Commission was an advisory body and not a constituent assembly and the final decision lay with the President who alone had received the mandate from the people.

Habibur Rahman revealed that expert constitutionalists, both Paki-

stani and foreign, would be consulted. Later he said the constitution would probably be drafted by a foreign expert. Zakir Husain also said that the services of foreign experts, assisted by Pakistani jurists, would be secured for drafting the document. On the eve of the submission of the Commission's report to the President in early May 1961, it was reported that the services of a foreign expert—preferably British or Australian—would be utilized for the final draft.

Quayle's presence at the constitution-signing ceremony was apparently the first public acknowledgement of the identity of the foreign constitutional expert. Three weeks later Quayle received public recognition for his part in writing the Pakistani Constitution when Manzur Qadir, in an address to senior West Pakistan officials, said that he would like to thank publicly the Australian expert who had assisted in the compilation of the new constitution. Later, in answer to reporters' questions, Qadir paid "rich tributes" to the expert who was "sent by the Australian government in an honorary capacity as a goodwill gesture towards Pakistan." Quayle, he said, "made a very great and real contribution" and "worked round-the-clock for two months."[7]

In May 1961 Zakir Husain had disclosed that when a decision on the Commission's recommendations had been made by the President a public announcement would follow. Ibrahim thought the President might announce the fundamentals of the constitution by the middle of August 1961. By early September the date favored for the President's announcement was October 27, the third anniversary of the Revolution. Within three weeks an "authoritative spokesman" from the secretariat at Rawalpindi said President Ayub Khan would make public his decisions regarding the future constitution in November. The President also thought in early October that he would be able to give the broad features of the future government in November. But October was the month in which President Ayub made his speech in East Pakistan acknowledging the justification of the east wing's economic grievances. The communiqué issued at the close of the Governors' conference, just ten days later, said that instead of giving the broad outlines in November as promised the President would announce the constitution in its entirety in March 1962. In November it was made clear that the announcement and promulgation of the constitution would be simultaneous.

Of the three English language dailies consulted, *Dawn* had four short articles on the Commission's report on an inside page on March 2, the same date as the publication of the provisions of the constitution. These were from the Pakistan Press Association (PPA). Its next issue contained an article from the Associated Press of Pakistan (APP). The

*Morning News* and the *Pakistan Observer* contained nothing on the subject on the first day, but the next day both printed articles, whose source was also the APP, on the report's recommendations. The Indian paper, the *Statesman,* contained a short article which gave the principal recommendations. Only the *Morning News* published any of the text. From March 14 through April 16, this newspaper published the Introduction, Chapters I through V and Chapter VII. This series ended with Article 124 out of a total of 221 articles. The chapters published dealt with most of the controversial issues, but failed to include Chapters IX and X on the judiciary and fundamental rights. The published report was made available to the public March 1. It began with an introduction which listed the terms of reference, discussed the method of distribution of the questionnaire and the number of replies, explained the method of inquiry used in the Commission's interviews, reiterated that the Commission was unfettered and concluded with remarks on the gravity and scope of the task. It stated that 9,000 questionnaires were printed in English and 19,000 in Urdu and Bengali. There were 9,269 replies. The Commission had interviewed 565 persons, primarily those selected by the divisional commissioners and some individuals who were anxious to express their views.

The chairman and members were understandably sensitive on the issue of the Commission's autonomy, as there were rumors that the Commission was expected to endorse a scheme already drawn up. The chairman sought to dispel this notion at the first meeting and was pleased when the President said in a speech that the Commission had "full freedom and full powers to make such recommendations" as it considered proper for Pakistan. The Commission asserted that the members reached their conclusions "independently and to the best of [their] judgment," and that the public's point of view was given as much attention as the delegation presenting the government's views. Furthermore, the President in one speech said, "We shall accept the Commission's recommendations even if they are different from my ideas, provided that they are better than mine and good for the country." The Commission explained, "This provides a complete answer to the question . . . as to why the Commission has interviewed so many persons and is writing a report when the President is not bound to accept its recommendations."[8]

The report followed the order of the questionnaire but was more carefully organized. In each chapter the opinions expressed to the Commission were analyzed. The government's point of view was presented, and the Commission's recommendations and reasons for them were discussed. The failure of the parliamentary form of government

in Pakistan was considered in the first chapter. The Commission concluded that "the real causes . . . were mainly the lack of leadership
resulting in lack of well-organized and disciplined parties, the general
lack of character in the politicians and their undue interference in the
administration."[9] The second chapter, "Certain points of general
importance arising for consideration in connection with the steps to be
taken to prevent a recurrence of the causes determined in the previous
chapter," recommended that moral training be included in the educational system and that students study the lives of national and
religious heroes and people whose lives exemplified service to others.
The Commission recognized that education is a long-range measure,
however, but meanwhile saw no alternative to recommending a representative form of government.[10]

Chapters III, IV and V dealt with the parliamentary vs. the presidential form of government, the unitary vs. the federal pattern of
organization, and unicameral vs. bicameral legislature. Chapter VI
considered the checks and balances of the American system. Chapter
VII discussed universal vs. qualified franchise, direct vs. indirect elections, Basic Democracies, political parties, and the first elections under
the forthcoming constitution. To summarize, the Commission favored
a presidential form of government with a federal structure; a central
legislature with two houses; and direct election of the president, vice-
president, lower house and provincial assemblies by restricted adult
franchise.

Other chapters dealt with the president and vice-president (qualifications, terms of office, powers and duties), the judiciary, fundamental
rights, the services, Islamic provisions, the method of amending the
Constitution, and transitional procedures. The closing chapter stated
that all the conclusions were unanimous except for a few points on
which dissenting notes by Sardar Habibullah were appended. As to
whether the Commission had adhered to the original terms of reference, the report said:

> 218. This report answers fully the questions raised in the original
> terms of reference. As far as the additional term of reference, received
> after the Commission had started its work, our answer is that our
> recommendations should be given effect to as early as possible. . . .
> We shall be failing in our duty if we do not once again emphasize
> the urgent necessity of return to the representative form of govern-
> ment. We have made pointed reference to this in the introductory
> chapter . . . as well as in the chapter dealing with the electorate.
> While expressing the opinion that the Basic Democracies would not
> be a suitable electorate for the Parliament and the Presidency, we
> have, nevertheless, recommended the first Parliament being elected

by such an electorate solely because it is only by such an electorate that a representative government can be brought into existence before the end of this year.

219. . . . We do not claim that the scheme we have suggested is perfect. As a matter of fact, we have already stated that it is not a foolproof scheme but, having regard to our present circumstances and the experiences we have had since Pakistan came into being, we think it is the most feasible. The responsibility under the system of government we have recommended, rests heavily on the President as far as the administration goes, and on the legislature as far as legislation and appreciation of the administration are concerned.

The report closed with expressions of gratitude to the Commission's advisers and assistants and with a prayer to Allah "that the new constitution [might] preserve the representative form of government and maintain the principles of justice and freedom."[11]

The "Summary of the Constitution" released throughout the two provinces on March 1 explained that the new Constitution provided for "a federal unicameral legislative setup and a Presidential form of government."[12] In addition to the central legislature, each province was to have a legislature. The President would appoint the governors of the provinces and the governors would appoint provincial ministers with the concurrence of the President. Dacca was to be "the principal seat of the Central Legislature" and Islamabad "the principal seat of the Central Government." Urdu and Bengali would be the national languages. Provisions were made for over-riding the President's veto on legislation, for amending the Constitution, and for impeachment of the President. The legislature was made responsible for seeing that no law violated the fundamental rights enumerated as Principles of Law-Making. No court would be able to challenge the validity of a law made by any legislature. No taxation could be levied without the consent of the national assembly. A schedule enumerating the matters over which the center would have exclusive jurisdiction was included. Residual powers were vested in the provincial legislatures.

After presenting the salient features of the Constitution, the summary considered at greater length the Preamble, the sixteen Principles of Law-Making, and the twenty-one Principles of Policy. These principles provided chiefly that no law could be repugnant to Islam; all citizens were equal before the law; provincial parity was to be maintained in all spheres of the central government insofar as possible; freedom of expression and association were to be restricted only by such considerations as security of the state, public order, etc.; and an advisory council of Islamic ideology would be set up to ensure that no law was made in violation of Islamic principles. The remainder

of the summary dealt with the qualifications and powers of the President, the composition and powers of the central legislature and provincial assemblies, financial procedures (including taxation and budget, National Finance Commission and National Economic Council), and the advisory council of Islamic ideology.

The actual Constitution is not, of course, organized in the order in which the summary was written. The Constitution consists of a Preamble and twelve parts. Part I is entitled The Republic of Pakistan and Part II contains the Principles of Law-Making and of Policy.[13] Parts III and IV deal with the center and provinces respectively, while Part V concerns provisions applicable to both center and provinces and Part VI defines the relationship between the center and the provinces. Elections, the Services of Pakistan, the Comptroller and Auditor-General, and Islamic Institutions comprise Parts VII through X. Part XI is the procedure for amending the Constitution. Part XII is concerned with miscellaneous subjects, such as the capitals, national languages, tribal areas and transitional provisions.

*Dawn, Morning News* and the *Pakistan Observer* each treated the news of the long awaited Constitution differently. The *Morning News* was the most exuberant. A banner headline, "New Pak Constitution," was followed by four three-column wide headlines—"Presidential System of Government," "Central and Provincial Legislatures," "Electoral College of 80,000 Basic Democrats," and "Dacca Principal Center of Parliament." A picture of Field Marshal President Mohammad Ayub Khan in military uniform was centered on the upper half of the page. The entire first page except for two brief news articles and one small advertisement dealt with the Constitution or related subjects.

The Karachi *Dawn* carried a smaller banner headline, "Federal Constitution Enacted." The two-column secondary headlines were "Presidential Form Chosen" and "Ayub Explains Salient Points." A picture of President Ayub signing the Constitution was centered on the upper half of the front page. Five small articles and two advertisements were the only non-constitution material on *Dawn's* front page.

"Constitution Announced" was the brief five-column headline in the Dacca *Pakistan Observer*. Scattered over the page were other stories, such as "President Explains Salient Features," "Steps for Holding Elections" and "Constitution at a Glance." What distinguished the treatment of this major event by the *Pakistan Observer* from those of *Dawn* and the *Morning News* was the fact that not one headline gave any clue as to the nature of the Constitution, even in regard to the most controversial items. Yet it contained essentially the same total news content as the other two papers.

Included with the March 2 edition of *Dawn* was an eight-page supplement containing the full texts of the Constitution, the President's
broadcast and the summary of the Constitution. In addition inside
pages carried six smaller articles relating to the Constitution and an
editorial entitled, "Let Us Work It." Acknowledging that opinions on
the Constitution were bound to differ, *Dawn* urged "all patriotic
people to realize that it [was] a sincere fulfillment of the pledge given
by the architect of the Revolution . . . ; that it [was] a voluntary
handing over of considerable powers in the administrative and legislative fields to larger bodies chosen from among the people . . . ; that
it [was] now a beginning based on bitter experiences of the past and
therefore an attempt to ensure that those experiences [would] not
be repeated. . . ." The editorial writer felt that "the provision of practical means" to enable Muslims "to order their lives in accordance
with the principles and concept of Islam" was "the most satisfying
feature of the Constitution." The concluding note was one of "sadness
and disappointment that the framers of the new Constitution had
failed, as had the 1956 Constitution, to provide for "One Country, One
People, One Government, One Legislature and One Purse . . . through
an undiluted unitary form of government."

The *Morning News* also published the texts of the President's broadcast and the summary, as well as the first of four installments of the
Constitution. It included five articles of the "hail and welcome" type
("Chittagong hails Constitution") and a two-column editorial, "A
Charter of Democracy," which expressed the opinion that the Constitution opened "a new era of democratic hopes." It further said that
President Ayub, although a soldier by training and profession, was
"by temperament and conviction" a democrat. The editorial endorsed
the decision to have a presidential system on the grounds that it alone
"could provide a unifying and cohesive force." Proof of the President's
response to the wishes of the people, especially the East Pakistanis,
was "the wide measure of autonomy conceded to the Provinces," the
*Morning News* declared. More authority had "devolved on them than
they [had been] able to enjoy under the previous constitution" and the
"choice of Dacca as the legislative capital of the country" was a tribute
to the political consciousness of the province. It pointed out that the
Constitution would enable East Pakistan to reach economic parity
with West Pakistan. The editorial commended the inclusion of fundamental rights in the Constitution but conceded that opinions might
differ "as to the advisability of empowering the Legislature to safeguard
them." In any event, the new constitution would be "universally ac-
claimed as a charter of democracy."

Promulgation of the Constitution did not automatically lift martial law as this was to be done on the first day that the Central Legislature met. Hence, discussing the Constitution was still prohibited and any adverse reactions were worded cautiously.

The summary of the Constitution and the President's broadcast were also published in the *Pakistan Observer*. The text of the Constitution was presented in a piecemeal fashion. It began in the edition of March 3 and was spread out over nine installments. Perseverance, industry and a real determination were required to get any meaning out of it. For instance, one of the nine installments began on page five, continued on page two, and concluded on page six.

The *Pakistan Observer* was most eloquent by its silence. The March 2 issue did not even contain an editorial acknowledgement of the announcement of the Constitution. No editorial opinion was expressed until March 23. Then the writer merely reviewed the occasion of the Lahore Resolution and ended with a renewed pledge "to maintain the integrity, solidarity and sovereignty of Pakistan and rededicate ourselves to the cause of freedom, truth and democracy, participating to the best of our ability in all the efforts aimed at promoting social justice and the general welfare of the people." A March 24 editorial reviewed the activities of the "good" politicians before independence —reforms in land tenure in Bengal, regulation of money-lenders, etc.— and of the "bad" politicians after independence who retained "the petitioning mentality of British days." The editorial concluded,

> We have now a new system. But exactly how that system will work will depend on the spirit in which it will be worked. Ultimately every country gets the kind of government it deserves. And as we have said in the past, the real meaning of a constitution can only be unfolded by experience and with experience the gradual awakening of public opinion. It is the constitution which is adjusted to the people and not the other way about.

The *Morning News,* during the period between March 5 and 10, had more than two dozen items concerning the laudatory reactions of individuals and groups. The general consensus was that it was the best constitution possible in the prevailing circumstances and everyone should give it a chance. Nurul Huda, the President of the Pakistan Bar Association, said that "for the first time East Pakistan [had] got the essence of almost everything it wanted."[14] Others commented favorably on the provisions for women's rights, fundamental rights, and the Islamic features. Twenty leading *ulema* of Bannu promised their support for the new Constitution.[15]

The only adverse note in the general outpouring of congratulations

was the disappointment expressed by the fundamentalist Muslim, Maulana Maudoodi, over the provision for indirect elections. The first sign of what would become an overwhelming demand also appeared:

> Ex-politicians who stand discredited for their disruptionist activities are conspicuously silent for the time being, but Raja Ghazanfar Ali presumably echoing their sentiments has appealed to the President to give general pardon and amnesty to all those politicians who have been disqualified under EBDO.[16]

When the East Pakistan Governor visited Lahore he answered reporters' questions by saying, "generally speaking, the reaction was favorable" in the east wing. But he added that the Constitution was a wide subject and there was always a section which did not like certain things.[17]

The constitutional emphasis on a strong center elicited comments from both East Pakistani papers. A *Morning News* article of March 14 stated:

> These Articles will naturally be interpreted to mean executive and legislative control by the Center, especially the President, over the provinces. . . . These are devices by which the President will keep the provinces in check, if need be. These provisions may appear to be an infringement upon the rights of the provinces under the federal system, but a closer scrutiny reveals that some other federal governments are exercising the same measure of executive and legislative control over the provinces . . . India, for example. . . .
>   Also in the legislative field the over-riding rights of the Central Legislature have been clearly enunciated and preserved. . . . This provision [for legislation on other than Third Schedule] is sufficiently wide to enable the Central Government to enter the arena of provincial legislation if and when necessary.

A writer in the *Pakistan Observer* of March 23 commented that:

> In distributing executive powers between the Center and the Provinces the federal principle seems to have yielded to that on which a unitary state is based. Thus, though separation of powers (with some modifications) has been recognized, more powers and wider responsibilities appear to have been concentrated in the Central Executive. Apparently a strong government at the Center will emerge which is expected to concern itself only with matters of national importance. The President does not resemble a constitutional monarch, like that of England; but shall wield greater power than the President of the United States of America is seen to possess and enjoy. The President shall not only reign but rule.

This then was the immediate and for the most part carefully uncritical reaction of a number of individuals and groups to the provisions of the new Constitution. How the Constitution reflected President

Ayub's views on the desired form of government for Pakistan and how it was modified by public opinion are considered in the following chapter.

## NOTES

1. *Dawn* (Karachi), March 2, 1962, p. 1.
2. None of the newspapers mentioned that the President had previously recorded his speech.
3. See Appendix C for President's broadcast.
4. Government of Pakistan, *Report of the Constitution Commission, 1961* (Karachi, 1962), p. 2. See Appendix E for excerpts.
5. *Morning News* (Dacca), March 3, 1962, p. 1.
6. *Dawn*, April 30, 1961, p. 1.
7. *Ibid.*, March 21, *Morning News*, March 23, 1962.
8. *Report of the Constitution Commission*, p. 3.
9. *Ibid.*, p. 13.
10. *Ibid.*, p. 15.
11. *Ibid.*, pp. 138-139.
12. The following discussion of the announcement of the Constitution was drawn entirely from the March 2 editions of *Dawn, Morning News,* and *Pakistan Observer* (Dacca) unless otherwise noted.
13. See Appendix F for text of the Preamble and Principles of Law-Making and of Policy.
14. *Morning News*, March 3, 1962, p. 10.
15. *Ibid.*, March 7, 1962, p. 8.
16. *Ibid.*, March 4, 1962.
17. *Ibid.*, March 10, 1962, p .1.

# CHAPTER XIII

# ANALYSIS

WHEN Ayub Khan assumed control of Pakistan in October 1958 and promised the restoration of democracy and a new constitution suited to Pakistan's needs, his ideas on these subjects did not spring full-blown with his new title. As early as October 1954, in fact, General Ayub had written a plan for the type of governmental organization which he felt would be fitting and workable for Pakistan. When, therefore, as the head of the revolutionary regime, he began to expound his views publicly, many of his ideas displayed the quality of deep-rooted convictions. His thinking of 1958 had altered on two major points, however, for by that time he was calling urgently for a unitary system and a strong center. When West Pakistan had consisted of three provinces, plus several princely states and tribal areas, its need for integration was overwhelming. Once this change had taken place the next logical step would be to aspire to a completely unified government. The principle was the same but the units to be merged had necessarily changed. President Ayub Khan's later desire for combining East and West Pakistan into a unitary government was a natural extension of the principle involved in working for One Unit in West Pakistan. The idea of a strong center may seem incompatible with President Ayub's earlier belief that the center should deal only with inter-provincial communications, defense, foreign affairs and currency. Combined with his emphasis on decentralization, however, and with final control in the President's hands, there is no inconsistency in his point of view. Many things happened in the political sphere after 1954 which could account for his view that the center should be as strong as possible while allowing for some democratic exercise of power. But despite these changes in General Ayub's thinking it would seem that he was not entirely candid when, in October 1958, he asserted that his views were not yet formed.

The recommendations enunciated by President Ayub from October 1958 to February 1960 were: (1) a unitary structure, (2) a unicameral legislature of 150 members, (3) a presidential system, (4) a strong

central government for policy-making and supervisory functions but with decentralization of powers to provinces, divisions and districts, (5) no political parties functioning for the first elections under the new constitution, (6) indirect elections for the legislature and the president, (7) the electoral college to be composed of the elected members of Basic Democracies would be elected by universal adult franchise, (8) politicians should be prohibited from indulging in malpractice, (9) sovereignty should be exercised jointly by the executive and parliament, and (10) the constitution should reflect Islamic principles in a modern context. The most important obvious omission in this outline is the broad area which includes the rule of law, the guarantee of fundamental human rights and the independence of the judiciary. It appears that Bhutto made the first positive remark concerning this area in May 1961 when he said that no constitution could be complete without explicit provision for fundamental human rights.

Public opinion under Martial Law was revealed by: (1) the nature of the questions posed by newspaper reporters in interviewing government officials, (2) expressions by lawyers and judges of discontent with the restrictions of martial law, (3) published responses by Chaudhri Mohamad Ali and several East Pakistanis to the Constitution Commission's questionnaire, (4) "constructive" editorials which incidentally revealed facts not publishable as news, (5) foreign journals and newspapers, especially the Calcutta *Statesman* and (6) the tabulation in the *Report of the Constitution Commission 1961*—although this was not available until after the announcement of the Constitution—of the opinions of the 6,269 persons who answered the questionnaire and of the 565 who were interviewed.

How the sometimes divergent views of the President, expressions of public opinion and recommendations of the Constitution Commission were resolved is revealed by an examination of the Constitution.

*Form of Government*

The President wanted a presidential form. Of the opinions expressed before the Commission or in answer to the questionnaire, 21.3 per cent favored the "pure parliamentary pattern" and 29.3 per cent wanted some form of a parliamentary system; 47.4 per cent wanted a presidential system; the remaining 2 per cent suggested "dictatorship on lines of the Khilafat."[1] Most of the religious extremists in this latter category said if this were not practicable they would prefer the presidential system.[2] Hence public opinion was divided fairly equally between the parliamentary and presidential systems.

The Constitution Commission considered all aspects of the parliamentary vs. the presidential form. On the former it concluded, "In our opinion we shall be running a grave risk in adopting the parliamentary form, either in its purity or with the modifications suggested, and we do not think that we can afford to take such a risk at the present stage."[3] "We should have a form of government where there is only one person at the head of affairs with an effective restraint exercised on him by an independent legislature, members of which, however, should not be in a position to interfere seriously with the administration by exercising political pressure for their personal ends."[4] In order to minimize the chance of misunderstanding, that chapter of the *Report* ended with the following note of warning:

> We should however, like to sound a note of warning. Our recommendation . . . does not mean that we regard it as a fool-proof scheme, which would avoid any constitutional breakdown in future. We recommend that form of government because on a careful consideration of the possibilities and the probabilities of the situation and the experience we have gained during the past few years since Independence, we consider that it is a safer form to be adopted in our present circumstances. We are certainly not pessimistic about the future, but we are convinced that unless we evolve a system of checks and balances, which, while preventing deadlocks between the legislature and the President, provides a healthy restraint on the exercise by the executive of its powers, there will be difficulties in working this form of government also.[5]

The Constitution provided for a presidential system with the office of president combining the powers formerly exercised by both president and prime minister.

## Unitary vs. Federal Structure

The insistence on the unitary form was one of President Ayub's strongest demands. The published replies from East Pakistan to the Commission's questionnaire almost unanimously favored the federal form of government. Of the statements made before the Commission and the written replies to the questionnaire, 65.5 per cent favored the federal and 34.5 per cent the unitary form.

The Commission members could scarcely have gone more thoroughly into this problem than they did. "There is no part of the subject of our inquiry which seems to us to present greater difficulties," they admitted, "than the question whether the form of government should be unitary or federal as, in the controversy, feelings appear to run high."[6] A great deal of attention was given to East Pakistan's grievances against

West Pakistan. The West Pakistani members of the Commission were perhaps surprised to learn that "the witnesses examined in East Pakistan gave . . . the impression that they had very strong feelings in this matter."[7] Having given their "anxious consideration" to all the proposals put forth by the government delegation as well as those advanced by the people the Commission recommended "that the government should be of the same pattern as that of India and Canada [that is, federal] and not unitary as in Great Britain." It further recommended that whatever the defects of the One Unit scheme, it was safer to continue with the two units as they were at the time of the abrogation of the 1956 Constitution.[8]

The first words of the Constitution, after the Preamble and the Principles of Law-Making and of Policy, were:

> (1) The State of Pakistan shall be a Republic under the name of the Republic of Pakistan.
> (2) The Republic shall consist of
> (a) the Province of East Pakistan and the Province of West Pakistan; and
> (b) such other States and territories as are or may become included in Pakistan, whether by accession or otherwise.

Had a unitary form been adopted, such as was envisaged by the President, there would have been no provincial legislatures. There is evidence to indicate that the provincial advisory councils were being groomed under Basic Democracies to continue to play their initial role —advisory to the governor but with no legislative power—in a unitary system of government.

Except for the single phrase in the Preamble, that "Pakistan should be a form of federation," one can search the Constitution in vain for any such terms as "federal," "federation" or "federated units." One might infer from the fact that Pakistan was to consist of two provinces that it was a federal form of government. The Constitution itself was not explicit on this point. The comparable article of the 1956 Constitution had said: "Pakistan shall be a Federal Republic to be known as the Islamic Republic of Pakistan." Just as the Chief Martial Law Administrator had removed from the earlier Constitution the word "Islamic" by means of the Laws (Continuance in Force) Order 1958, now in the 1962 Constitution "Federal" was similarly disposed of.

### The Legislature

Having recommended "a strong central government in a quasi-federal structure," the Constitution Commission considered the relative merits of a bicameral vs. a unicameral legislature. Of the respondents

to the Commission's questionnaire, 74.1 per cent were in favor of a unicameral legislature, while 25.2 per cent spoke on behalf of a bicameral system. A small percentage mentioned an advisory council, a point of view not shared by the Commission because "it [is] necessary to have a legislature with effective powers." It was noted also "that no great state of the present day . . . [is] satisfied with a unicameral legislature."

The government delegation in its first interview pressed for a unicameral legislature. Not meeting with much sympathy from the Commission, the spokesmen returned later with the suggestion of an upper house elected on the basis of functional representation. The Commission advocated a bicameral legislature, with the upper house composed of persons in "mature age groups of meritorious personalities," and the lower house to be elected "on the basis of parity between the two wings."[9] In this one regard, at least, the Commission proved that it was neither "counting heads" nor being "fettered" by the government, for both the government and the majority of the people wanted a unicameral legislature.

The majority of opinions was in favor of a unicameral body for the provincial legislature and the Commission shared this view. It recommended that each provincial legislature should have 100 seats, three of which should be reserved for women. The Commission observed:

> The reservation of seats for women, in both the central and the provincial legislatures, would not debar their election from the general constituencies, but we think that the chances of their being so elected are rather slender. That is the reason why we have accepted the opinion of the majority that there should be reservation of seats for women.[10]

As the Punjab contained more than half of the total population of West Pakistan, it was arranged in 1955 that for ten years the Punjab would have only 124, or forty per cent, of the 310 seats in the provincial assembly. The Commission felt this allocation should continue for seven years from the date of promulgation of the new Constitution.

The Constitution provided that the National Assembly should consist of the president and one house of 156 members, one-half to be elected from each province, with three of the seats from each province to be reserved for women (Articles 19 and 20). The provincial assemblies were to consist of the governor and one house of 155 members, with five seats reserved for women. Special arrangements were made so that no more than forty per cent of the West Pakistani representatives would be elected from the territory formerly known as the Punjab. The Constitution specified ten years, rather than seven recommended by the Commission, for the duration of this system.

*Division of Powers*

In a federal system the division of powers between the center and the provincial governments determines whether the center is weak or strong. This strength or weakness partially derives from the scope and nature of the subjects on which each Legislature is authorized to enact legislation. The Commission felt it could not accept the recommendation of the official delegation "that the Center should not have a list of subjects on which it could legislate but that the Constitution should provide that it would legislate on every subject including those on the Provincial List." The Commission thought such a provision "would aggravate the suspicion and doubt already existing in East Pakistan which . . . it [was] extremely unwise, if not hazardous, to ignore."[11]

As many as 41.1 per cent of the opinions favored giving the center only three spheres of responsibility—defense, foreign affairs and currency. The reason most frequently given for this point of view was that the 1940 Lahore Resolution spoke of independent states and that therefore the provinces should be autonomous. The Commission felt it was "extremely unwise and unrealistic to insist on a literal following" of the Lahore Resolution because

> the East Pakistan envisaged in the Lahore Resolution was the whole of Bengal and Assam which could have been an autonomous province as it would have had industries and large economic resources. It could not have been anticipated at that stage that the former Bengal and Punjab provinces would be divided and Pakistan would get, as its eastern half, the unindustrialized portion of Bengal. . . . If, at the time of the Lahore Resolution, it could have been foreseen that ultimately a division would take place and that the present East Pakistan would be the only portion of Pakistan in the East, the Muslim League would not have thought of regarding it as an autonomous province because, without industrial development, it is impossible for East Pakistan to sustain itself as an independent unit.[12]

Pointing out that the tendency in most federal governments today is "towards increasing the powers of the Central Government," the Commission observed that for a program of economic development, "concentration of power should be in the Center as that alone can be regarded as a unit in the international field. . . . Wherever economic planning is urgently required as in Pakistan," the *Report* continued, "it is impracticable to have a form of government with autonomous units joined together for a limited purpose. . . . Neither East nor West Pakistan can develop itself without guidance and assistance from the Central Government."[13]

The Commission recommended that:

there should be a Federal list containing the subjects in which the Center alone can legislate, another list of subjects in respect of which both the Center and the provinces have concurrent powers and a third list of subjects on which the provinces alone can legislate. . . . We are also in favor of retaining the provision of the late Constitution that, if a state of emergency is declared by the President, the parliament shall have the power to legislate on any of the subjects of the Provincial List.[14]

A few changes were recommended but, by and large, the three lists recommended by the Commission remained fairly close to those of the 1956 document.

The Constitution, however, treated the matter quite differently from the Commission's recommendations. It contained only one list of subjects, known as the Third Schedule, on which the central legislature should have exclusive power to make laws. But it also provided that whenever the national interests of Pakistan—in relation to the security, economic stability, or achievement of uniformity between the wings— might require it the central legislature could enact laws on any subject. The Constitution further empowered the central legislature to make laws concerning the Islamabad and Dacca Capital Territories, as well as any non-provincial portion of Pakistan. A provincial legislature could make laws on any subject not enumerated in the Third Schedule (Article 133).

## The Electorate

The Commission considered four points concerning the electorate: (1) universal or restricted franchise, (2) direct or indirect elections, (3) joint or separate electorates, and (4) political parties.

Public opinion, as expressed in replies to the questionnaire and in interviews, favored direct universal franchise for the legislature but indirect election through an electoral college for the President. The Commission attributed these views to the fact that such provisions were laid down in the 1956 Constitution. The official delegation felt that both the President and members of the parliament should be elected, indirectly, by the members of Basic Democracies who had themselves been elected by universal franchise. The Commission recommended:

that the President, owing to the extraordinary position he occupies under the presidential system, bearing very heavy responsibilities, should command the confidence of the people, and that such confidence would be forthcoming only by a direct election.[15]

The Commission felt that since the late constitution had conferred universal suffrage it would be unwise to take away that right, although

an 85 per cent illiteracy in Pakistan weighted the scales heavily in favor of restricted franchise. Hence they recommended that suffrage should be restricted to those citizens who had attained a certain standard of literacy and possessed some property. They thought, in addition, that the president, the vice-president and members of the assemblies should be directly elected at the same time and by the same electorate.[16]

The Constitution provided (Articles 155, 157 and 158) that each province should be divided into 40,000 electoral units. All adults in each electoral unit were to elect an elector for that unit. The electors from both provinces would form the electoral college for the president and the national assembly. This procedure is exactly that which was employed in the initial elections to Basic Democracies and resulted in the electoral college which had given the overwhelming vote of confidence to President Ayub.

Apparently President Ayub Khan had no strong feelings as to whether the citizens should vote in a joint electorate with the same list of candidates or whether there should be separate electorates with a certain number of seats reserved for the various minorities. In the interests of national unity, however, it would have been consistent for him to have favored the joint electorate. The Commission observed that this had been a question of "paramount importance" in undivided India and the questions had remained unresolved in the 1956 Constitution because "the controversy became so keen."

Opinions expressed on the subject were 55 per cent in favor of joint electorate with no reservations and 40 per cent for separate electorates. The position of the minority community in East Pakistan—especially the role of the caste Hindus and scheduled castes—influenced the recommendation by the Commission: that the president, vice-president, members of the lower house of the central legislature and of the provincial assemblies should be elected directly on a restricted adult franchise; the elections of legislators for the two provincial assemblies and the lower house of the national assembly were to be on the basis of separate electorates. The Commission consented to the use of the electoral college for the first election as otherwise the elections might not take place until 1963.[17]

The Constitution provided that the election of a president should be decided by the electoral college as a whole; election to the national assembly or to a provincial assembly should be decided by the electors in each constituency (Articles 165, 168); all elections were to be held under the joint electorate system; there were to be 150 constituencies for the provincial assembly and 75 constituencies for the central legis-

lature in each province; and separate constituencies would be set up for election to the seats reserved for women (three and five for the central legislature and each provincial assembly, respectively).

### Political Parties

Despite President Ayub's strong negative stand on the subject, the Commission apparently assumed the eventual emergence of parties to be inevitable. The questionnaire asked: "If you recommend parliamentary form of government what steps do you suggest to secure stability of government while . . . checking undue interference with the day-to-day administration on account of party considerations?" The official delegation told the Commission that it was necessary only to provide that there should be no political parties, although they recognized that "like-minded persons would get together and discuss political problems." The Commission retorted, "Are we to understand that [like-minded people] can assemble and discuss . . . but are not bound to act in accordance with that decision?" After citing learned scholars on the inevitable role of political parties in a representative government, the Commission concluded:

> Having regard to the necessity of parties and the important fact that, if there are no parties, it would not be possible to work the representative form of government, we strongly recommend the complete suspension of the said Martial Law Regulation. If we want to have a democratic form of government, our endeavor should be to create conditions in which parties will soon come into existence in the form of government we have recommended. . . .[18]

Both the summary of the Constitution and the text of the President's broadcast said that political parties were banned. The Constitution, however, put it quite differently. Article 173 provided:

> Except as permitted by Act of the Central Legislature, any person who, in connection with an election required to be held under this Constitution, holds out himself or any other person as being a member of, or as having the support of, a political party or any similar organization shall be punishable in such manner as may be prescribed by the Act of the Central Legislature. . . .

In his broadcast on March 1, 1962, President Ayub explained that "because of the sad experience of political parties in the past . . . and the fact that the Martial Law has to stay until the National Assembly takes over, the coming elections will be held on the basis of personal merit." However, he recognized that "like-minded people in the Assemblies" might form groups. If political parties had to be revived,

it would be "only with the permission of the National Assembly," thus ensuring that the number of parties would be limited and that they would have "healthy national programs."

It was hoped that the Constitution would eliminate or at least seriously cripple the power of politicians. Former politicians disqualified by EBDO or by any other law were not allowed to seek assembly seats (Article 103). Any politician suspected of engaging in malpractice in the future would be referred to the Supreme Court or High Court, depending on whether he was a member of the National or Provincial Assembly (Article 113). The Constitution provided that the law would ensure opportunities for the candidates to meet the relevant members of the electoral college (Article 173).

### The Judiciary

President Ayub felt that legal processes ordinarily took too long and were too expensive for the common man and he concluded that the legal system should be simplified and decentralized. Questions 24 and 25 of the Commission's questionnaire dealt with the jurisdiction of the Supreme Court and the High Courts; the terms of office, appointments, etc. of the judges of these courts; and the offices of attorney-general and advocates-general. The relevant articles in the 1956 Constitution were given in the annexure and the public was asked, "Would you adopt these provisions or do you consider any change necessary?" Ninety-eight per cent of the opinions favored incorporating the provision for maintaining the independence of the judiciary by giving judges security of tenure.[19] Opinions on judiciary provisions were presented before the Commission by the Lahore Bench of the West Pakistan High Court, the Dacca High Court, the Karachi Bench of the West Pakistan High Court, the Supreme Court, the Law Commission, the Attorney-General and, of course, the official delegation.

The Commission recommended seven judges, but believed Parliament should have the power to increase the number if necessary.[20] The Constitution provided that the number should be determined by law or be fixed by the President (Article 49). The Commission suggested that the President should have exclusive power in the appointment of judges. The Constitution provided that the Chief Justice of the Supreme Court should be appointed by the President, and other judges by the President in consultation with the Chief Justice. The Commission recommended Islamabad as the seat of the Supreme Court but assumed that until the Court could be permanently situated there it would remain at Lahore. It also recommended that the Court should sit at Karachi at least once a year and at Dacca at least twice a year.

The Constitution provided that Lahore should be the principal seat for the West Pakistan High Court with permanent seats at Karachi and Peshawar. Dacca was named the seat of the High Court for East Pakistan.

The Commission expressed dismay at the reduction of the powers of the Courts under the military regime and wanted previously exercised powers returned to the High Courts. The Commission, however, agreed with the official delegation that it was not necessary for the Supreme Court to have original jurisdiction over fundamental rights since there was right of appeal to the Supreme Court against the judgment of a High Court.

The *Report* concluded this subject by re-emphasizing the fact

> that the independence of the Judiciary should be maintained, as had been the practice from a long time, and any inroad into it, that has been found necessary during the present authoritarian regime, should not be treated in future as a precedent. Government should not take any step which is likely to affect the prestige of the Courts adversely. It must be realized that an independent Judiciary adds to the strength of the administration, and no effort should be spared to keep up its prestige and position. According to the Quran, the sayings of the Prophet, the Islamic traditions and the present-day canons of the democratic free world, an independent Judiciary is a pre-requisite for a just and good government.[21]

The Constitution provided three jurisdictions to the Supreme Court: (1) original jurisdiction in any dispute between the Central Government and a Provincial Government, or between the two Provincial Governments, (2) appellate jurisdiction to hear and determine appeals from judgments and sentences of a High Court, and (3) advisory jurisdiction when the President wanted the Supreme Court's decision on any question of law. A great curb on the powers previously enjoyed by the courts was contained in Articles 6 and 8 which empowered the legislature concerned to decide whether a law violated the Principles of Law-Making (that is, fundamental rights) or the Principles of Policy. The validity of a law could be called in question neither by the Supreme Court nor by the High Courts on the grounds that it was not in accordance with the Principles of Law-Making or of Policy. It was demonstrated earlier how the judges chafed during Martial Law at the non-justiciability of fundamental rights. Now that principle was incorporated in the basic law of the land.

## Fundamental Rights

In answer to Question 22 as to whether fundamental rights should be enumerated in the Constitution or left to "the fundamental good

sense of the legislature," opinion was 98.3 per cent in favor of their inclusion in the Constitution.[22] The official delegation suggested that "the rights of the State over the people" and the people's obligation to the state should be specifically mentioned. The Commission, it seems, was shocked by this proposal. They were "unable to appreciate the difficulty felt by the official delegation" in this regard and asserted that since the state was supreme it was the individual who should have his rights assured against the state, and not vice versa.[23]

The sixteen Principles of Law-Making contained in Article 6 of the Constitution provided, first, that no law should be repugnant to Islam. Although this principle was not included in the earlier Constitution's list of fundamental rights, it was included under the Islamic provisions. The Principles further provided for equality of citizens, freedom of expression and association, freedom of movement and of acquiring property, freedom of religion and, in fact, included the complete 1956 list of fundamental rights except for the significant omission mentioned above, that of granting power to the Supreme Court to guarantee these rights.

Despite the Commission's disapproval, the Constitution's Article 3 said that "loyalty to the Republic is the basic duty of every citizen," and Article 4 declared that "obedience to the law is the basic obligation of every citizen. . . ."

### Islamic Provisions

One of the terms of reference by which the Constitution Commission was guided was how "a democracy adapted to changing circumstances and based on the Islamic principles of justice, equality and tolerance" might best be assured.

Question 23 of the questionnaire asked if the preamble from the 1956 Constitution should be included in the new constitution. This preamble pointed out that Quaid-e-Azam Mohammad Ali Jinnah had declared "that Pakistan would be a democratic state based on Islamic principles of social justice" and it was the purpose of the Constituent Assembly to frame a constitution

> Wherein the principles of democracy, freedom, equality, tolerance and social justice as enunciated by Islam, should be fully observed; [and]
> Wherein the Muslims of Pakistan should be enabled individually and collectively to order their lives in accordance with the teachings and requirements of Islam, as set out in the Holy Quran and Sunnah. . . .

Ninety-six per cent of the opinions were in favor of incorporating this preamble.[24]

Question 34 asked if any special provisions were necessary "to assist the Muslims in the study of the basic values of Islam and of their application to the changing conditions of life." The opinion of a very small minority "that religion should not be brought into the political field" was carefully considered but the Commission finally recommended that the preamble should be incorporated in the new Constitution.[25]

This chapter of the *Report* revealed how profoundly the members of the Commission felt about their religion and especially how concerned they were about the tendency of the younger generation to prefer a secular state. The Commission approved supporting research and instruction in advanced Islamic studies and recommended that continuation of the Islamic Research Institute be made obligatory. The final item relating to Islamic provisions dealt with bringing the law into conformity with the Quran and the Sunnah.[26] Because of the wide diversity of opinion on these basic matters, the *Report* recommended that a commission should be constituted to draw up principles "which should be regarded as the standard to which the laws of the country should conform. . . ." Furthermore, it urged that cooperation in this project should be sought throughout the entire Muslim world.[27]

The 1962 Constitution contains a preamble very similar to that of the 1956 Constitution. It is somewhat shorter but it contains the Islamic provisions. The very first of the Principles of Law-Making is, "No law should be repugnant to Islam" (Article 6). And the first of the Principles of Policy deals with the Islamic way of life. Muslims should be enabled to order their lives in accordance with the tenets of Islam; the teaching of the Holy Quran should be compulsory for Muslims; Islamic moral standards should be promoted among Muslims; and the proper organization of *zakat, wakfs* and mosques should be ensured.[28] Article 9 specified that the President should be a Muslim.

Part X of the Constitution concerns Islamic institutions. An Advisory Council of Islamic Ideology and an Islamic Research Institute were provided for. The functions of the Council were (1) to recommend means by which Muslims could live in accordance with the tenets of Islam and (2) to advise the legislatures or executives on any question of "whether a proposed law disregards or violates or is otherwise not in accordance with the Principles of Law-making." The function of the Islamic Research Institute was to undertake research and instruction in Islam in order to assist "in the reconstruction of Muslim society on a truly Islamic basis" (Article 207).

*Basic Democracies*

The concept of Basic Democracies was President Ayub's answer to what form of democracy would suit the genius of Pakistan. He felt that if this system were successful in Pakistan it might well point the way to self-government for other developing countries which had tried unsuccessfully to operate parliamentary democracy. Although the Commission did not want the elected members of Basic Democracies to serve as an electoral college, it declared that the Basic Democracies scheme was "of considerable importance and very useful as far as local government [was] concerned."[29] The Constitution set up an election procedure which, without mentioning Basic Democracies by name, described the scheme that had been employed in the vote of confidence for the President.

*Fiscal Arrangements*

The last promise made by the government just prior to the announcement of the Constitution had been that some portion of the Finance Commission's report would be incorporated into the basic law. The Constitution Commission's questionnaire had included nothing about financial provisions. The members of the Commission attempted to discuss the problem but were hampered by the unwillingness of the Government to make any suggestions for financial provisions should the form of government prove to be federal. The Commission, then, could only recommend that the provisions of the 1956 Constitution, which had been drawn up for a federal form of government, be adopted. It also recommended the formation of a National Economic Council consisting of the President, the Vice-President, three ministers from the central government, two ministers from each province and the two provincial governors.[30]

Article 144 of the new Constitution provided for a National Finance Commission consisting of the ministers in charge of the portfolios of finance in the central and provincial governments, and others to be appointed by the President after consultation with the governors. The Finance Commission's task would be to recommend to the President the distribution between the central and provincial governments of the proceeds from income tax, sales tax, export duty on jute and cotton, excise duties and other taxes as might be specified by the President. It was also to consider the center's making grants-in-aid to the provinces, the borrowing power of the three governments, and any other financial matter referred to the Commission by the President.

Clause 5 of Article 144 describes the procedure for determining the allocation of the provincial funds to be shared between East and West Pakistan:

> As soon as is practicable after receiving the recommendations of the Commission referred to . . . the President shall, after considering the recommendations, specify by Order the share of the proceeds of the taxes referred to [above] which is to be allocated to each Provincial Government, and that share shall be paid to the Government of the Province concerned. . . .

The other important task of the Finance Commission was to submit to the President, not later than six months before the end of any plan period (such as the second five-year plan) a report on progress made during that period towards achieving parity of per capita income through the allocation of the resources of Pakistan, including foreign exchange (Article 145). The National Economic Council was to review the over-all economic position of Pakistan, formulate plans for the economic development of the nation and determine the proper allocation of resources to the provinces.

## National Capital and Languages

The Constitution named Islamabad as the seat of the central government. Dacca was to be the second capital and the seat of the National Assembly.

Bengali and Urdu were named as the national languages, although English would continue to be used for official purposes until arrangements could be made for its replacement, some time in 1972.

## Transitional Provisions

The Commission stated that it would not be necessary for the President to stand for election as he had received a mandate and, in addition, "his continuance in office was necessary to facilitate the transition from an authoritarian regime to a representative form of government." The President, furthermore, should continue in office not only until the new Constitution had come into force but until the end of the first term of three years.[31] The Commission had previously recommended using the elected Basic Democracies members as an electoral college simply because the election commission could not prepare for the elections before 1963. For that reason it was suggested that the first term be set at three years instead of the four-year term which the Commission was recommending.[32] The Constitution, how-

ever, provided five-year terms for the President and the legislatures, and stated that "Field Marshal Mohammad Ayub Khan, Hilal-i-Pakistan, Hilal-i-Jura'at, shall . . . become the first President of Pakistan under this Constitution on the commencing day" (the first day on which the Central Legislature should meet). His first term was set at three years and sixty days, and the first term for members of the assemblies was set at three years.

Under the transitional provisions of the Constitution governors, judges of the Supreme Court and High Courts, and anyone in the service of Pakistan just prior to the announcement of the Constitution were to continue in office under the same terms. The Commission recommended that the martial law regulations, except those relating to land reform, should stand repealed on the first day Parliament met. Article 225 of the Constitution said all existing laws would remain in force, with the exception of the Proclamation of October 7, 1958, and four laws including the Laws (Continuance in Force) Order 1958, and all martial law regulations would be repealed except five which included the West Pakistan Land Reforms Regulations.

## NOTES

1. The Khilafat or Caliphate was "the spiritual headship of Islam as formerly residing in the person of the Turkish Sultan." *Webster's New International Dictionary,* Second edition, 1936.

2. Government of Pakistan, *Report of the Constitution Commission, 1961* (Karachi, 1962), p. 19.

3. *Ibid.,* p. 20.

4. *Ibid.,* p. 28.

5. *Ibid.,* p. 31.

6. *Ibid.,* p. 34.

7. *Ibid.,* p. 36.

8. *Ibid.,* p. 40.

9. *Ibid.,* pp. 45-47.

10. *Ibid.,* p. 49.

11. *Ibid.,* p. 42.

12. *Ibid.,* pp. 40-41.

13. *Ibid.,* p. 41.

14. *Ibid.,* p. 42.

15. *Ibid.,* p. 64.

16. *Ibid.,* pp. 65-69.

17. *Ibid.,* pp. 71-77.

18. *Ibid.,* pp. 79-80.

19. *Ibid.,* p. 89.

20. *Ibid.,* p. 91.

21. *Ibid.,* p. 100.

22. *Ibid.,* p. 101.

23. *Ibid.,* p. 104.

24. *Ibid.,* p. 114.

25. *Ibid.,* p. 120.

26. *Sunnah* refers to the custom or tradition that has developed with regard to "the theory or practice consecrated by Mohammad's example." *Encyclopedia of Islam* (Leyden and London, 1913-1934), IV, 555.

27. P. 124.

28. *Zakat* is "the alms tax, one of the principal obligations of Islam." *Wakf* refers to property the income of which goes to "a work pleasing to God," such as the upkeep of mosques or other good works. *Encyclopedia of Islam,* IV, 1202, 1096.

29. *Report,* pp. 70-71.

30. *Ibid.,* pp. 131-133.

31. *Ibid.,* p. 134.

32. *Ibid.,* p. 77.

# CHAPTER XIV

# GAINERS AND LOSERS UNDER THE
# NEW CONSTITUTION

PAKISTAN's 1956 Constitution had been worked out in the full glare of publicity. It had been subjected to the demands of various regions, orthodox Muslim groups, and ambitious politicians. President Ayub Khan was determined that the new Constitution Commission and the subsequent cabinet committees should be as free as possible from the pressures of interest groups and public discussion of the issues. While it was possible to keep the deliberations of the Commission and sub-committees from the press and the public, it was not possible to suppress all expressions of public opinion. The *ulema* were vocal on the subject of Islamic provisions, even though their criticisms were seldom published. Lawyers and judges were outspoken on the rule of law and independence of the judiciary. East Pakistan's demand for economic justice was eventually discussed in the newspapers. Inevitably the impact of these feelings and ideas was felt by the constitution makers. What then did the new Constitution mean to the various groups and individuals?

Least is known about the reaction of the large bulk of the population. Just as in the revolutionary takeover, when "the ostensible equanimity with which the public reacted" was, according to the correspondent of the *Statesman* on October 15, 1958, one of the "most remarkable features of the change-over," so a new constitution was probably felt to make but little difference in their lives. Largely illiterate, their contact with government for centuries had been chiefly as taxpayers. They had been given a measure of participation in self-government and local economic development planning through Basic Democracies. But, except for the Basic Democrats, nothing further was expected of the masses regarding the acceptance or rejection of the Constitution or the election of various assembly members. They had voted for their electors in January 1960 and no further political decisions were expected of them until the next Basic Democracies elections to be held in 1965.

## Politicians

For the most part the politicians had been effectively silenced either through EBDO or under such regulations as the Security Act or the Prevention of Prejudicial Acts Order. Several former politicians had enjoyed the unexpected opportunity of seeing their views on the constitution published in the newspaper, but that period lasted less than a month. Land reforms in West Pakistan had political as well as economic implications by "paralyz[ing] the political power of landlords in that area."[1] The banning of political parties proved disabling but even more crushing was the elimination of the parliamentary system itself. From the politician's point of view, "the inability of the legislature to force ministerial changes made it 'powerless' and certainly less attractive as a field of political action."[2] The *Statesman* on March 5, 1962, commented, "That Pakistan's new Constitution would make things difficult for previous political leaders, on whom the present regime has never ceased to blame all the country's previous shortcomings, was a foregone conclusion."

Despite the restrictions, Suhrawardy and Ghaffar Khan had played the game of politics and had lost. Most of the former politicians, however, discreetly waited for the lifting of Martial Law.

## Ulema

The orthodox Muslim leadership had found it difficult to agree on what would constitute an Islamic state. From 1948 until 1954 they had labored to identify the requirements for an Islamic constitution. The abrasion of politics had forced many compromises along the way. By 1954 the *ulema* reluctantly admitted that, under the draft constitution, "Pakistan would, in theory at least, be an Islamic state, and that the BPC [Basic Principles Committee] report as amended was an Islamic constitution."[3] However, the dissolution of the constituent assembly was a repudiation of the draft constitution and "it seemed that the struggle for an Islamic constitution had ended in a defeat for the religious interests."[4]

The second constituent assembly was not asked for a draft constitution but the government prepared its own draft[5] and on March 23, 1956, this constitution went into effect. Binder points out[6] five sections of the 1956 Constitution which might be taken to represent the gains of the religious groups: (1) the Preamble, (2) the name— Islamic Republic, (3) the Head of State must be a Muslim, (4) the Directive Principles of State Policy, and (5) provisions for establishment of an Islamic teaching and research organization and imple-

mentation of the "repugnancy" clause. Binder called the 1956 Constitution a "watered-down version" of the *ulema's* agreed amendments to the Basic Policies Committee Report.[7]

Despite the facts that the first Principle of Law-Making under the 1962 Constitution declared, "No law should be repugnant to Islam," and an Islamic Advisory Council and an Islamic Research Institute were to be set up, there were no mandatory provisions relating to "repugnancy."[8] The Islamic parties had wanted some requirement that would assure the conformance of laws to Quranic injunctions. Article 198 (3) of the 1956 Constitution had called for the appointment of a commission to bring existing law into conformity with Islam and compile for the guidance of the assemblies, "such Injunctions of Islam as [could] be given legislative effect." This report was to have been submitted in five years "and the Assembly after considering the report [should] enact laws in respect thereof."

In explaining this aspect of the constitution President Ayub said, "Whilst making laws, the President and the legislatures have been enjoined to seek [the Advisory Council's] advice for giving them an Islamic bent."[9] Article 5 of the Constitution declared: "It is the responsibility of each legislature to ensure" that no proposed law should disregard or violate the Principles of Law-Making. Since, however, Article 6 leaves the decision of whether a law violates the principles up to the legislature, rather than the courts or the Islamic Advisory Council, the effect of Article 5 is considerably weakened. It is a voluntary decision on the part of executives or legislators as to whether a contemplated law is submitted to the Advisory Council of Islamic Ideology, and equally voluntary as to whether the advice tendered is accepted. Thus, while the responsibility for guaranteeing fundamental rights was placed with the Islamic Advisory Council, no provision was made for enforcement.

The President declared that it would be wrong to superimpose a higher power on a broad-based and elected assembly representing the people.[10] Manzur Qadir also defended the provision that legislatures need not be bound by the advice of the Islamic Advisory Council because, he said, nothing could shackle the will of the people.[11] He further contended that the Constitution included "definite checks and balances" to prevent the violation of those principles.[12] He did not, however, point to the relevant articles.

## Lawyers and Judges

The rule of law, the independence of the judiciary, and the guarantee of fundamental human rights were the main points emphasized

by lawyers and judges for incorporation in the Constitution. The "rule of law" meant abolition of Martial Law, the institution of duly elected assemblies for enacting legislation, and the right of individuals to be represented by counsel in a courtroom presided over by a duly qualified magistrate. The "independence of the judiciary" meant, in part, the assurance to judges of financial security, prestige and tenure, with all ranks of judicial officers a part of the judiciary system rather than under executive control. It also meant freedom for the courts to interpret the law without interference from the executive or legislative branches. The Commission had assumed that the High Courts would retain the power to protect individual rights. Instead the Constitution entrusted this important power to the law-makers. On this the *Statesman* commented:

> Perhaps the most insidious aspect of the new basic law is the limita-
> tion of the powers of the judiciary, the more so as it is indirectly
> linked with the process of safeguarding whatever fundamental rights
> the Constitution has conferred. . . . The legislatures have been held
> responsible for seeing that no legislation is enacted which violates
> these rights. Yet the judiciary, it would appear, has not the power
> to interfere if the legislatures fail to safeguard them.[13]

The extent to which the Constitution limited the powers of the Courts is shown by the following provisions:

"The validity of a law shall not be called in question on the ground that":

Article 6 (2)—"the law disregards . . . the Principles of Law-Making";

Article 8 (2)—"it is not in accordance with the Principles of Policy";

Article 134 (2)—"the legislature by which it was made had no power to make the law."

Finally, in his explanation of the powers of the judiciary, President Ayub stated that the function of the courts would be "to take notice of and to rectify any breaches of the law." Any person would have the right to go to court with a grievance whether "against a private person, a public servant, an official agency, or a department of the Government." To ensure that the courts understood their situation with regard to fundamental rights, he stated bluntly, "No court, however, shall be at liberty to refuse to enforce a law because it is of the opinion that the law is not in accordance with the Principles of Law-Making. The relevant opinion for this purpose is the opinion of the law-makers and nobody else."

Two years earlier Z. H. Lari, the President of the Karachi High Court Bar Association, had listed several provisions essential to "willing acceptance" of any constitution: (a) fundamental rights enforcable through courts, (b) independent judiciary, (c) supremacy

of parliament, (d) direct elections based on adult franchise, (e) elections to all offices and legislatures after withdrawal of martial law, and (f) authority to Parliament and Parliament alone to change the constitution.

Lari's opinions about the new Constitution were published in the *Statesman* on March 6. He expressed satisfaction that a Constitution had been announced "with the assurance that it [would] be enforced some time." He criticized it because the Supreme Court was not made "the final arbiter in all juridical matters" and because control over the main budget was withdrawn from Parliament. He also observed that under the new basic law writ jurisdiction had been substantially curtailed, direct elections were not provided, and political parties were banned. Considering the list of provisions he felt were essential he might also have noted the supremacy of the executive and the continuance of martial law until after the first elections. On the basis of these criteria it seems safe to say that the Constitution did not find "willing acceptance" by the bar and the bench. Mr. Lari, with apparent resignation, commented, "A democratic set-up, however imperfect and deficient, is to be welcomed as a step towards rehabilitation of real democracy." In spite of its limitations he felt that the Constitution "should be worked out and amended in the process."[14]

## Intellectuals

The group known as "intelligentsia" is difficult to define. In general it included those with higher education, a westernized attitude toward government and science, and the belief that Islam should be adjusted to suit the needs of the twentieth century. President Ayub Khan was certainly an intellectual as were a great many of the officers of the armed services and higher civil services, lawyers and judges, élite of the press, politicians and university professors. Yet, from the President's usage, it would seem that the term "intelligentsia" did not include all of these people; it might narrow down to include only ex-politicians, lawyers and those whose suggestions regarding political matters were at variance with the wishes of the ruling powers. In any case, it is significant that the intellectuals as a class—at least "some sections" of them—were the only group, except politicians, to which President Ayub made direct reference in his speech explaining the new Constitution. In discussing indirect elections, the President stated:

> While saying this, I am conscious of the fact that some sections of the intelligentsia and those with vested interests may have cause

to complain. I do not see any reasons why a suitable formula cannot be evolved later which will give them a feeling of full participation. The need of today, however, is that the Constitution should be brought in quickly, and that can be done only if the electoral college of Basic Democracies is used for the elections.

*Dawn* on October 27, 1960, referred to the "loose-thinking intellectuals and malcontents." The *Pakistan Observer,* however, frequently in its editorials urged full participation in national development by those who had ability to contribute. *Dawn* found the Islamic provisions "the most satisfying feature of the Constitution" but was disappointed that "an undiluted unitary form of government" was not provided. The *Pakistan Observer's* negative reaction to the new Constitution may well have reflected the attitude prevalent among East Pakistani intellectuals.

*East Pakistan*

East Pakistan posed a problem to Ayub Khan, as it had to his predecessors, from the earliest days of Martial Law. On his first visit to the east wing, two weeks after becoming Chief Martial Law Administrator, he began to speak at once of the necessity for "a sense of single nationhood." During his few years as President he accomplished more for the economic development of East Pakistan than had any former government.[15] It is of particular interest, therefore, to note what concessions were included in the Constitution for this province.

East Pakistan's demands were for a parliamentary and federal form of government, in which the prime minister was responsible to the legislature; an equitable share in economic development and the fiscal resources of the government; and participation in all branches of the civil and armed services. The insistence on a federal form could not be shaken. The East Pakistani members of the Commission had unanimously refused to sign a report that included the unitary form as a recommendation. The Commission's *Report* warned that East Pakistan had very strong feelings on this matter. The Constitution consequently provided for a form of federalism within a presidential system but the lack of autonomy gave little satisfaction to the eastern province.

While a new constitution could not insure equitable allocation of resources, civil service positions or industries, it could spell out the policies and specific means by which the Government hoped to achieve these goals. The 1962 Constitution contained certain provisions which

could be interpreted as concessions to East Pakistan. Four of the twenty-one Principles of Policy are relevant. Numbers six and seventeen state that people of all areas "should be enabled to participate fully in all forms of national activities, including employment in the service of Pakistan" and in the defense services of Pakistan. The well-being of all people should be secured "by raising the standard of income of the common man," declared the ninth Principle, and "by preventing the undue concentration of wealth . . . in the hands of a few." Parity between the provinces in all spheres of the central government was the goal expressed in the sixteenth Principle of Policy. The provisions for the Supreme Court to sit in Dacca at least twice in each year, and for Dacca to be the second capital and seat of the National Assembly, have been mentioned. Provincial control of the railways was made a constitutional matter by empowering the President to arrange for this transfer by July 1, 1962.

Fiscal arrangements in the Constitution included provisions for a National Finance Commission and a National Economic Council. The Finance Commission was to recommend to the President the division between the center and the provinces of revenue from certain taxes but it was left to the President to specify the share to be allocated to each province. A primary objective of the National Economic Council was to ensure that per capita income disparities between the provinces were removed and that the resources of Pakistan were allocated in such a way as to achieve this "in the shortest possible time."

It is necessary to refer to the 1956 Constitution to determine whether or not these provisions of the 1962 Constitution which are here interpreted as concessions to East Pakistan were, in fact, modifications introduced by the military regime. In 1947 Pakistan adopted an interim constitution based on the Government of India Act 1935. The 1956 Constitution generally followed the interim constitution but added the Directive Principles of State Policy and certain Islamic provisions.

The 1956 Constitution provided that no citizen should be discriminated against "on the ground only of race, religion, caste, sex, residence or place of birth" in appointment to the service of Pakistan (Article 16). In the "Principles of Social Uplift" (Article 28) the State was enjoined to "enable the people of different areas to participate fully in all forms of national activities, including employment in the service of Pakistan." The sixth Principle of Policy in the 1962 Constitution is almost an exact quotation from Article 28 of the 1956 Constitution. The ninth Principle of Policy in the 1962 Constitution, concerning raising the standard of living of the common

man and preventing the concentration of wealth is identical with Article 29 (a) of the earlier Constitution. Similarly the new Constitution's sixteenth and seventeenth Principles of Policy, dealing with parity between the provinces in the central government and in the defense services, are almost exact repetitions of Article 31 of the 1956 document. Only with regard to the achieving of parity is there any difference of wording. Where the previous Constitution states, "Steps shall be taken to achieve parity . . . ," the new Constitution declares, "Parity . . . should as nearly as is practicable, be achieved. . . ." Both Constitutions assured West Pakistan of parity in representation in the National Assembly despite the fact that it comprised only 46 per cent of the population. Thus no new concessions to East Pakistan appeared in the Principles of Policy.

Article 118 of the 1956 Constitution and Article 144 of the new document provided for a Finance Commission. These articles were identical except for the order in which the taxes (which were to be divided between the central government and the provinces) were listed and the inclusion in the 1962 Constitution of the corporation tax. In both constitutions the President was to specify the share of the divisible pool to be allocated to each province. Both constitutions also provided for a National Economic Council. Whereas the earlier document said ". . . the Council shall aim at ensuring that uniform standards are attained in the economic development of all parts of the country," the new Constitution declared that a "primary object" of the Council should be "to ensure that disparities between the Provinces" were removed and the resources allocated between the provinces "in such a manner as to achieve that object in the shortest possible time," thus strengthening this provision. Furthermore, under the 1962 Constitution, the National Economic Council was to submit an annual report on the progress achieved in attaining this objective. The Finance Commission was also to review the progress made in this field six months before the end of every plan period.

In contrast with the 1956 Constitution's permissive wording—that "Parliament may by law provide for the transfer of the railways in each Province to the Government of the Province" (Article 132)—is the mandatory provision of the 1962 Constitution: "The President shall, on or before the first day of July 1, 1962, provide for the transfer . . . of the railways in each Province to the Government of the Province" (Article 233).

Naming Dacca as the second capital might seem an innovation in the new Constitution. However, the military regime had decided as early as June 1959 that a second capital should be built there.[16]

According to the then Governor, Mr. Zakir Husain, five hundred acres had already been acquired at Tejgaon for that purpose by December of that year.[17]

Thus only three new concessions were granted East Pakistan by the 1962 Constitution: Dacca as the principal seat of the National Assembly; the removal of economic disparities as the primary objective of the National Economic Council; and provincial control of the railways.

### President Ayub Khan

To what extent did the President realize his ambitions in the provisions of the 1962 Constitution? Over and over again President Ayub had emphasized that politicians and political parties had been responsible for the breakdown of democracy. He held the parliamentary system to blame for the country's deterioration, since a president as head of state plus a prime minister as chief executive divided the power and, after Jinnah and Liaquat Ali Khan, led to a power struggle. Furthermore, under the parliamentary system the prime minister was dependent on the goodwill of the legislators who were continually indulging in political maneuvers. Tribalism, parochialism, and provincialism had created barriers between segments of the population and prevented the achievement of a unified nation.[18]

President Ayub believed that a stable government and a unified nation were Pakistan's most pressing needs. He instituted his plan for accomplishing these objectives by throwing out or drastically changing everything that had proved unworkable—political parties, provincial legislatures, the British judicial system, and the whole parliamentary form of democracy. The President intended to reach his goal through a government with one executive and one legislature. When adamant resistance to the unitary plan developed, especially in East Pakistan, he was forced to concede to a modified form of federalism, but with greatly reduced provincial autonomy. Nevertheless he maintained his determination to create a strong central government through an executive with legislative powers, a legislature with overriding powers, and weak provincial legislatures. Under the 1962 Constitution, any subject not reserved for the center could be acted upon by the provincial legislatures. But the weakness of the provinces was that they were not given exclusive power to enact laws on any matter.

In contrast, the central legislature was given forty-eight subjects on which it alone was empowered to act. In addition, when the national interests of Pakistan were concerned, the central legislature could also

make laws relating to the security of Pakistan, including economic and financial stability, and any matter related to the achievement of uniformity in the different parts of Pakistan. It was also the central legislature's duty to resolve any conflict between the governor and the provincial assembly when the president was appealed to either by the governor or the speaker (Article 74). An unusual power given to the National Assembly was the privilege of deciding whether or not its laws violated the Principles of Law-Making or the Principles of Policy (Articles 6 and 8).

One check on the assembly's legislative power was Article 26 which provided that no bill relating to preventive detention should be introduced in the central legislature without the previous consent of the President. Another limitation concerned voting on the budget: recurring expenditures might be discussed but could not be voted on by the assembly and new expenditures would be submitted to the assembly in the form of demands for grants. The President explained this arrangement during his Constitution broadcast:

> In order to reduce chances of conflict between the Assembly and the President and to prevent paralysis of the administration and to ensure continuance of on-going schemes, it has been laid down that the previously passed budget shall not be altered without the permission of the president, and new taxation shall not be levied without the consent of the National Assembly. This is based on the theory that the President is finally responsible to the country for administration and the members of the National Assembly represent the feeling of the people who have to pay taxes.

East Pakistan considered this provision a setback to achieving parity in development financing since West Pakistan already had many on-going projects whose budgets were now constitutionally assured.

The powers of the president and the prime minister under the 1956 Constitution were, in the 1962 Constitution, merged into the office of president, legally making the office one of the most powerful presidencies in the world. In times of war or internal crisis he was enabled to use dictatorial powers. It was certainly no exaggeration when one newspaper declared that the "bias" in the new Constitution toward the center "appeared to be prominent."[19] Specifically, the powers of the President included the supreme command of the defense services (Article 17), the power to grant pardons and suspend any sentence passed by court or tribunal (Article 18), and the power to appoint and direct the governors of the provinces (Article 56). He was also to concur in the governors' ministerial appointments (Article 82). Legislative power was granted to the President when the National

Assembly was not in session if he was "satisfied that circumstances exist[ed] which render[ed] immediate legislation necessary." He was also given the power to veto bills presented to him by the National Assembly. To pass a bill over the President's veto would require a two-thirds majority approval by the Assembly (Article 27). The President could summon and prorogue the Assembly and, within limits, dissolve the Assembly but he would have to cease holding office within four months after the dissolution. He might, however, be re-elected (Articles 22, 23).

The only checks on the President's power lay in the National Assembly's right to pass a law over his veto and its power to impeach the President for violation of the Constitution or "gross misconduct," or to remove him because of physical or mental incapacity (Articles 13 and 14). A three-fourths majority vote would be necessary to remove the President from office. If less than one-half of the Assembly voted for the President's removal, the original signatories of the resolution would "cease to be members of the Assembly forthwith" (Article 13).

The *Statesman* on March 3, 1962, considered "the provision regarding the impeachment of the President significant and interesting. It [was] probably the only serious check on the executive head of the country." It continued:

> Through the unusually far-reaching powers reserved for the Head of State, it has paved the way for any one individual (like President Ayub Khan himself) not necessarily a professional politician, to wield immense and possibly damaging power in the future. It requires no effort of memory to recall the contribution made by another 'non-political' President to the problems of pre-1958 Pakistan.

A critique from a university professor in Australia declared:

> The new Constitution has been styled as prescribing a presidential form of government in Pakistan, but it would be misleading to compare it with the American system. Beyond vague similarities, there is very little in common between the two, for the American President is not nearly as powerful as his Pakistani counterpart. Nor can even President de Gaulle, under the Constitution of the Fifth Republic, match the Pakistan President's authority. Presidential appointments do not require endorsement by the National Assembly. Neither Presidential nor Cabinet actions can be subjected to questioning by the committees or other agencies of the legislatures. With his emergency powers, the President's powers come close to being all-embracing. . . . The wide authority given to the President almost makes him a constitutional dictator. . . . At best Ayub's Constitution . . . introduces an authoritarian regime of the old British colonial type.[20]

This opinion paralleled that of an eminent Pakistani who felt the form of government provided by the Constitution was "a British

administrator's dream." Another observer described the Pakistan Constitution by asserting that it embodied "elements of the 1956 Constitution, plus an attempted polygamous marriage of the Basic Democracies Program, the parliamentary system of Great Britain and the presidential system of the United States."[21]

An American political scientist analyzed the 1962 Constitution as a "simple executive-legislature-voter relationship" with an "independent and unified national leadership responsible to his electorate." This commentator added that "four very controversial matters in the Constitution" represented departures from the recommendations of the Constitution Commission:

> First, in order to make possible a closer relationship between candidate and voter, the legislative and presidential franchise was limited to an electoral college made up of some 80,000 Union Councillors (themselves elected by universal adult suffrage). Second, in order to prevent manipulation of the voters by anti-national elements, political party participation in the electoral process was banned except as authorized by act of the central legislature. Third, in order to prevent a hostile Assembly from coercing the independent executive by withholding appropriations, the fiscal powers of the Assemblies were limited to approving or disapproving increases over the previous year's budget. Fourth, in order to prevent judicial process from thwarting policy laid down by public representatives in legislation or from obstructing the smooth working of the administration, no justiciable fundamental rights were included in the Constitution and the courts were denied the right to strike down laws as unconstitutional or *ultra vires*. Thus once passed by an Assembly and approved by the President or Governor, a law was to become effective and could be challenged only through the political process.[22]

Because of East Pakistan's strong opposition to a unitary government, the President had compromised for elected provincial legislatures. But all of President Ayub Khan's other objectives—a strong central government with a presidential system, a unicameral legislature, a ban on political parties at least until after the first elections, provisions for dealing with assembly members who engaged in malpractices, and indirect elections through an electoral college composed of the elected members of Basic Democracies—were attained through the new Constitution.

### NOTES

1. Khalid B. Sayeed, "Collapse of Parliamentary Democracy in Pakistan," *Middle East Journal,* 13 (Autumn 1959), 389-406.
2. Richard Wheeler, "Pakistan: New Constitution, Old Issues," *Asian Survey,* III, 2 (February 1963) 107-115.

3. Leonard Binder, *Religion and Politics in Pakistan* (Berkeley and Los Angeles: University of California Press), 1963, p. 337.

4. *Ibid.,* p. 362.

5. Keith Callard, *Pakistan: A Political Study* (London: George Allen and Unwin, Ltd., 1958), p. 121.

6. *Op. cit.,* pp. 369-374.

7. *Op. cit.,* p. 240.

8. Provisions for enforcing the "repugnancy" clause had been one of the knottiest problems to be worked out in 1953. Binder, *op. cit.,* pp. 286-291.

9. Broadcast of March 1. Unless indicated otherwise, all statements attributed to the President in this chapter have the same source.

10. *Pakistan Observer,* March 6, 1962, p. 1.

11. *Dawn,* March 18, 1962, p. 1.

12. *Ibid.,* March 7, 1962, p. 1.

13. March 3, 1962.

14. As a candidate for the National Assembly, Mr. Lari said he would like to make fundamental rights justiciable and to entrust the Supreme Court with powers to adjudicate in case of a constitutional conflict. However, Mr. Lari was defeated. *Statesman,* April 17 and May 1, 1962.

15. Government of Pakistan, Bureau of National Reconstruction, *A Pledge Redeemed,* (Karachi, 1962), p. 4.

16. *Dawn,* June 13, 1959, p. 1.

17. *Statesman,* December 4, 1959, p. 1.

18. Foreign observers corroborated President Ayub's version of the situation. An editorial in the Calcutta *Statesman* (December 18, 1958) remarked that the predecessors of the military regime in Pakistan "were so full of corruption and intrigue that the survival not merely of a democracy in Pakistan but even of Pakistan itself had come to be in doubt." An English writer observed that as early as 1953 "Pakistan had proclaimed her political and economic bankruptcy," brought about by the failure of parliamentary democracy. Poorly organized political parties and the "havoc" they wrought were largely instrumental in producing the "confused state of affairs" which "gave a free rein to a leadership which had lost all sense of purpose and direction except that of personal aggrandizement." "The New Constitution," *Round Table,* 52 (1961-62), pp. 291-294. Numerous other statements supporting this point of view could be cited.

19. *Morning News,* March 14, 1962.

20. D. P. Singhal, "The New Constitution of Pakistan," *Asian Survey,* II, No. 6 (August 1962), 15-23.

21. Louis Dupree, "A Note on Pakistan," *American Universities Field Staff Report,* South Asia Series, VII, 8 (Pakistan: August 1963), 13.

22. Wheeler, *op. cit.,* pp. 108-109.

# EPILOGUE

THIS FINAL WORD is not intended to continue the discussion of government propaganda vs. public opinion *vis-a-vis* the new Constitution, but merely to follow through to the end of Martial Law.

Immediately after the announcement of the Constitution the Government launched a massive publicity campaign to inform the public about its provisions and to attempt to assure the people's approval. The foremost speakers who traveled the provinces to inform the people, and hopefully gain their approval, of the Constitution were President Ayub Khan and Manzur Qadir. Other members of the cabinet, A. K. Khan, Z. A. Bhutto and Zakir Husain, also made speaking tours in what was called "a vocal mass contact."[1] In a radio broadcast the day after the announcement of the Constitution the new election commissioner, Akhtar Hussain, promised that elections would be held in an orderly manner, that ballots would be cast in secrecy and undue influence would not be permitted.[2] The date for elections to the National Assembly was set at April 28 and for provincial assembly elections at May 6. By March 11 a number of candidates in the Rawalpindi area had embarked on their campaigns,[3] within a week the country was "in the grip of election fever,"[4] and the tempo of campaigning gained momentum rapidly.

Shortly after the transitional provisions of the Constitution went into effect President Ayub said that in the near future he would explain to the public what his program as President would be.[5] He subsequently chose March 23, Lahore Resolution Day, to, as he said, "place before the nation the objectives and requirements of Pakistan as I see them, so that the people, the electorate and the prospective candidates should know what guidelines I intend to follow." In the Manifesto he summarized the objectives of his administration:

> . . . Islamic ideology, security, stability, unity, discipline, progress and prosperity at home; peace and prestige abroad; economic de-

211

velopment, social reforms, social justice, equality of opportunities
and the reconstruction of a society which can sustain a workable
pattern of democracy under the umbrella of enlightened moral,
political, cultural and spiritual values . . .

and he discussed the means of achieving these goals:

. . . our faith in the Constitution, responsive masses, responsible
leadership, competent legislators, strong and stable Governments,
competent powerful defence forces, clean and quick administration,
cheap and ready justice, multi-dimensional programs of development in education, industry, commerce and agriculture, individual
and collective austerity, integrity, homogeneity, service of man, fear
of God and a relentless passion for work, ceaseless work and nothing
but work.[6]

Student agitation had not ceased with the trial of the eleven persons which ended on March 3 when the court reserved judgment. Ten
days later the eleven were found guilty only on the third count, that
of attending a procession of a political nature. The court then pronounced sentences but immediately afterward the president of the
three-member military court "announced that the GOC and Martial
Law Administrator of East Pakistan was graciously pleased to grant
pardon to all the eleven persons."[7] However, this gesture on the part
of the Government did not pacify the general student population.
On March 24 a large number of students attempted to form a procession but they were restrained by the police and 207 persons were
arrested.[8] All were released within a few days except ten students who
were charged under Martial Law Regulations 13, 24, and 29—obstruct-
ing government officials from performing their duties, raising objectionable slogans and being members of an unlawful procession.[9] The
cycle seemed about to be repeated as student strikes once more began
to spread all over the province.

At this point, seven former politicians of East Pakistan joined forces
to prepare a statement which was published on April 14. The signatories, representing various pre-revolutionary parties, included three
former chief ministers, Nurul Amin, Ataur Rahman Khan* and Abu
Hossain Sarkar;* an important central ex-minister, Hamidul Huq
Chowdhury; two former provincial ministers, Mahmud Ali and Syed
Azizul Huq,* and Pir Mohsenuddin. Their statement declared that
with the union council members about to participate in the forthcoming National Assembly elections, in which a little over 500 voters from
each constituency would represent a population of 650,000 in East
Pakistan and 500,000 in West Pakistan, "mass opinion [would] hardly

---

* Disqualified by EBDO.

count." Under such circumstances "to keep detained quite a number of leading public men" and students "look[ed] not only extremely harsh and illogical but unjust." These men asked the government to "release immediately all the political prisoners," for they felt that such action would "create an atmosphere congenial to the cause of true democracy in the country."[10] This demand was supported by some union councillors of Lahore and Gujranwala, lawyers of Sylhet and Khulna and several assembly candidates from Lahore.[11]

After the April 28 elections a deputation of the newly elected members of the National Assembly submitted a petition to the Martial Law Administrator, Major-General Khwaja Wasiuddin, asking him to grant a reprieve to all the students held by the government. General Wasiuddin recommended to the President that this petition be granted. On May 3 President Ayub Khan, a government press release stated, "granted clemency to all the students arrested under Martial Law Regulations in connection with their recent agitation."[12]

With Martial Law only partially lifted newspapers were not quite sure how free they were to express opinions, either their own or those of others. Therefore, early mentions of policies opposed by the government were cautious. The *Pakistan Observer* of March 26 quoted a speaker at a youth forum sponsored by the Bureau of National Reconstruction on the matter of the revival of political parties. But questions concerning political parties posed to President Ayub and Manzur Qadir elicited strong replies on the undesirability of these democratic necessities and the mere trickle of published items favorable to political parties represented only a token of the strong public opinion on this subject.

Interest in the coming elections was intense. The election rules were announced March 26 and early in April relaxation of the martial law regulation regarding meetings and processions was announced.[13] Three members of the President's cabinet, A. K. Khan of Chittagong, Habibur Rahman of Bogra and Z. A. Bhutto of Sind, decided to stand for election,[14] as did Mohammad Ali of Bogra, a former prime minister and, at that time, Pakistan's ambassador to Japan.[15] In West Pakistan, Z. H. Lari, a lawyer, and Begum Saeeda Qazi Isa, whose husband had been disqualified by EBDO, decided to enter their names for the elections.[16]

Nominations were to be filed no later than April 4.[17] Altogether, approximately six hundred candidates were nominated for the one hundred fifty seats to the National Assembly.[18] Only two hundred forty-seven of the three hundred thirty-five candidates nominated from East Pakistan were found to be qualified.[19] The first government-

sponsored election meeting was held in Dacca on April 13 and all such meetings were concluded by April 20.[20] On April 28, 37,672 union councillors of East Pakistan cast their ballots for members of the National Assembly. Mohammad Ali and Habibur Rahman received the highest percentage of votes cast.[21] The general pattern in East Pakistan indicated that Muslim Leaguers had staged a comeback.[22] Successful candidates in West Pakistan were Ghulam Ali Talpur, a former central minister and key figure in Republican Party circles, and Choudhury Mohammad Husain, who had recently acquired control of the *Pakistan Times* in Lahore. When it became clear that former Muslim Leaguers constituted the largest group in the Assembly the *Morning News* of April 30 predicted, "Things are destined to take a definite shape in the course of the next few weeks preceding the first session of the National Assembly."[23]

The number of pre-revolutionary politicians elected to the Assembly must have come as a shock to the President. The agitation for parties generally, capped by the publicly acknowledged intention of the former Muslim Leaguers to reorganize,[24] resulted in President Ayub's promulgating an ordinance prohibiting the unregulated activity of political organizations.[25]

Elections for the provincial assemblies took place on May 6. In West Pakistan the majority of the successful candidates "came from the rank of hitherto lesser known persons" but a substantial minority represented former political party members.[26] In East Pakistan there were nine hundred and ninety-six candidates for one hundred and forty-nine seats and the polling was heavy. The results in this wing introduced many new faces to the political arena; nevertheless, there was also a large number of experienced politicians as well as some members of Basic Democracies.[27] The elections to the seats reserved for women took place on May 27 for the provincial assemblies and May 29 for the National Assembly.[28]

The President announced that his cabinet would consist of eight ministers, four to be chosen from each wing, and an equal number of parliamentary secretaries. The speaker would be from East Pakistan since the President was from the west wing.[29] He had already named Abdul Qadir and Mohammad Munir as Ministers for Finance and Law, respectively,[30] and as the opening of the Assembly in Rawalpindi approached there was "renewed activity" among National Assembly members "in search of group alignments."[31]

As a prelude to the enforcement of the new Constitution President Ayub Khan's Martial Law Cabinet resigned on the evening of June 7. Early on the morning of June 8 the members started filling the audi-

torium of Ayub Hall. The President arrived at 8:30 a.m. where Akhtar Hussain, the Chief Election Commissioner, was waiting to receive him. After recitations from the Quran the President addressed his audience. At exactly 8:37 a.m. Chief Martial Law Administrator and Field Marshal President Mohammad Ayub Khan declared the lifting of Martial Law "amidst loud cheers from all sides of the House." The members were then sworn in, each in the language of his choice—English, Bengali or Urdu. At 5:45 p.m. Ayub Khan was sworn in as the first President of the Republic of Pakistan under Section 226 of the Constitution by Chief Justice of the Supreme Court, A. R. Cornelius.[32] Through his voluntary termination of the military dictatorship, President Ayub Khan had succeeded in executing a bloodless military coup, in ruling by Martial Law for forty-four months and in restoring constitutional government to Pakistan.

## NOTES

1. *Dawn,* March 5, 1962, p. 1.
2. *Morning News,* March 3, 1962, p. 3.
3. *Ibid.,* March 12, 1962.
4. *Ibid.,* March 19, 1962, pp. 1, 8.
5. *Pakistan Observer,* March 12, 1962, p. 1.
6. Khan, Md. Ayub, *Speeches and Statements* (Karachi: Pakistan Publications, July 1961-June 1962), IV, 187-194.
7. *Pakistan Observer,* March 13, 1962.
8. *Ibid.,* March 25; *Dawn,* March 26, 1962.
9. *Pakistan Observer,* March 26; *Morning News,* March 30, 1962.
10. *Pakistan Observer,* April 14, p. 1; *Statesman,* April 16, 1962.
11. *Morning News,* April 17; *Pakistan Observer,* April 21, 26, 28, 1962.
12. *Pakistan Observer,* May 4, 1962.
13. *Ibid.,* April 2, 1962.
14. *Morning News,* March 25; *Statesman,* April 7, 1962.
15. *Pakistan Observer,* March 30, 1962, p. 3.
16. *Morning News,* March 12, 31, 1962, p. 6.
17. *Pakistan Observer,* March 30, 1962.
18. *Statesman,* April 7, 1962.
19. *Ibid.,* April 9, 1962.
20. *Ibid.,* April 15, 1962, p. 9.
21. *Morning News,* April 29, 1962.
22. *Pakistan Observer,* April 30, 1962.
23. According to the *New York Times,* International Edition (May 6, 1962), forty-four per cent of the newly elected members belonged to proscribed political groups. The *Statesman* (June 2, 1962) said, however, that nearly seventy of the 150 members (forty-six per cent) were former Muslim Leaguers with perhaps forty additional ex-politicians whose affiliations had been with other parties.

24. *Pakistan Observer,* May 3, 1962, p. 1.

25. *Ibid.,* May 11, 1962, p. 1.

26. *Morning News,* May 7, 1962.

27. *Pakistan Observer,* May 7, 1962.

28. *Ibid.,* May 28, 30, 1962. This reverse order was followed because it was the duty of the provincial assembly to elect the women to the reserved seats in the National Assembly.

29. *Ibid.,* May, 20, 1962.

30. *Morning News,* May 19, 1962.

31. *Pakistan Observer,* June 6, 1962.

32. *Ibid.,* and *Morning News,* June 9, 1962, p. 1; Khan, Md. Ayub, *op. cit.,* IV, 243-252.

# APPENDICES

A. Members of the Cabinet of President Ayub Khan
   (1) As inducted October 27, 1958
   (2) As reallocated January 7, 1960
   (3) As inducted February 17, 1960
   (4) As reallocated April 21, 1960
   (5) As of June, 1960
   (6) As of January, 1962

B. "A Short Appreciation of Present and Future Problems of Pakistan," by General Mohammad Ayub Khan

C. Questionnaire of the Constitution Commission

D. Text of President Ayub Khan's Broadcast on the Constitution, March 1, 1962

E. Selected Excerpts from the *Report of the Constitution Commission, 1961*
   (1) Form of Government—Unitary or Federal
   (2) Fundamental Rights and Directive Principles
   (3) Preamble and Islamic Provisions

F. Selections from the Text of the 1962 Constitution of the Republic of Pakistan
   (1) Preamble
   (2) Part I—The Republic of Pakistan
   (3) Part II—Principles of Law-Making and of Policy

Members of the Cabinet of President Ayub Khan
(1) As inducted October 27, 1958

Gen. Mohammad Ayub Khan — Chief Martial Law Administrator, President, and with portfolios of Defense and Kashmir Affairs

Manzur Qadir — Foreign Affairs

M. Shoaib — Finance

Lt. Gen. Mohammad Azam Khan — Rehabilitation

Lt. Gen. W. A. Burki — Health and Social Welfare

F. M. Khan — Communications

Habibur Rahman — Education, Information and Broadcasting; and soon added, Minority Affairs

Lt. Gen. K. M. Sheikh — Interior

Abul Kasem Khan — Industries

Hafizur Rahman — Food and Agriculture

Zulfiqar Bhutto — Commerce

Maulvi Mohammad Ibrahim — Law

Akhtar Hussain — Governor, West Pakistan

Zakir Husain — Governor, East Pakistan

(2) As reallocated January 7, 1960

Mohammad Ayub Khan — Defense and Kashmir Affairs

Manzur Qadir — Foreign Affairs and Commonwealth Relations

M. Shoaib — Finance

Lt. Gen. Mohammad Azam Khan — Rehabilitation and Works, Food and Agriculture, and Irrigation

219

Lt. Gen. W. A. Burki               Health, Labor and Social Welfare
F. M. Khan                         Railways and Communications
                                   (including Shipping)
Habibur Rahman                     Education
Lt. Gen. K. M. Sheikh              Interior
Abul Kasem Khan                    Industries
Hafizur Rahman                     Commerce
Zulfiqar Bhutto                    Information & Broadcasting, National Reconstruction, Village-AID, Basic Democracies, Tourism and Minorities

Maulvi Mohammad Ibrahim            Law

Akhtar Hussain                     Governor, West Pakistan
Zakir Husain                       Governor, East Pakistan

## (3) As inducted February 17, 1960

Mohammad Ayub Khan                 Defense and Kashmir Affairs
Manzur Qadir                       Foreign Affairs and Commonwealth Relations
M. Shoaib                          Finance
Lt. Gen. Md. Azam Khan             Rehabilitation, Works and Water Resources, Food and Agriculture

Lt. Gen. W. A. Burki               Health, Labor and Social Welfare
F. M. Khan                         Railways and Communications
Habibur Rahman                     Education
Lt. Gen. K. M. Sheikh              Interior
Abul Kasem Khan                    Industries
Hafizur Rahman                     Commerce
Zulfiqar Bhutto                    Information and Broadcasting, and Minority Affairs

Mohammad Ibrahim                   Law

Akhtar Hussain                     Governor, West Pakistan
Zakir Husain                       Governor, East Pakistan

March 1960 the Ministry of Information and Broadcasting became the Ministry of National Reconstruction and Information; it remained with Mr. Bhutto.

April 1960 Lt. Gen. Azam Khan became Governor of East Pakistan. His portfolios went to Interior Minister, Lt. Gen. Sheikh.

## (4) As reallocated April 21, 1960

| | |
|---|---|
| Mohammad Ayub Khan | Cabinet Division, Defense, Establishment |
| Manzur Qadir | Foreign Affairs and Commonwealth Relations |
| M. Shoaib | Finance |
| Lt. Gen. W. A. Burki | Health, Labor and Social Welfare |
| F. M. Khan | Railways and Communications |
| Habibur Rahman | Education and Minority Affairs |
| Lt. Gen. K. M. Sheikh | Food and Agriculture, Interior, Rehabilitation and Works, States and Frontier Regions |
| Abul Kasem Khan | Industries |
| Hafizur Rahman | Commerce (including Tourism) |
| Zulfiqar Bhutto | National Reconstruction and Information, Kashmir Affairs, Fuel, Power and Natural Resources and Projects Division |
| Mohammad Ibrahim | Law |
| Akhtar Hussain | Governor, West Pakistan |
| Lt. Gen. Md. Azam Khan | Governor, East Pakistan |
| Zakir Husain | On leave |

## (5) As of June 1960

| | |
|---|---|
| Mohammad Ayub Khan | Cabinet Division, Defense and Establishment Division |
| Manzur Qadir | Foreign Affairs and Commonwealth Relations |
| M. Shoaib | Finance |
| Lt. Gen. W. A. Burki | Health, Labor and Social Welfare |
| F. M. Khan | Railways and Communications |
| Habibur Rahman | Education and Minority Affairs |
| Lt. Gen. K. M. Sheikh | Food and Agriculture, Rehabilitation and Works, States and Frontier Regions |

| | |
|---|---|
| Abul Kasem Khan | Industries |
| Hafizur Rahman | Commerce (including Tourism) |
| Zulfiqar Bhutto | Fuel, Power and Natural Resources, and Projects Division |
| Md. Ibrahim | Law |
| Akhtar Hussain | National Reconstruction and Information, and Kashmir Affairs |
| Zakir Husain | Interior |
| Malik Amir Mohammad Khan | Governor, West Pakistan |
| Lt. Gen. Md. Azam Khan | Governor, East Pakistan |

On April 18, 1961, Habibur Rahman became Minister of National Reconstruction and Information, and Akhtar Hussain assumed the portfolios of Education and Scientific Research, Kashmir Affairs and Minority Affairs. During this period the Ministry of Foreign Affairs became the Ministry of External Affairs and the name of the Ministry of the Interior was changed to Ministry of Home Affairs.

## (6) As of January 1962

| | |
|---|---|
| Mohammad Ayub Khan | Defense |
| Manzur Qadir | External Affairs |
| M. Shoaib | Finance |
| Lt. Gen. W. A. Burki | Health, Labor and Social Welfare |
| F. M. Khan | Railways and Communications |
| Habibur Rahman | National Reconstruction and Information |
| Lt. Gen. K. M. Sheikh | Food and Agriculture |
| Abul Kasem Khan | Industries |
| Hafizur Rahman | Commerce |
| Zulfiqar Bhutto | Fuel, Power and Natural Resources |
| Md. Ibrahim | Law |
| Akhtar Hussain | Education and Scientific Research, Kashmir Affairs, and Minority Affairs |
| Zakir Husain | Home Affairs |
| Malik Amir Mohammad Khan | Governor, West Pakistan |
| Lt. Gen. Md. Azam Khan | Governor, East Pakistan |

Before the lifting of Martial Law June 8, 1962, the following changes in personnel occurred: (1) Abdul Qadir became Finance Minister 1/30/62 when Shoaib was appointed a Director of the World Bank. Shoaib remained as Minister of Economic Affairs until his departure in May. (2) Ibrahim's resignation from the Cabinet was accepted 4/18/62 and Manzur Qadir took over the Law portfolio. (3) Ghulam Faruque became Governor of East Pakistan May 10, 1962, and Azam Khan was transferred.

# A Short Appreciation of Present and Future Problems of Pakistan

## By General Mohammad Ayub Khan*

From pp. 86–93 of *My Chief,* by Colonel Mohammad Ahmad
(Lahore: Longmans, Green and Co., 1960)

## THE AIM

1. The ultimate aim of Pakistan must be to become a sound, a solid and a cohesive nation to be able to play its destined role in world history. This can be achieved only if as a start a constitution is evolved that will suit the genius of the people and be based on the circumstances confronting them, so that they are set on the path of unity, team work and creative progress.

2. Before such a constitution can be devised, it is obvious that certain preliminary steps will have to be taken that will provide the setting for the unhindered evolution of such a constitution. Taking of such preliminary steps therefore becomes the *immediate* aim of Pakistan.

## FACTORS

*General*

3. (a) The people of Pakistan consist of a variety of races each with its own historical background and culture. East Bengalis, who

---

* Written in London October 4, 1954.

constitute the bulk of the population probably belong to the very original Indian races. It would be no exaggeration to say that up to the creation of Pakistan, they had not known any real freedom or sovereignty. They have been in turn ruled either by the caste Hindus, Moghals, Pathans or the British. In addition, they have been and still are under considerable cultural and linguistic influence. As such they have all the inhibitions of downtrodden races and have not yet found it possible psychologically to adjust to the requirements of their newborn freedom. Their peculiar complexes, exclusiveness, suspicion and a sort of defensive aggressiveness probably emerge from this historical background. Prudence, therefore, demands that these factors should be recognized and catered for and they be helped so as to feel equal partners and prove an asset. That can be done only if they are given a considerable measure of partnership.

(b) The population in West Pakistan, on the other hand, is probably the greatest mixture of races found anywhere in the world. Lying on the gateways to the Indian sub-continent, it was inevitable that each successive conquering race should have left its traces here. Consequently, this forced mixture of races has fusion of ideas, outlook and culture, despite linguistic variety obtained. Strategically and economically too, this area is destined to stand or fall as a whole. Lying as it does in the basin of the Indus river and its tributaries, its future economic development must be considered as a whole to achieve maximum results. All this indicates therefore that West Pakistan, in order to develop properly and prove a bulwark of defense from the North or South, must be welded into one unit and all artificial provincial boundaries removed, regardless of any prejudices to the contrary, which are mostly the creation of politicians rather than real. When doing this, however, regard must be had for the prejudices and fears of people and their future balanced development. This unit should, therefore, be so subdivided that each sub-unit embraces a racial group or groups with a common economy, communications and potentiality for development, and administration decentralized in them to the maximum possible.

(c) The creation of one unit in West Pakistan, however, is possible only if the biggest constituent is prepared to show large-heartedness and make a sacrifice for the common good. Punjab is the biggest and most important province in West Pakistan with more than half its population. If she insists on proportionate representation, the others will, at once, shy off. Besides, no coalition can work with one dominant partner. Therefore, for its preservation and the glory of Pakistan, Punjab should be asked to accept forty per cent representation in the

legislature of this unit, others having representation in proportion to their population. But before such a unit can be brought into being, the existing provincial and States' legislatures and cabinets will have to be done away with so as not to interfere and impede reorganization.

*Deductions from the above*

(1) Call East Bengal one unit and give it as much partnership as possible.

(2) Reorganize West Pakistan into one unit and give it similar partnership as above.

(3) Abolish present provincial Ministries and legislatures to speed up reorganization.

(4) Subdivide each unit into convenient sub-units, each embracing a racial group or groups with common economy, communications and prospective development. Administration to be decentralized in these subunits as much as possible.

(5) In order to remove any fear of domination, Punjab to be asked to accept forty per cent representation in West Pakistan unit legislature.

(6) Both East and West units to have their own legislatures.

4. Given the above, the fear of one unit dividing or dominating others would disappear; harmonious and unfettered development in each unit will be possible, fear of provincialism will be reduced to the minimum; saving in man-power in eliminating so many top-heavy provincial administrations would be effected; expense of administration would be reduced to the minimum and the danger of politicians interfering with the local administrators curtailed. In other words, very valuable gains would have been made by such a reorganization.

## THE ADMINISTRATIVE STRUCTURE OF EACH PROVINCIAL UNIT

5. Having created two provincial units in Pakistan, the next question is to determine the structure of administration in each unit. Before answering such a question, it would be appropriate to reiterate the fact that our eventual aim must be to develop democracy in Pakistan, but of a type that suits the genius of the people. Our people are mostly uneducated and our politicians not so scrupulous. The people are capable of doing great things, but they can also be easily misled. Unfettered democracy can, therefore, prove dangerous, especially now-a-days when Communism from within and without is so

quick to make use of its weaknesses. We, therefore, have to have a controlled form of democracy with checks and counterchecks. This indicates that legislature finds [sic] the Cabinet, whose actions are controllable by a Governor, who in turn is controlled by the Head of the State (President); in certain circumstances, the Governor having the power to remove Ministers or the Ministry. He should also be in a position to protect the rights of the Services and have them carry out their obligations.

6. Connected with the elections of legislatures is the question of franchise. It is too late now to resile from universal suffrage, however great its shortcomings may be. The answer would be to provide checks here too, so as to prevent its becoming irresponsible. We must not forget that democracy is a means to an end and not an end by itself and that there is no set pattern of democracy that can be applied to every country without modifications. It would be advisable, there-fore, to enable people to elect a college of people in each sub-unit, who in turn elect members for the Provincial and Central legislatures. Such an electoral system would be more easily manageable and would make for a good deal of responsibility.

7. As to the size and type of provincial and central legislatures, opinions may differ, but the need for strict economy in men and money would indicate that one legislature for each province, of about 150 members each, would do. Similarly, the central legislature, of which mention will be made later, should not be of a strength more than that.

8. Whilst talking about administration there is the problem of our legal system, which is most expensive, ineffective, dilatory, tyrannical and totally unsuited to our genius. This will need complete overhaul and to be made humane, quick and cheap. The answer would seem to lie in having a *Jirga* cum judicial system and revision of evidence and procedural laws with only one right of appeal. The highest judicial court for dealing with cases other than constitutional will have to be created in each sub-unit. The federal or the provincial High Courts should deal only with cases of a constitutional nature.

*Deductions from the above*

(1) In each province there should be one legislature of about 150 members each, headed by a Cabinet. There should be a Governor in each Province appointed by the President with powers of control over the Cabinet and the Services.

(2) The electoral system should consist of election of electoral col-

leges in each sub-unit by universal suffrage; these colleges to elect members for the provincial legislature, the central legislature and also to elect the President, of which mention will be made later.

(3) The legal system should be simplified and decentralized to sub-units: introduction of *Jirga* cum judicial system to be examined.

(4) Government Servants' Conduct Rules should be revised so as to make summary dealings in cases of rewards and punishment possible.

## THE STRUCTURE OF THE CENTER

9. Having created two units of the country, their federation on an equal basis without fear of domination of one over the other becomes a practical proposition. This federation should consist of one legislative house of about 150 strong, equally divided amongst the two units, headed by a Cabinet. This cabinet should have executive powers as voted by the legislature, subject to some effective control by the President, who should be elected. The President should be made the final custodian of power on the country's behalf and should be able to put things right in both the provinces and the Centre should they go wrong. Laws should be operative only if certified by the President except in cases where they are passed by three-fourths majority. No change in the constitution should be made unless agreed to by the President. In case of serious disagreement between the President and the legislatures, provision should be made for fresh elections of either one or both. Acceptance of the Mohammad Ali Formula for election of the President and passing of laws would perhaps be necessary.

10. For reasons given before, the provinces should have as much partnership as possible and that means that in addition to the subjects already in their hands, Communications, except inter-provincial, Industries, Commerce, Health, etc., should be handed over to the Provinces, leaving Defense, Foreign Affairs and Currency in the hands of the Centre.

11. The quick development of our resources and raising the standard of living of our people is one of the main problems which Pakistan has to solve. This can be done effectively only if we overhaul our educational system to prepare our manpower for the task and to have well-controlled and well-financed organizations to undertake major development projects. That indicates organization of Development Boards rather on the P.I.D.C. fashion for education, cottage industries, land and power and hosts of other things in each Province. This arrangement will help relieve local administrations of a lot of headaches and will ensure quick development.

12. But nothing much will be gained unless we carry out land reforms in a scientific fashion. Possession of vast areas of land by a few is no longer defensible nor is acquisition of land without compensation. The Egyptian example is a very good one; they allowed the owner a certain limit of holding, buying the rest for distribution amongst peasants, who will pay the cost in seventy yearly instalments.

13. It was mentioned earlier that the President should be made the repository of power. He can discharge this duty only if the Services are made directly responsible to him. To do that, a system of Joint Staff headed by a Supreme Commander will have to be introduced. The Supreme Commander should be appointed by the President. In addition to other duties, he should be made the Defense Member and an ex-officio member of the Cabinet. This will not only knit the Services together and lead to economy in pooling things common to all the Services, but would put a stop to any attempt by politicians to interfere in the internal affairs of the Services to promote their personal interests.

14. The experience of the last seven years has shown how dangerous the use of ambiguous clichés can be. Everybody said we should have an Islamic Democracy without ever defining what it was and how it differed from the normally understood democracy. Perhaps it is not possible to define it. Would it, therefore, not be correct to say that any variety of democracy when worked in the spirit of the Quran can be called an Islamic Democracy? We shall perhaps do better and avoid many pitfalls if we accept this concept.

## OUTLINE PLAN

15. As a preliminary, abolish provincial Ministries and legislatures in West Pakistan and create one Province of it under a Governor with the requisite staff.

16. Create sub-units in East Bengal and West Pakistan equivalent to a Commissioner's Division, each Division containing racial group or groups with common language, common economy and communications and common development potential. Decentralize administration so that the Head of the Division becomes the king-pin of administration.

17. Overhaul the legal system so as to make it cheaper and quicker, placing the highest appellate court in a Division, except for cases involving points of constitutional law, for which a Federal Court or a High Court in each Province should suffice. A *Jirga* cum judicial system should be evolved and procedural law simplified.

18. Create Development Boards in each Province covering Education, Water and Power, Land Reforms and Development, Cottage Industries, etc.

19. Create a Joint Staff for the three Services headed by a Supreme Commander who in addition to other duties should be the Defense Member and be the ex-officio member of the Central Cabinet coming finally under the President.

20. The Central Government to consist of one Legislature consisting of about 150 members equally divided between the two Provinces, a Cabinet and the President. The President to have overriding powers to assume control should things go wrong in the Provinces or the Centre. To avoid undue domination of the one Province over the other, apply the Mohammad Ali Formula to the election of President and passage of Bills.

21. The Provincial Government in East Bengal to consist of a legislature of about 150 members headed by a Cabinet with a Governor appointed by the President: the Governor to have some measure of control over the Cabinet and the Services. Same arrangement should apply in the Province of West Pakistan, except that the representation of the present Punjab to be forty per cent and the rest of the seats divided amongst others in accordance with their population.

22. Provinces to have maximum partnership possible, the Centre dealing only with Defence, Foreign Affairs, Currency and such communications as are inter-provincial.

23. The Government Servants' Conduct Rules should be revised so as to make summary awards or punishments possible.

24. The suffrage should be adult franchise, who should be called upon to elect an electoral college in each division, who will then elect the President and members of the Central and provincial legislatures.

25. Finally hope and pray that this Constitution is worked in the spirit of the Quran. If so, our solidarity, strength and future is assured.

Questionnaire of the Constitution Commission (not including the Annexures) as published in *Report of the Constitution Commission, 1961,* pp. 143-146.

In answering these questions you are requested to keep in view the terms of reference given to the Commission, a copy of which is annexure 'A'.

Q. 1. What, in your opinion, were the nature and causes of the progressive failure of the parliamentary pattern of democratic government in Pakistan leading to the abrogation of the Constitution of 1956 (hereinafter referred to as the late Constitution)?

Q. 2. What steps do you suggest for preventing a recurrence of the said, or like, causes?

Q. 3. In the light of your conclusions on the aforesaid questions: (a) do you recommend the parliamentary pattern or prefer the presidential form of government? (b) are you in favour of unitary or federal form of government? (A short note on the abovesaid forms of Government is appended as annexure 'B').

Q. 4. If you recommend parliamentary form of Government what steps do you suggest to secure stability of government while at the same time effectively checking undue interference with the day-to-day administration on account of party considerations?

Q. 5. As in the Presidential form of Government there is separation of powers with the result that the executive and the legislature are independent of each other, it is necessary to devise a system for securing co-ordination between the separate branches and thus to avoid deadlocks. If you favour the presidential form do you think the system of checks and balances provided in the American Constitution (annexure

'B') would adequately meet our needs particularly in the matter of money bills, foreign relations and appointment of Ministers, Ambassadors and other high officers of the executive and the Armed Forces, or would you suggest any modification thereof?

Q. 6. If you are in favour of the unitary form, please indicate the changes in the present administrative structure which, in your opinion, it will be necessary to make.

Q. 7. If you prefer the federal form of government (a) what should be the federating units; (b) what form of government would you suggest for each of the units; (c) how would you distribute legislative power between the centre and the units; and (d) what provisions do you suggest for the administration of the federal capital?

Q. 8. Are you in favour of the President having powers of legislation; if so, under what circumstances may he exercise them?

Q. 9. How should the President be elected? (1) Do you recommend election (a) by adult suffrage, or (b) by restricted adult suffrage; e.g., literacy, property qualification, etc. or (c) by an electoral college? (2) If you are in favour of (b) how would you restrict the suffrage? (3) If you prefer (c) do you recommend the adoption of the electoral college by which the President has been recently elected (i.e. elected members of the local councils under the Basic Democracies Order, 1959—annexure 'C') and if not, what other electoral college would you suggest?

Q. 10. Annexure 'D' reproduces the provisions of the late Constitution regarding the qualifications, terms of office, removal, etc., of the President. Are you in favour of adopting these provisions or would you modify them? If you are in favour of the presidential form do you suggest that there should be a Vice-President and if so, how is he to be chosen and what should be his duties and powers?

Q. 11. Are you in favour of the unicameral or bicameral legislature? What should be the strength and how would you determine it?

Q. 12. How should the members of the legislature be elected? (1) Do you recommend election (a) by adult suffrage or (b) by restricted adult suffrage; e.g., literacy, property qualification, etc. or (c) by an electoral college? (2) If you are in favour of (b) how would you restrict the suffrage? (3) If you prefer (c) do you recommend, for the legislature, the electoral college by which the President has been recently elected (annexure 'C'); if not, what other electoral college do you suggest?

Q. 13. The question as to whether elections should be held on the principle of joint, or separate, electorate was left by the late Constitution, to be determined by Parliament. This was ultimately decided by resolutions of the Central and Provincial Assemblies, the consequent position being that the principle of joint electorate was adopted. Are you in favour of this decision or would you suggest any modification?

Q. 14. What should be the qualifications for membership of the legislature? If you are in favour of a bicameral legislature, what should be the constitution of the upper house? (a) Should it be by election based on the principle of functional representation, as well as by nomination for securing a place in it for distinguished persons of experience and knowledge (annexure 'E'), or (b) should it be wholly elected in the same manner as the lower house, the candidates having higher qualifications than those of the lower house?

Q. 15. What should be (a) the respective powers of the two houses and their duration, (b) their relations inter se and (c) their relations with the President?

Q. 16. If you are in favour of the federal form would you recommend (i) the unicameral or (ii) bicameral legislature for the federating units; i.e., the Provinces?

Q. 17. If you are in favour of a bicameral legislature for the Provinces what should be (a) the respective powers of the two houses and their duration, (b) their relation inter se, and (c) their relations with the head of the Province; i.e., the Governor?

Q. 18. If you are in favour of an unicameral legislature what should be the relations of the Provincial legislature with the Governor?

Q. 19. Are you in favour of the Governor having powers of legislation; if so, under what circumstances may he exercise them?

Q. 20. Article 70 of the late Constitution (annexure 'F') contains provisions dealing with the qualifications for and the mode of resignation as well as the term of office, etc. of a Governor. Would you adopt the said provisions or do you consider any change necessary?

Q. 21. Are you in favour of the same protection being given to the Governor as was done in the late Constitution (please refer to Article 213 in annexure 'D')? Would you extend such protection even if the form of government is to be unitary?

Q. 22. Do you think it necessary that the fundamental human rights should be precisely formulated in the new Constitution as was done in the late Constitution (annexure 'G')? Or do you consider that the assurance of such rights can safely be left, as in the United Kingdom, to the fundamental good sense of the legislature and the operation of recognized principles through the wisdom and experience of courts?

Q. 23. Do you consider it necessary to retain in the new Constitution the preamble and the specific terms of guidance for the future legislature and government contained in the late Constitution (annexure 'H')?

Q. 24. Annexure 'I' reproduced the provision of the late Constitution relating to the jurisdiction of the Supreme Court and the High Courts as well as the qualifications, terms of office, appointment and removal

of the judges of these courts. Are you in favour of adoption of the same provisions or do you consider any change necessary?

Q. 25. Annexure 'J' reproduces provisions of the late Constitution regarding the Attorney-General and the Advocate General. Have you any suggestions to make in this respect or would you adopt these provisions?

Q. 26. Articles 179 to 183 of the late Constitution are reproduced in annexure 'K'. These articles deal with the conditions of service, tenure, recruitment and discipline, etc., of the services. Do you consider these provisions adequate or would you like to modify them; if the latter please indicate the changes desired.

Q. 27. In France, there is a thoroughgoing system known as Droit Administratif (Administrative Law) under which (a) the relations of Government with its own public servants, with members of the public in the discharge of their official functions are controlled and regulated by a system of Administrative Courts at the apex of which is the Council D'Etat (Council of State). This council is composed of persons of distinction from all walks of life and besides acting as the final court of decision in the matters indicated above also acts in an advisory capacity towards the government in many important fields (annexure 'L'). The operation of this system is regarded as entirely satisfactory in France.

Do you consider that the introduction of this system in modified form would be of advantage to this country as well?

Q. 28. Annexure 'M' gives the provisions of the late Constitution with regard to the Public Service Commissions. Would you recommend the same provisions or consider any change necessary?

Q. 29. Should the conduct of elections at all levels be entrusted to the Pakistan Election Commission and should it be made responsible for taking all steps necessary for the preparation for, and conduct of elections and by-elections?

Q. 30. Should the electoral rolls be prepared and revised by the Election Commission? Is it necessary for the Election Commission to control the preparation of electoral rolls for the Basic Democracies and to supervise elections thereunder or should the executive perform these duties?

Q. 31. Should the appointments of the Chief Election Commissioner and the Election Commissioners be made by the President in his discretion, or subject to the approval of the legislature, or would you suggest any other method of appointment or any other provision to safeguard the independence of the Election Commission?

Q. 32. Article 142 of the late Constitution (annexure 'N') deals with

the Delimitation Commission. Would you adopt the same provisions or would you alter them?

Q. 33. Annexure 'O' reproduces provisions of the late Constitution relating to certain measures to be taken in times of war or internal disturbances. Do you consider these provisions adequate or would you alter them?

Q. 34. Do you think it necessary to incorporate any provisions in the new Constitution to assist the Muslims in the study of the basic values of Islam and of their application to the changing conditions of life? If so, what special measures do you suggest in this regard?

Q. 35. The late Constitution reserved seats for women in each of the Provincial and National Assemblies for ten years from the Constitution Day. Do you think such reservation necessary?

Q. 36. What special provisions would you suggest for the scheduled castes and backward classes?

Q. 37. Annexure 'P' reproduces the provisions of the late Constitution with regard to Excluded and Special Areas. Do you suggest any change in these provisions?

Q. 38. What provision would you suggest for the amendment of the Constitution? Would you prefer amendment by a simple, or a larger, such as $\frac{2}{3}$rd or $\frac{3}{4}$th majority vote?

Q. 39. What other suggestions would you make for establishing "a democracy adaptable to changing circumstances and based on the Islamic principles of justice, equality, and tolerance" (annexure 'A')?

Q. 40. Have you any other suggestions to make, relevant to the terms of reference (annexure 'A')?

## Text of President's Broadcast on the Constitution, March 1, 1962

ASSALAMO ALAIKUM.

My fellow countrymen, I want your attention to what I am going to say as it vitally affects your future and that of the country. The subject matter of my talk is our future Constitution.

On the 8th October, 1958, I gave a radio talk and made certain solemn promises. God has been kind in enabling me to fulfill most of those. Amongst the remaining, the most important is the one relating to the Constitution. In this connection I used the following terms—

> Let me announce in unequivocal terms that our ultimate aim is to restore democracy but of the type that people can understand and work. When the time comes your opinion will be freely asked. But when that will be, events alone can tell. Meanwhile, we have to put this mess right and put the country on an even keel.

Today, I consider myself fortunate to be in a position to say that the Constitution is now ready and I am now going to promulgate it.

As you know, a great deal of thought and effort has gone into the collection, examination and formulation of proposals leading to the decisions incorporated in the new Constitution.

On the 17th February, 1960, the Constitution Commission of Pakistan, composed of eminent men from various walks of life, was appointed to advise how best to secure a democracy adaptable to changing circumstances and based on the Islamic principles of justice, equality and tolerance; the consolidation of national units; and a firm and stable system of Government.

After examining 6,269 replies to its questionnaire and interviewing 565 persons in both wings of the country, the Commission submitted its report on the 6th May, 1961.

Since its submission, the Report has been examined in every possible detail by several committees appointed by the Cabinet and also by the Cabinet as a whole. The decisions as finally drafted are the outcome of all these exhaustive examinations, and represent, as far as humanly possible, the results of mature and honest assessment of the lessons of our past, the experience of the last 3½ years and the requirements of the foreseeable future.

I am grateful to all those who helped me in evolving this scheme. My special thanks are due to ex-Chief Justice, Mr. Shahabuddin, the Chairman of the Constitution Commission, who produced an excellent report, which will be published and which served as the working draft. I am also grateful to Mr. Manzur Qadir who took infinite pains in helping me in the production of the final draft. I have come across very few people who can surpass the sincerity, integrity and patriotism of these two.

The Constitution is being published in English, Bengali, and Urdu in simple language and in large numbers for wide distribution and understanding. People can be expected to defend it only when they understand its meaning and spirit. I hope most of you will acquire copies in due course and study it in full. Here, I shall only attempt to give you its outline and salient points:

(1) Our aim is to have representative institutions based on the will of the people. They shall be the final arbiters of who shall govern them and how. In other words, people shall have the right to hire and fire their rulers. This is basic.

(2) There will be a President, a Central Legislature and a Legislature in each Province, headed by an appointed Governor. Their normal term will be 5 years but for the coming elections only their term will be 3 years as recommended by the Constitution Commission.

(3) The above will be elected by an electoral college consisting of the elected members of Basic Democracies, who in turn will be elected by universal adult franchise.

(4) The judicial power has been vested in the Supreme Court in the Centre and the High Courts in the two Provinces.

(5) There will be only one list of subjects of national character, which will be the exclusive concern of the Centre. All other subjects will be left to the Provinces. However, the Centre would be able to legislate in the Provincial field, where matters relating to Security, Co-ordination of Economic Development and Co-ordination between the two Provinces is involved. Such occasions should be rare. Even in these cases, execution will rest with the Provinces. The under-

lying theme is that what can be done on a Provincial basis ought to be done on that basis.

(6) The principles of policy have been included in the Constitution and the responsibility of observing them has been placed upon each organ of the State and on each individual discharging any function on behalf of the State, so far as they concern him. To enable Muslims to lead their lives according to the teachings of Islam, to safeguard the rights of the minorities, to promote the interests of backward areas, to attain balanced development of all parts of Pakistan, to observe parity between the two Provinces, are some of the principles of policy. These principles of policy are by and large substantially the same as the Directive Principles in the last Constitution.

(7) Fundamental rights have been made the principles of law-making and every care taken that the law-makers observe them.

(8) Since it is in the interest of the country that proper men are elected for the Presidentship and the Legislatures, the State shall give all facilities to candidates to project themselves to the voters and the voters to assess the merits of the candidates.

(9) Political parties are banned unless allowed for by an act of the National Assembly.

(10) In order that Muslims are enabled to lead their lives in accordance with the teachings of Islam, provision has been made to set up an "Advisory Council of Islamic Ideology." This body will consist of eminent men in theology, law, economics, administration, etc. and will be supported by the Islamic Research Centre. Whenever in doubt Legislatures and the President will consult this body to make sure that laws conform to the requirements of Islam and observe the fundamentals of law-making. The advice of the Council will be made public.

(11) The Constitution will be capable of amendment if ⅔ of the National Assembly and the President agree. Three-fourths majority of the House will over-ride the President's veto, unless he refers the matter to a referendum or dissolves the Assembly and seeks re-election himself.

(12) This, in brief, is the outline of the Constitution. I shall now touch on each institution.

## PRESIDENT

(13) The President shall be a Muslim and will be head of the Executive Government. He will appoint Ministers to help him discharge his duties. Those Ministers appointed from the Legislature shall resign their seats from the House. The Ministers shall, however, have the right

of attending the House without the right to vote. To assist the Ministers, Parliamentary Secretaries from amongst the Legislature will be appointed. They will retain their membership of the House.

(14) The bills passed by the Assembly would require the assent of the President. The President's veto can however be over-ridden by $\frac{2}{3}$ majority of the Assembly.

(15) When the Assembly is not in session, the President can make Ordinances for not more than six months. These will lapse after six months unless passed by the Assembly as laws.

(16) The President can dissolve the Assembly under certain circumstances, in which case he too will have to seek re-election for continuance.

(17) The President can be impeached by the Assembly by $\frac{3}{4}$ majority for misconduct. He can be similarly removed for physical or mental incapacity. However, to prevent irresponsible moves of this nature, the movers will cease to be members of the National Assembly if they fail to get the support even of $\frac{1}{2}$ of the members.

(18) In the event of the President becoming a casualty or during his absence from the country or removal, the Speaker of the National Assembly will officiate. A convention will be established that if the President is from West Pakistan, the Speaker will be from East Pakistan and vice versa.

(19) The President can be elected only for two terms unless specially permitted by the joint session of the members of the National and Provincial Assemblies. There is also a provision for screening of the Presidential candidates by these bodies. Only a limited number will be allowed to contest to ensure that whoever wins the elections would be an appropriate person.

## NATIONAL ASSEMBLY

(20) The National Assembly will consist of 150 general members, 75 from each Province. They will be elected by the elected members of Basic Democracies. In addition, there will be 6 women members, 3 from each Province. The electoral college for them will be the Provincial Assemblies. This has been done to save them having to cover vast constituencies. In addition, women can also contest for general seats if they wish.

(21) The National Assembly is the source of law.

(22) In order to reduce chances of conflict between the Assembly and the President and to prevent paralysis of the administration and to ensure continuance of on-going schemes, it has been laid down that

the previously passed budget shall not be altered without the permission of the President, and new taxation shall not be levied without the consent of the National Assembly. This is based on the theory that the President is finally responsible to the country for administration and the members of the National Assembly represent the feeling of the people who have to pay taxes.

(23) To check misconduct on the part of members of the House, the Speaker will have the power to refer such cases to the Supreme Court for disciplinary action.

(24) Because of the sad experience of political parties in the past and the fact that if allowed to re-emerge today they cannot be any different from what they were before, and the fact that the Martial Law has to stay until the National Assembly takes over, the coming elections will be held on the basis of personal merit. The criteria will be the candidate's faith in Pakistan, its ideology and his known personal conduct and behavior. Would he help in building a united, disciplined and stable Pakistan or not? To my mind, there can be no criterion better than this to judge a person's worth. Certainly no party manifesto can be better than this.

(25) In our case, political party activity only divides and confuses the people further and lays them open to exploitation by the unscrupulous and demagogues. So I believe that if we can run our politics without the party system, we shall have cause to bless ourselves though I recognize that like-minded people in the Assemblies will group themselves together. That is not serious, but what is dangerous is for these groups to have tentacles in the country. However, should this experiment prove unworkable, which I don't believe, then the party system could be revived only with the permission of the National Assembly. This will ensure that the parties are limited in number and have respectable and healthy national programmes.

(26) It is sometimes argued that the canvassing for candidates, and especially for the Presidential candidates, will become difficult without the assistance of a party organization. That undoubtedly is a problem and that is why the Constitution has provided that the State assist the candidates for projecting themselves to the electoral college.

## PROVINCIAL GOVERNORS

(27) They will be appointed by the President and shall be responsible to him for the good government of the Provinces in accordance with the Constitution. They too will appoint Ministers with the concurrence of the President. The relationship of the Governors and their Ministers

with the Provincial Assemblies will be similar to that obtaining between the President, his Ministers and the National Assembly. They can appoint Parliamentary secretaries as in the Centre. In order to prevent abuse, the number of Parliamentary Secretaries, both at the Centre and Provinces, shall not exceed the number of Departments.

## PROVINCIAL ASSEMBLIES

(28) Each Assembly shall consist of 150 general members. In the West Pakistan Assembly, 40 per cent of the members will be elected from the old Punjab and Bahawalpur and the remaining 60 per cent from the other areas. This arrangement will obtain for 10 years or 2 normal election periods. In addition, there will be 5 women members in each Assembly. They will be elected by their respective Provincial Assembly.

## JUDICIARY

(29) The responsibility for ensuring that no law is made which is contrary to fundamental human rights has been placed upon the law makers. Principles have been enunciated for the law makers which they are under obligation to observe. The first of these principles is that no law shall be made that is repugnant to Islam. The second is that all citizens shall be treated alike in all respects. There are 15 such principles of law-making set out in the Constitution. In case the Centre or the Provincial Legislature is in doubt whether a provision in any proposed law is or is not repugnant to Islam or at variance with any other principle, it has been made possible for it to refer the question for advice to a body set up under the Constitution to be called the "Advisory Council of Islamic Ideology." A position has thus been brought about under which the functions of the Courts will be to take notice of and to rectify breaches of the law. Any person who has not been treated in accordance with law or who is treated otherwise than in accordance with law will have the right to go to a Court with his grievance whether it is against a private person, a public servant, an official agency or a department of the Government. No Court, however, shall be at liberty to refuse to enforce a law because it is of the opinion that the law is not in accordance with the principles of law-making. The relevant opinion for this purpose is the opinion of the law-makers and nobody else.

Fundamental rights have thus been secured in the Constitution without the complication of all laws never reaching the stage of complete certainty because they remain perpetually susceptible to challenge in

a Court of Law. Though it is frequently said that this challenge guarantees rights of the citizens in actual practice it is usually only a rich litigant who can afford to engage the best available legal talent to throw out a challenge to a law for getting rid of something that operates to his disadvantage, irrespective of whether it is to the advantage of the community at large or not, and frequently holds up indefinitely the implementation of beneficial schemes. The scheme adopted in the Constitution brings our position on the same lines as the position existing in England.

(30) Judiciary will have its own built-in arrangement for maintaining internal discipline.

## SERVICE RIGHTS

(31) Service rights have been guaranteed to public servants in the usual way. In respect of dismissal, removal, reduction in rank, stipulated pay, stipulated pension and the age of super-annuation, any public servant has been given the right to go to the High Court in a jurisdiction which up to now has been called Writ Jurisdiction. In respect of other matters, however, like leave, transfer, promotion, etc., the public servant is only under the disciplinary control of a departmental nature, but it has been provided that he must have the right to at least one departmental appeal.

(32) That completes the broad description of the institutions. I shall now draw your attention to the salient points of the Constitution and the reason why they have been adopted.

(33) We have adopted the Presidential System as it is simpler to work, more akin to our genius and history, and less liable to lead to instability—a luxury that a developing country like ours cannot afford. The other alternative was the Parliamentary System. This we tried and it failed. Not that there is anything inherently wrong with it. The trouble is that we have not yet attained several sophistications that are necessary for its successful operation. For it to work you need democratic institutions right down to villages, trade unions, and co-operatives on large scale to give people training in the spirit of give and take and dispassionate consideration of problems. You need a much higher level of education, prosperity, public spirit and integrity. Above all, you need really cool and phlegmatic temperament, which only people living in cold climates seem to have. Also it requires long periods of probation. For instance, the British took 600 years of trial and tribulations to reach this stage. Looking around the world you notice that this system has only worked successfully in Britain and the Scandinavian

countries. Elsewhere it has not taken real roots. Even France which gave birth to liberal philosophy has not been able to work it. So, don't let us kid ourselves and cling to clichés and assume we are ready to work such a refined system knowing the failure of earlier attempts. It will be foolhardy to try it again until our circumstances change radically.

In that system, the Chief Executive—the Prime Minister—must have the support of a majority of the members of the House, at all times. If Parliamentary traditions have taken root in a country, any member of the House, who withdraws his support, after pledging it, will have to account for it before the bar of public opinion.

In our conditions, however, there is no mechanism which will automatically operate to prevent members from selling their support or from charging a price for continuing to give support. The whole process of Government thus becomes liable to be subverted in the first instance, to placating those members without whose support the government in power would fall. The only insurance against such an eventuality in our conditions is to release the Chief Executive from the obligation of having to be sustained artificially so as to enable him to get on with the functions entrusted to him for the benefit of the people at large.

(34) Our system of Basic Democracies is probably unique. It is already breeding pride, hope, sense of participation and responsibility in large numbers of people and laying a real base for a democratic society. We should do all we can to nurse it. In addition, the elected members from amongst them will be called upon to act as an electoral college as described already. In other words, the broad masses of people elect the electoral college who in turn elect National and Provincial institutions. The reason for this is simple. We are recognizing an obvious truth that the ballot can only produce a true answer if those exercising it are asked questions [on a] level with their horizon and knowledge. If this is done, by and large the question will be right. The election to Basic Democracies has proved it, and I have no doubt that, Insha-Allah, the general elections will confirm it. Whilst saying this, I am not claiming that some voters will not go wrong, but in human affairs a 100 per cent result is unrealistic to expect, especially where a society has not yet matured. Anyhow, the voters will be less liable to be exploited and misled in this system than in direct elections where they were driven as cattle to polling booths. In fact, the direct elections amongst us were far less direct than the system I am now proposing. In that all you had to do was to get hold of or fix a few leading people, and the rest then followed them. This won't happen and can't happen in my system as everyone of these voters is a person of substance in his

community. Another reason for adopting the indirect election system
is that if we were to have direct adult franchise, the elections would be
delayed for another year or two for preparing fresh electoral rolls as the
present ones are some years old. Besides, that system of elections is far
too expensive. It was estimated that the 1958 general elections would
have cost the country around six crores of rupees. Can this country
afford such a waste?

While saying this, I am conscious of the fact that some sections of the
intelligentsia and those with vested interests may have cause to complain. I do not see any reasons why a suitable formula cannot be evolved
later which will give them a feeling of full participation. The need
of today, however, is that the Constitution should be brought in
quickly, and that can be done only if the electoral college of Basic
Democracies is used for the elections. Any innovation or addition at
this stage will be time-consuming and will delay the Constitution, which
obviously is undesirable from every angle.

I might also add that in future there will be no nominations to Basic
Democracies. Consequently, their number will increase from 80,000 to
120,000, unless it is decided to enlarge it still further.

(35) Friction between the executive and the legislative often arises
over money bills with damaging effects on the administration and
development projects. Our Constitution, by dividing the budget between committed and fresh taxation and making the President dominant in one and the legislature in the other, will obviate or eliminate
unnecessary clashes. I would not be a bit surprised if this formula is
being tried for the first time.

(36) The wish to get good people elected is universal, but in actual
fact the community makes no real attempt to help them. In our Constitution, the State will assume the responsibility of helping candidates
project themselves before the electorate, who must, of course remain
free to elect as they like.

(37) In a Presidential System so much depends on choosing the right
man as the President. So the community must make certain that only
suitable candidates are allowed to contest. In our case, a joint session
of the National and Provincial Assemblies will screen candidates.
Normally three candidates will be allowed to contest unless the sitting
President is also eligible and willing to contest, in which case the number will be four.

(38) We are an ideological state and the basis of our nationality
is the ideology of Islam. Whilst making material progress, we naturally wish to do so under the umbrella of Islamic spiritual and moral
values. To achieve this is a continuous process and affects every aspect

of life. We have therefore provided an organization called the "Advisory Council of Islamic Ideology." This body will consist of experts from many fields and it will be backed by eminent research scholars. Whilst making laws, the President and the Legislatures have been enjoined to seek their advice for giving them an Islamic bent. By this process and the fact that religious education has been made compulsory up to 8th class, the curriculum in religious institutions in general and the Auqaf institutions in particular is being revised and balanced, we hope to attain our goal in due course in a well considered and sound fashion.

(39) Notice the processes laid down for the amendment of the Constitution. The variation takes into consideration the importance of different parts. Unless the President and the National Assembly agree on ⅔ majority, the process becomes more difficult so as to prevent changes being made without due consideration and in haste. In cases requiring major structural changes, it may even be necessary to refer the matter to people for a referendum. My view about the Constitution is that it should not be made too difficult. This is the only way stability, natural evolution and freedom from revolutions can be ensured. I believe also that in a society like ours, which is launching forth on wide education, industrialization and modernization and is becoming dynamic, it would be necessary to look into the Constitution every twenty years or so to make it conform to social, economic and political changes. I would commend this for the consideration of future generations. Meanwhile, this Constitution can only stand as a whole. If any attempt is made radically to change any of its main elements, the rest can't stand. This must be understood clearly.

(40) This Constitution expects positive results from the institutions. Having created them, it expects them to function freely within the law and produce results. It also provides built-in disciplinary arrangements in order to prevent abuse of law and transgressions and breakdown. In other words, the Constitution gives free field to do good, but it will not feel shy to curb evil. It embodies a blending of democracy with discipline, the two prerequistes to running a free society with stable government and sound administration.

This in brief is the philosophy behind some of the salient points in the Constitution. These salient points are my humble contribution and are based on long association with the administration at the highest level, detailed knowledge of the country and the people, wide study, deep and prolonged thought and a burning desire to help the people in building the country into a sound, vigorous, progressive and powerful State. I believe in every word of this Constitution and

have complete faith in it. I believe also that the country can reach its cherished goal by following it. I therefore commend it to you all with fervent prayers that God in His infinite mercy grant us wisdom, courage and faith to work the Constitution truly and loyally for our betterment and the betterment of future generations and above all for vindication of faith and belief of those who under the great leadership of Quaid-i-Azam Mohammad Ali Jinnah, struggled so hard and suffered so much for the creation of Pakistan. Amen!

PAKISTAN PAINDABAD.

Selected Excerpts from the *Report of the*
*Constitution Commission, 1961*

(1)                          Chapter IV

## FORM OF GOVERNMENT—UNITARY OR FEDERAL

### ANALYSIS OF VIEWS

55. In the questionnaire, the difference between federal and quasi-federal was not pointed out, but the trend of opinion clearly shows that the federal form was regarded, by those who replied to the questionnaire, as equivalent to the form adopted in the late Constitution, and that was also the standard kept in view by those who made statements before us. On an analysis of the various opinions, both in the statements recorded by us and the replies to the questionnaire, we find that the preponderance of view is in favour of the federal form with a centre as strong as, if not stronger than, that of the late Constitution. Tabulating the opinions, irrespective of their being in favour of a parliamentary or a presidential pattern, we find that 65.5% were in favour of the federal and 34.5% in favour of the unitary form. Regarding the units of the federation, 88.4% were for the two units as they existed at the time of abrogation of the late Constitution—East and West Pakistan—while 8.6% favoured the breaking up of the One Unit, 2.3% wanted to break up both East and West Pakistan into several units, while .7% suggested that East Pakistan should be broken up into units but the One Unit of West Pakistan should be preserved. As regards the distribution of powers, which gives an indication as to whether it should be a federation of a strong, or a loose, type, the opinions were as follows. Distribution of powers as per the late Con-

stitution was favoured by 53.5%, while 8% were for giving the Centre more subjects than as in the late Constitution; 3.2% were for giving the residuary powers also to the Centre, while 1.2% wanted to empower the Centre to withdraw powers from the provinces. Thus 61.5% were in favour of a Centre as strong as, if not stronger than, that of the late Constitution, while 38.5% opined that the provinces should be autonomous, the powers of the Centre being confined to Defence, Foreign Affairs, and Currency. Of the witnesses examined before us, however, there were only 23 who were in favour of such a weak Centre —18 from East Pakistan and 5 from West Pakistan. The rest of the opinions on this subject came from the replies—765 out of a total number of 1,357 from East Pakistan and 194 out of 794 from the West.

56. Views expressed in favour of a unitary government may be stated as follows. Pakistan was demanded, and achieved, on the fundamental basis that the Muslims of the sub-continent constituted a nation and were, therefore, entitled to the right of self determination in areas where they were a majority. That being so, it is but necessary to have one government though the two wings are separated by over a thousand miles of foreign territory. The differences in language and the regional interests, which have existed and unfortunately been encouraged during the past years, can best be subordinated to the national interest only by having a unitary form of government. The official delegation strongly advocated this type and, in doing so, pointed out that a very disquieting feature of the political development in this country over the past years was the growing power of the provinces in opposition to the authority of the Centre, resulting in administrative friction. It was also stated that, in the provincial legislatures, the Centre used to be attacked by the provincial ministers in order to divert the attention of those who were inconvenienced by the faulty administration of the province.

57. As against the unitary form, the following views were expressed for a federal form. A unitary form of government is practicable if the country is one compact area. The geographical position of the two wings of Pakistan makes the federal form inevitable as, otherwise, administrative difficulties would arise apart from confirming the people of the East wing in their present feeling of being treated as a Colony, as the Capital is situated in West Pakistan. As regards administration, a high degree of decentralisation would be necessary and, if there be no provincial legislature, with powers of criticising the administration, the officers would become autocratic. One parliament would find it difficult to legislate for the entire country, especially during emergencies. The manner in which the development of East Pakistan was

handled in the past has shaken the confidence of that province in the Centre, and to overlook the distrust and suspicion that has crept in would be extremely unwise.

### DISCUSSION OF THE PROBLEM

58. There is no part of the subject of our enquiry which seems to us to present greater difficulties than the question whether the form of government should be unitary or federal as, in the controversy, feelings appear to run high. That was apparently the reason why 595 replies took the extreme view in favour of a very weak Centre, while, during our enquiry, when the several aspects of the question were fully discussed with the witnesses, only 23 favoured that view. It will be convenient to consider this minority view after dealing with the main question of a unitary form of government versus the federal variety of the late Constitution.

59. It is necessary, at the outset, to refer to certain facts which constitute the background to the main issue. After 1857, when the British Sovereign took over from the East India Company, a unitary form of government was established in British India. As a result of the reforms introduced in 1919, the provinces were given certain powers and, very soon, the demand for more powers for the provinces assumed an important role in the general scheme of agitation till at last provincial autonomy became the objective. Though the majority community, while referring to the future Constitution of India, had expressed itself in favour of a unified, strong Central Government, yet its immediate objective was provincial autonomy as the first practical step towards independence. The Muslim community was all along for provincial autonomy in order to avoid domination by the majority community. Thus political activity centered round the provinces getting all the powers to manage their provincial affairs, but this goal was not reached though the Government of India Act, 1935, except in certain matters, gave the provinces extensive powers. When, out of the undivided India, two self-governing dominions emerged, the system of government was still of a federal variety with a very strong Centre. The people of East Pakistan, who had worked whole-heartedly for the achievement of Pakistan, finding themselves free from the domination of the Hindus, were quite prepared to follow the Quaid-e-Azam for strengthening their newly-won independence. In spite of the country being divided into two parts, separated by more than a thousand miles of foreign territory with the capital located in West Pakistan, a feeling of oneness was very much in evidence when the Quaid-e-Azam visited Dacca for the first time after Pakistan was achieved. During his stay in East Pakistan,

people came from remote places in the interior to see the Father of the Nation. Addressing them, the Quaid-e-Azam,* amongst other things, referred to East Bengal's feeling of isolation from the rest of Pakistan and said:

> I have only come here for a week or ten days this time, but in order to discharge my duty as the Head of the State, I may have to come here and stay for days, for weeks and similarly the Pakistan Ministers must establish closer contact.

These were the words of a statesman, and, had he lived longer, he would have not only implemented them but would have brought about such a change of heart that the present feeling, amongst the people of East Pakistan, that their province is regarded as a colony would not have arisen. It is regrettable that, after his death, his proposal of the Head of the State or ministers staying in East Pakistan for longer periods, was not given effect to. The visits of the Heads of the State, and the central ministers, were only for short periods and at no time did any minister of the Centre stay there for even a month continuously. It is a matter for serious consideration whether the President and the Vice-President should not stay in Dacca, by turns, for at least a few weeks at a stretch, and that it should also be arranged amongst the ministers, that one or two of them, by turns, should similarly, stay there at least during that portion of the year when the President, or the Vice-President, does not do so. The object of the suggestion is to have a part of the central administration working in the province so that the people may not feel that they are isolated because the capital is located in West Pakistan. We understand that there is a proposal to set up a subsidiary capital at Dacca but we have not, before us, any definite scheme and we do not know as to what exactly would be the effect of such a capital. We suggest that there should be a section of the Central secretariat, especially of those departments dealing with nation-building activities, stationed at Dacca so that delays in administration may be avoided. We do not propose to draw up a scheme ourselves but we feel that, if the suggestions that we make in this regard are accepted, and, as a result thereof, a machinery is always available to the people of the province, it will have a healthy effect on the public mind and will go a long way to remove the feeling of isolation. As regards the session of the Parliament, we would adopt Article 50 (1) of the late Constitution, under which at least one session in each year was to be held at Dacca. We understand from one of the members of the

---

* "Speeches by Quaid-e-Azam Mohammed Ali Jinnah, Governor-General of Pakistan," p. 63.

Commission that a scheme for establishing a marine academy in Chittagong, which had been previously sanctioned, is now being given up.
If this is so, we would suggest that government should reconsider that
decision.

60. However, the fact of the location of the capital of the country
in the Western part, far away from the Eastern province, and the strik-
ing disparity between the two wings in the matter of industrialisation,
was exploited by the politicians of the day, and by certain non-Muslim
elements. The latter being unable to reconcile themselves to the idea
of Pakistan, created, amongst the people of East Pakistan, the impression that, as a result of neglect by the Central Government, their
province, in spite of its superiority in numbers as well as its capacity
to earn more foreign exchange, was far behind the other part of the
country in the field of development. Such propaganda met with success,
as the people, having emerged out of a condition of utter dependence,
saw and heard that in West Pakistan the progress in the industrial field
was greater than in their own province. During the British days, the
policy of the undivided Bengal government seems to have been not to
industrialise East Bengal. It is remarkable that, although that province
is the main jute growing area, all the jute mills were, at the time of
Independence, in and around Calcutta. In the Punjab, on the other
hand, industrial development had gone on and a number of non-
Muslims, who had established factories, migrated to India when the
division took place and the evacuee property was occupied by the
refugees as well as by local persons who started working the existing
industries. As a result of there already being industries in existence in
West Pakistan, further industrial progress was quicker in that area than
in the East where they had to make a start for the first time. Having
regard to the fact that the work of industrialisation could be handled
more rapidly in the West than in the East, larger amounts were allocated by the Centre to the Western wing. From information laid before
us it is seen that in 1948-49 and 1949-50 though 8 crores and 21 lacs
were allotted to East Pakistan as against 13 crores and odd given to
the West, nothing was drawn by the East Pakistan government whereas
West Pakistan utilised about 11 crores out of the amount allotted to
them. In 1950-51, 1951-52, and 1952-53, East Pakistan utilised fully
the amount given to them, but in 1953-54, 1954-55, and 1955-56, the
amount that was actually drawn by the government of East Pakistan
out of the amount allotted came up to only about 50%. In 1956-57,
while 20 crores and 69 lacs was the amount sanctioned, the amount
drawn was only 8 crores 47 lacs. In 1957-58, it was a little higher. It is
significant that, in the budget speeches for 1949-50 and 1950-51, there

was no real complaint against the Centre with regard to these allotments. On the other hand, speaking on the budget estimates of 1951-52, the then Chief Minister acknowledged the help rendered by the Central Government to meet the financial difficulties, but in the speeches of the subsequent years there was a note of discontent.

61. There is a feeling in East Pakistan that the Centre delayed the financial sanction of the schemes in order to prevent the province utilising the allotments fully. The official point of view, on the other hand, is that there were, no doubt, cases of delay by the Centre, but the main reason for the province not having been able to use the full amount allotted to it was the delay in the preparation of schemes coupled with the fact that the provincial ministers did not consider promptly those schemes in which they, or their party, were not interested. In this connection, it was pointed out that the development of North Bengal was so badly neglected in the past by the party in power that the people of that region went to the extent of demanding that their part of East Pakistan should be made a separate province with a separate Governor. It was explained that schemes submitted to the Centre were defective owing to the dearth of experienced officers and that, on account of those defects, sanction was naturally delayed as the Centre could not allow expenditure without the central coordinating authority certifying that the schemes were in accordance with the plan.

62. As the witnesses examined in East Pakistan gave us the impression that they had very strong feelings in this matter and felt very much aggrieved, we, at first, thought of going into the question fully in order to determine which of these versions was true. But, on further consideration, we gave up that idea, as we felt that an inquiry at this stage would do greater harm than good. Prejudice which seems to have taken root, can, we think, be removed more by practical steps taken to dispel doubt and suspicion than by any verdict we can record on the events in the past. As for the work of development, there is the second five year plan, in which the respective spheres of development in the East and the West are clearly indicated, and we have been told on behalf of government that a scheme of devolution of funds had already been drawn up which would speed up the sanctioning of expenditure. The idea, which seems to have gained ground in some quarters in West Pakistan, that the people of East Pakistan would ultimately secede from the West should be dispelled as, in the nature of things, the average Muslim of East Pakistan cannot be thinking of placing himself in the position in which he was prior to Independence. Similarly, East Pakistanis should be assured that it is not true

that West Pakistan does not care for them or their interests. Unfortunately, a few instances of indiscretion, on the part of a few officers in the early years of Pakistan, created this impression amongst the intelligentsia, which seems to have been kept alive by certain parties bent on promoting friction between the two wings. To restore mutual trust and confidence between these wings, a system facilitating frequent visits by the various strata of intelligentsia from one side to the other would be, in our opinion, of great help. Similarly, frequent visits by the students, of either wing, to the other, will also help in the removal of misunderstanding.

63. But all these measures will take time to produce results and, till that stage is reached, the present state of feeling cannot possibly be ignored. Persons who advocated the unitary form of government regard the adoption of the federal form that existed at the time of the Revolution, or even before the late Constitution, as an adverse step as far as the relations between the two provinces are concerned, and they think that the unitary form is the solution. According to them, these prejudices will disappear if there is one uniform administration all over the country, whereas, if the old system is revived, the provincial feeling will gain strength. We are unable to agree with this view. There are two points which the framers of a constitution should always keep in view. One is that the scheme devised should be workable and the other that those for whom it is intended should be prepared to make it work. Any constitution lacking in these qualities will not be successful. It is our considered opinion that if we impose a unitary form ignoring the state of feeling in East and West Pakistan we would be driving the average Muslim of East Pakistan into the arms of the extremists and the disruptive elements which are active in that province. . . . The fact that 65.5% of opinion is in favour of a federal form is an indication of the inclination of the people and we feel that to ignore this preponderance of view would be an extremely rash step, especially when, even apart from the doubt and suspicion we have dealt with, the unitary form of government is not practicable in Pakistan.

64. Under a unitary form of government, there would be decentralisation on an extensive scale without a provincial legislature to act as a check on the officers in order that they may not become autocratic. When this aspect of the matter was put by the Commission to the witnesses who advocated the unitary form, including those who appeared on behalf of government, our attention was drawn to the Governor's Council constituted under the Basic Democracies scheme, and it was said that that body could be utilised by persons having grievances against officers for bringing their facts to the notice of the Governor.

But the Governor's Council, even if its members happen to be bold enough to criticise the officers of the province before the Governor, being a nominated body, will not command the confidence of the people, and, consequently, that body would not give satisfaction to the province. As for the parliament, where the representatives of both the regions will be present, it would hardly have time for questions to be asked with regard to administration as it would be the only legislature in a unitary form and, therefore, busy the whole time with legislation for the whole of Pakistan. In this respect, the case of West Pakistan is more in point. This province consists of four former provinces and the people of these regions complained to us that sufficient decentralisation had not yet been made, though, at the time of integration of these provinces into One Unit, it had been decided to decentralise the administration. As stated already, the majority opinion is in favour of retaining the One Unit and it is only 8.6% of the opinions that recommend the breaking up of the integrated province. We think that, whatever the defects in the present arrangement and however objectionable the methods of integration were, it would open the flood-gates of provincialism if we break up the integrated province at this stage. Decentralisation is the only remedy, and that would satisfy the majority who are only anxious for an arrangement that would avoid the inconvenience of their having to go to the headquarters of the province in matters in which, prior to the integration, they could get relief nearer home. If the administration on this account is decentralised on a large scale, then a provincial legislature becomes indispensable as a check on the arbitrary exercise by the executive of its extensive powers, but the unitary form does not provide for it.

65. The further proposals put before us on behalf of the government acknowledge the difficulty of the Central Parliament dealing with legislation for the entire country while sitting at the Capital. It was conceded that provincial matters could be better dealt with by the province concerned, and the suggestion was that powers should be given to the provinces, more or less on the lines of the late Constitution, subject to Railways and Industries being excluded from the Provincial List, and that the Centre should be empowered to legislate in respect of all subjects including those of the Provincial List. It was further suggested that, instead of provincial legislatures, each half of the parliament representing a province should act as a provincial committee to deal with provincial affairs at the headquarters of the province, and that the legislation passed by such committees should receive the assent of the President and not of the Governor concerned. It was

also said that this would save time and expense while retaining the appearance of a unitary form of government. In the same strain, it was proposed that there should be ministers appointed for the province but that their appointment should also be made by the President and not by the Governor.

66. Having given our anxious consideration to the above proposal, we find ourselves unable to recommend it. In our opinion, this scheme, besides creating difficulties, is the surest way of making the central legislature provincial-minded. What is required for the progress of our country is the inculcation of the habit of considering every question from a national point of view. This would need the members of the central legislature to be trained to look at questions affecting the country from the point of view of the whole of Pakistan. That being so, if, for nearly half of the year, each half of the parliament, instead of continuing to deal throughout with subjects of all-Pakistan importance, has to go back to the respective provinces to deal with provincial matters, what hope can there be of ever developing an all-Pakistan point of view? The result of these persons acting in the regional committees would be that, in course of time, everything they handle would be approached from the provincial angle. Apart from this, in the practical working of the scheme, there will be difficulties. For instance, if these regional committees have already legislated on any of the items of the Concurrent List and nullified even the veto by reiterating the legislation by a two-thirds majority, and it is considered by the President that the Centre should then legislate on that very subject or in a cognate matter, the said committees, who have already committeed themselves to one point of view, are least likely to change their mind and legislate to a different effect. When this aspect of the matter was put to the official delegation, the answer received by the Commission was that the provincial committees would not pass all measures unanimously, and that, if they pass a measure unanimously, the Centre should not venture to legislate again. But even if the local committees are not unanimous, they would at least have been in a majority and, if so, the minorities of the two committees cannot constitute a sufficient majority, when sitting together in the parliament to pass a different legislation. We are unable to understand the position that, if the provincial legislation has been passed unanimously, the Centre should not venture to legislate. If the Centre wants to legislate contrary to the provincial legislation, it must be because it considers such a course necessary in the interests of the country as a whole. We fail to see why we should adopt a system which could, under such circumstances, render the Centre helpless.

67. The establishment of the provincial committees, it was stated, would save expense and time. Separate provincial legislatures were objected to on the ground that they would give the people of the province an opportunity of criticising the Central Government, without justification, merely on provincial prejudice. We have considered these aspects very carefully. As far as expense is concerned, a democratic form of government is certainly more expensive than an autocratic one, and on the ground of expenditure alone we cannot refuse to have a legislature. But, in this case, there will be no saving of expense or time by the system of local committees, for the members of the parliament would be wholly occupied, either in the parliament with central legislation or in the provincial committees with provincial legislation and, wherever they may be, they will have to be paid. From this point of view, separate legislatures will not be costlier than the provincial committees. But the more serious objection is what we have already stated, namely, that we will, by this system, be forcing every member of the central legislature to become thoroughly provincial-minded. As regards the tendency to be provincial in criticism, we think that, having regard to the feelings that prevail at present, which would take some time to subside, it would be safer to provide for a safety valve in the provincial field. We should like to emphasise that, for the safety, as well as the progress of this country, it is essential to have an Assembly with a broad national perspective. If there be no provincial legislature where provincial matters can be discussed from a provincial angle, the parliament itself would be converted into a provincial Assembly, and a member, who while sitting in the committee has approached the questions from a provincial point of view and spoken in that connection with a provincial bias, would be inclined to do the same in the central parliament, even with regard to a matter which concerns the entire country. If the system of government we were recommending were parliamentary, the objection to having separate provincial legislatures might have been on stronger grounds as, in that case, the majority party in the legislature would be able to interfere with the administration. There were instances of the provincial government discouraging outside capital from coming into the province of East Pakistan during the period under review. But under the system we are recommending, the Governor, not being elected by the province but appointed by the President, would act as his agent and the administration would be run under his direction. Even with these provincial legislatures, the character of government will not be strictly federal as there will be some control by the Centre both in the legislative and the executive fields. It would be a federal government of the Indian

pattern. As for the proposal regarding the appointment of provincial ministers, and the giving of assent to provincial legislation, it will be convenient to discuss it in the chapter dealing with checks and balances.

68. We, therefore, recommend that the government should be of the same pattern as that of India and Canada and not unitary as in Great Britain. The next question is whether there should be two units as at the time the late Constitution was passed, or, the One Unit should be broken up into its former provinces. As has been set out in the analysis of opinions, the preponderance of view is in favour of retaining the two units, East and West Pakistan and, as already stated, only a small minority advocated the breaking up of the One Unit. As we have already observed, whatever defects the One Unit scheme may have it is safer to continue it. We, therefore, consider that the units should be as they were at the time the late Constitution was abrogated.

(2) Chapter X

## FUNDAMENTAL RIGHTS AND DIRECTIVE PRINCIPLES

### NECESSITY FOR FUNDAMENTAL RIGHTS

160. Reconciliation of the liberty of the subject with the authority of the state has been a problem throughout the ages. The struggle for liberty, to start with, was against arbitrary power and unjust laws. Since political power remained with the King, or with an oligarchy, the attempt of the people was to secure self-government. But when that goal was reached, it was realised that the self-rule was not, in effect, a rule by the whole people but only by a majority which may have ideas different from those of minorities within the same people. Nevertheless, the Parliament remains supreme in England and no attempt has been made to restrict its power to pass laws, with the result that any law infringing the essential human rights, guaranteed by the Magna Carta, can be passed in England and the courts cannot declare it void, and yet it was never feared by the British people that their Parliament would misuse its supremacy. But the United States of America, after it became independent and framed a constitution of its own, brought certain basic human rights into its constitution (by amendment). Most of the constitutions, that came into existence after the first World War, followed this example. In the constitutions of Eire, India and in the late Constitution, fundamental rights are specific and protected.

161. The question to which this chapter relates is whether the

provisions of the late Constitution, which enumerate the fundamental rights, should be incorporated in the new Constitution or, the assurance of such rights can safely be left, as in the United Kingdom, to the fundamental good sense of the legislature and the operation of the recognised principles through the wisdom and experience of courts. Preponderance of opinion (98.39%) is in favour of the first alternative and we are of the same view. We do not think we can follow the example of England in this regard because, there, the tradition that had grown, and the genius of the people, make it almost certain that the Parliament, though it is supreme in the sense that it can pass any law, which the English courts have no power to declare as void, would not infringe the fundamental rights except in grave emergency and that, too, only to the extent strictly necessary. . . . At the time the Government of India Act, 1935, was on the anvil, it was proposed that the fundamental rights should be enumerated in the constitution but the Statutory Commission was not in favour of it, one of the reasons given being that the Princely States in India were against such rights being formulated and it was considered that it would be anomalous if such a declaration had legal force in only part of the area of the federation. However, one or two legal principles were embodied in the constitution. . . . The position, however, changed with the coming in of Independence, as those principles were no longer legally binding on the new legislatures, and, had they enacted legislation infringing the basic human rights, the courts could not have declared them void. The late Constitution specified and protected these rights, obviously because one could not be certain that our legislature would so soon acquire the sort of intuition which enables the British people to react almost instinctively against interference with fundamental liberties. For the same reason, the relevant provisions of the late Constitution should, we think, be adopted in the new Constitution. Sufficient has been said in the earlier chapters to indicate how utterly lacking we are in those traditions which guide the British people in the art of legislation and government. Unless, therefore, the power of the legislature is restricted . . . any law passed by it, which contravenes any of the provisions enumerating the fundamental rights, as well as any existing law which is found to be inconsistent with those provisions, cannot be declared void to the extent of the inconsistency. This provision as well as the other Articles seem to be adequate, to safeguard the fundamental rights and, as we have already indicated, the preponderance of view is in favour of adopting these provisions. . . .

164. It was suggested to us during the inquiry that the right of representation by a counsel should be given as a fundamental right

in civil matters also. Under Article 7 of the late Constitution, such a right was given to every person only in criminal matters. A provision to this effect was not made with regard to civil matters, apparently because it was not anticipated that the right of representation in such matters would be taken away, and the present suggestion is made obviously in view of some recent legislation curtailing this right. In this connection, we have also received a reference from the East Pakistan government suggesting that the Commission should consider whether even Article 7 of the late Constitution, as it stands, that is confining the right of representation to criminal cases should be made applicable to the Chittagong Hill-tracts. It is surprising that this reference has been made only in the month of February this year [1961], although the Commission held its sessions for over two months in East Pakistan last year. We have, however, examined the question and our considered opinion is that not only is there no reason to take away the right which the late Constitution conferred on the people of the Chittagong Hill-tracts with regard to criminal cases, but that it is necessary that we should extend the same right in civil matters also. From the papers before us it appears that, in criminal cases, while the prosecution is conducted by Police officers trained for the purpose, the accused persons have to defend themselves and no pleader is allowed to appear on their behalf. The ground on which this obviously inequitable procedure is justified is that the people of the Hill-tracts are mainly truthful and, if legal aid is given, they would be inclined to be untruthful—a proposition to which we cannot possibly subscribe. However, it is clear from the letter of the Commissioner which is before us, that, at present, it is not only the people of the Hill-tract who reside in that area, but also some of the people of the rest of the province who have gone and settled down there, either for business or in connection with the industrial expansion in that area. Their percentage is shown to be about 15, apparently based on the last census figures, and we shall not be surprised if it has gone up in recent years. It is, in our opinion, imperative that the right of representation should be given to the people of this area not only in criminal, but also in civil, matters. We would, therefore, adopt Article 7 of the late Constitution with the modification that the right of representation would extend to civil matters as well; but we think we should make an exception in the case of conciliation proceedings in Industrial disputes and in arbitration in Co-operative society matters, as the appearance of Advocates in such cases may take away the special nature of those proceedings which are intended to effect reconciliation between parties on a broad equitable basis rather than on technical aspects of rights.

## OBLIGATIONS TO THE STATE

165. The official delegation was not against mention, in the Constitution, of the fundamental rights but they urged that there should be specific mention also of the rights of the State over the people and their obligations to it. In his statement before us, the leader of the delegation apprehended that enumeration of the fundamental rights may give the impression that the public have no obligation towards the State. We are unable to appreciate the difficulty felt by the official delegation. A study of the provisions of the late Constitution, relating to the fundamental rights clearly shows that, except with regard to the extent to which protection is given in those provisions, the obligation to obey the laws of the State, and orders issued thereunder, continues. These provisions limit the power of the legislature and of the executive, with regard to certain matters which are specified therein, but none of them give the impression to any person that he is under no obligation to obey the laws of the State. As the State is supreme, it is the subject who should have rights against it and not the State against the subject. We, therefore, think it unnecessary to enumerate the obligations to the State in the Constitution. As a matter of fact, no constitution has been brought to our notice wherein the State is given specific rights. The Soviet Constitution, and the Constitution of South Viet Nam, mention certain obligations of the subjects, but those obligations are covered by the general laws that are now in force in our country.

## DIRECTIVE PRINCIPLES

166. As regards the Directive Principles of State policy, to which the late Constitution has devoted a chapter, 97.14% of the opinions is in favour of the said provisions being incorporated in the new Constitution. The view of the microscopic minority of 2.45%, which stated that the incorporation of the said principles was unnecessary, is obviously influenced by the fact that they cannot be enforced in a court of law. They, however, overlooked the important fact that these directions, though they are not enforcable in law, still, have a great effect on future legislation. It is the fundamental principle of any civilised government that its legislators should act within the sphere, and the limits, fixed by the constitution under which they have been elected to office and although the constitution would not, by merely enunciating the directive principles, make it obligatory on them to follow it, nevertheless the very fact that they are mentioned as principles to guide their deliberations, does have an effect on their minds. We would, therefore, incorporate them in the new Constitution.

(3)                     Chapter XII

## PREAMBLE AND ISLAMIC PROVISIONS

### PREAMBLE

182. The preamble to the late Constitution begins in the name of Allah, the Beneficent, the Merciful; and the first proposition it enunciates is that sovereignty over the entire Universe vests in Allah alone and the authority to be exercised by the people of Pakistan within the limits prescribed by Him is a sacred trust. The second clause is a statement of the fact that the Quaid-i-Azam, the founder of Pakistan, declared that Pakistan would be a democratic state based on Islamic principles of social justice. Then follows a clause which is inapplicable in the present context as the constitution is to be promulgated by the President, and not framed by a Constituent Assembly. Under the fourth clause, the powers and authority of the state should be exercised through the chosen representatives of the people. This is followed by the clause which directs that the principles of democracy, freedom, equality, tolerance and social justice, as enunciated by Islam, should be fully observed. The sixth clause requires that the Muslims of Pakistan should be enabled, individually and collectively, to order their lives in accordance with the teachings and requirements of Islam as set out in the Holy Quran and Sunnah. Then come clauses which refer to the structure of government, and which preserve the integrity of the territories and safeguard the legitimate rights and religious liberty of the minorities and backward classes.

183. The preponderance of opinion (96.64%) is in favour of adopting this preamble. . . . A minority opinion did not consider it necessary to adopt this preamble, not because they disputed any of the propositions mentioned in it, but because, the majority in the country being of Muslims, an Islamic way of life is naturally expected of them. Some of them wondered if it was practicable to come up to the standard envisaged in the preamble, while others stated that, as its provisions cannot be enforced by law, it has only a sentimental value. Had the difference of opinion been confined to these points we could have closed our discussion at this stage in view of the desire of the over-whelming majority to adopt the preamble in the new Constitution. But, from the speeches delivered in 1949 when the Objectives Resolution, which was to the same effect as the Preamble in question, was introduced in, and passed by, the First Constituent Assembly (at the time the preamble in question was being discussed in the second Constituent

Assembly, the Hindu members appear to have abstained from attending the House), it appears that the position taken by the Caste-Hindu minority was that religion should be not brought into the political field. Some of the opinions we have come across (a very small minority) appeared to be to the same effect, their inclination being towards a secular state. We, therefore, consider it necessary to deal with this matter at some length.

184. There is nothing unusual in having a preamble to a constitution. On the other hand, a preamble is a natural beginning as it only sets out a goal for, or an ideal to be followed by, those who are adopting a particular constitution. It is true that whatever is stated in it is not enforcable in law and from that point of view it may be said that its value is mainly sentimental, but, as we have indicated in Chapter VIII, while dealing with the question as to whether the President should be a Muslim, the sentiment of the majority cannot be ignored. It is stated by some that it is not correct to say that the objective, from the outset, was that Pakistan should be an Islamic State, but that the main cause for the Pakistan movement was the desire to avoid domination by the Hindu majority, and in this respect reliance is placed on the absence of any reference to an Islamic State in the Lahore Resolution. The majority opinion, however, is otherwise and in its support various pronouncements of the Quaid-i-Azam as well as of the Quaid-i-Millat are pressed into authority. As to what exactly the view, in this regard, was at the inception is an academic question, because, even if it is taken that in the beginning the objective was not an Islamic State, it cannot be doubted that the majority in this country now desire an Islamic way of life, which, as stated in the second chapter, consists in an obligation not only to God, in the sense that we have to develop ourselves spiritually, but also towards humanity and society. To discharge the latter obligation, it is necessary that we should have discipline, a sense of common responsibility and of civic obligation.

185. The apprehension entertained by the Caste-Hindu minority, at the time the Objectives Resolution was discussed in the First Constituent Assembly, was that excesses might be committed in the name of religion if the constitution had an Islamic bias. It was not denied that the statement made in the first paragraph of the preamble, *viz.*, that the sovereignty of the universe vests in God and the authority given to the people of Pakistan is a sacred trust, was a correct proposition, but the argument was that religion was a matter of faith, while politics was a matter of reason, and that these two should not be mixed up and that, in case the religious point of view was brought into the constitution, people of a strong religious bent, if they attain ascendency, would act as fanatics. The remedy suggested by them, therefore, was

a secular constitution; but a mere declaration of secularity, is no guarantee that the rights of the minorities would be respected by the majority in actual practice. . . . As has been pointed out in Chapter VII of our report, the treatment accorded to the minority, or non-powerful group, in a state depends on the ideals which the majority, or those in power, set before themselves. If the people are religious in the sense that they allow religion to permeate their practical lives, as is the case with most of the countries in Asia, the ideals of the majority are coloured by the religion they follow. Even in a state which has declared itself secular, the minorities may suffer if the majority is influenced by an ideology which makes a distinction between man and man. As has been pointed out already, Islam permeates the life of a Muslim and does not allow politics to be kept apart from ethics as is the case in countries with secular constitutions. The non-Muslims in Pakistan need have no fear on this account as Islam gives them a guarantee of equality, freedom and justice, which is far more effective being a matter of ideology, than a mere declaration of secularity. . . .

188. . . . There can be no reasonable objection to the enunciation of the various propositions in the Preamble to which reference has already been made. In the second paragraph reference is made to the Islamic principles of social justice and in the fifth paragraph the principles of democracy, freedom, equality, tolerance and social justice are qualified by the words "as enunciated by Islam." Some of those, who are secular minded, inquire as to why these principles, which are expected of any modern nation, have been referred to in the Preamble, as well as in the terms of reference, as Islamic. The explanation for this is found in the opening speech of the First Prime Minister of Pakistan when the Objectives Resolution was introduced in the first Constituent Assembly. . . . The Prime Minister* observed:

> . . . When we use the word democracy in the Islamic sense, it pervades all aspects of our life; it relates to our system of Government and to our society with equal validity, because one of the greatest contributions of Islam has been the idea of equality of all men. Islam recognises no distinction based upon race, colour or birth. . . .

It may be pointed out here that there is a definite clause in this Preamble requiring the making of adequate provision for the minorities freely to profess and practise their religion and develop their culture.

189. We therefore, consider that the preamble to the late Constitution should be incorporated in the new Constitution with its third clause suitably re-drafted, as the constitution is to be promulgated by the President and not passed by an Assembly.

---

* "Constitutions of Nations" (Vol. II), by Amos J. Peaslee, pp. 693-694.

Selections from the Text of the 1962 Constitution
of the Republic of Pakistan

In the name of Allah, the Beneficent, the Merciful

## THE CONSTITUTION OF THE REPUBLIC OF PAKISTAN

(1)                                    PREAMBLE

Whereas sovereignty over the entire Universe belongs to Almighty Allah alone, and the authority exercisable by the people is a sacred trust:

And whereas the founder of Pakistan, Quaid-i-Azam Mohammad Ali Jinnah, expressing the will of the people, declared that Pakistan should be a democratic State based on Islamic principles of social justice:

And whereas the territories now and hereafter included in Pakistan should be a form of federation with the Provinces enjoying such autonomy as is consistent with the unity and interest of Pakistan as a whole:

And whereas it is the will of the people of Pakistan that—

(a) The State should exercise its powers and authority through representatives chosen by the people;

(b) the principles of democracy, freedom, equality, tolerance and social justice, as enunciated by Islam, should be fully observed in Pakistan;

(c) the Muslims of Pakistan should be enabled, individually and collectively, to order their lives in accordance with the teachings and requirements of Islam;

(d) the legitimate interests of the minorities in Pakistan (including their religious and cultural interests) should be adequately safeguarded;

(e) the fundamental human rights (including the rights of equality before law, of freedom of thought, expression, belief, faith and association, and of social, economic and political justice) should consistently with the security of the State, public interest, and the requirements of morality, be preserved; and

(f) the independence of the judicature should be ensured:

Now, therefore, I Field Marshall Mohammad Ayub Khan, Hilal-i-Pakistan, Hilal-i-Jura'at, President of Pakistan, in exercise of the mandate given to me on the Fourteenth day of February, One thousand nine hundred and sixty, by the people of Pakistan, and in the desire that the people of Pakistan may prosper and attain their rightful and honored place among the nations of the World and make their full contribution towards international peace and the progress and happiness of humanity, do hereby enact this Constitution.

Dated this first day of March, One thousand nine hundred and sixty-two, being the twenty-third day of Ramazan, One thousand three hundred and eighty-one.

PRESIDENT

(2) PART I—THE REPUBLIC OF PAKISTAN

1. (1) The State of Pakistan shall be a Republic under the name of the Republic of Pakistan.

(2) The Republic shall consist of—

(a) the Province of East Pakistan and the Province of West Pakistan; and

(b) such other States and territories as are or may become included in Pakistan, whether by accession or otherwise.

2. (1) To enjoy the protection of the law, and to be treated in accordance with law, and only in accordance with law, is the inalienable right of every citizen, wherever he may be, and of every other person for the time being within Pakistan.

(2) In particular—

(a) no action detrimental to the life, liberty, body, reputation or property of any person shall be taken except in accordance with law;

(b) no person shall be prevented from, or be hindered in, doing that which is not prohibited by law; and

(c) no person shall be compelled to do that which the law does not require him to do.

3. Loyalty to the Republic is the basic duty of every citizen.

4. Obedience to the law is the basic obligation of every citizen, wherever he may be, and of every other person for the time being within Pakistan.

(3) PART II—PRINCIPLES OF LAW-MAKING AND OF POLICY
CHAPTER I—PRINCIPLES OF LAW-MAKING

5. The Principles set out in this Chapter shall be known as the Principles of Law-making and it is the responsibility of each legislature to ensure that a proposed law is not made by it if the proposed law disregards, violates or is otherwise not in accordance with those Principles.

6. (1) The responsibility of deciding whether a proposed law does or does not disregard or violate, or is or is not otherwise in accordance with, the Principles of Law-making is that of the legislature concerned, but the National Assembly, a Provincial Assembly, the President or the Governor of a Province may refer to the Advisory Council of Islamic Ideology for advice any question that arises as to whether a proposed law disregards or violates, or is otherwise not in accordance with those Principles.

(2) The validity of a law shall not be called in question on the ground that the law disregards, violates or is otherwise not in accordance with the Principles of Law-making.

PRINCIPLES OF LAW-MAKING

1. —Islam.
No law should be repugnant to Islam.
2. —Equality of Citizens.
   1. All citizens should be equal before the law, be entitled to equal protection of the law and be treated alike in all respects.
   2. This Principle may be departed from where—
      (a) in the interest of equality itself, it is necessary to compensate for existing inequalities, whether natural, social, economic or of any other kind;
      (b) in the interest of the proper discharge of public functions, it is necessary—
         (i) to give to persons performing public functions powers, protections or facilities that are not given to other persons; or
         (ii) to impose on persons performing public functions obli-

gations or disciplinary controls that are not imposed on other persons; or

(c) it is necessary in the interest of the security of Pakistan or otherwise in the interest of the State to depart from this Principle, but where this Principle is departed from, it should be ensured that no citizen gets an undue preference over another citizen and no citizen is placed under a disability, liability or obligation that does not apply to other citizens of the same category.

3. This Principle shall not be construed as preventing a legislature from making laws different from laws made by any other legislature.

## 3. —Freedom of Expression.

1. No law should impose any restriction on the freedom of a citizen to give expression to his thoughts.

2. This Principle may be departed from where it is necessary so to do—

(a) in the interest of the security of Pakistan;

(b) for the purpose of ensuring friendly relations with foreign States;

(c) for the purpose of ensuring the proper administration of justice;

(d) in the interest of public order;

(e) for the purpose of preventing the commission of offences;

(f) in the interest of decency or morality;

(g) for the purpose of granting privilege, in proper cases, to particular proceedings; or

(h) for the purpose of protecting persons in relation to their reputation.

## 4. —Freedom of Association.

1. No law should impose any restriction on the freedom of citizens to assemble peacefully and without arms, or to form associations or unions.

2. This Principle may be departed from where it is necessary so to do—

(a) in the interest of the security of Pakistan;

(b) in the interest of public order;

(c) for the purpose of preventing the commission of offences;

(d) in the interest of decency or morality; or

(e) for the purpose of protecting persons in relation to their health or property.

## 5. —Freedom of Movement and Right to Acquire Property.

1. No law should impose any restriction—
    (a) on the freedom of a citizen to move throughout Pakistan or to reside or settle in any part of Pakistan; or
    (b) on the freedom of a citizen to acquire, hold or dispose of property in any part of Pakistan.
2. This Principle may be departed from where it is necessary so to do in the public interest.

6. **—Freedom to Follow Vocation.**
    1. No law should impose any restriction on the freedom of a citizen to engage in any profession, trade, business, occupation or employment, or otherwise to follow the vocation of his choice.
    2. This Principle may be departed from where it is necessary so to do—
        (a) in the interest of the security of Pakistan;
        (b) in the interest of decency or morality;
        (c) for the purpose of regulating, in the public interest, any profession or trade by a licensing system;
        (d) for the purpose of ensuring, in the public interest, that where a profession or trade requires special qualifications or skill, only persons possessing those qualifications or that skill engage in the profession or trade;
        (e) for the purpose of ensuring, in the public interest, that a trade, business, industry or service may be carried on by or on behalf of the State or an organ of the State to the exclusion, in whole or in part, of other persons; or
        (f) for the purpose of ensuring, in the public interest, the development of Pakistan and of its resources and industries.

7. **—Freedom of Religion.**
    No law should—
        (a) prevent the members of a religious community or denomination from professing, practicing or propagating, or from providing instruction in their religion, or from conducting institutions for the purposes of or in connection with their religion;
        (b) require any person to receive religious instruction, or to attend a religious ceremony or religious worship, relating to a religion other than his own;
        (c) impose on any person a tax the proceeds of which are to be applied for the purposes of a religion other than his own;
        (d) discriminate between religious institutions in the granting of exemptions or concessions in relation to any tax; or
        (e) authorize the expenditure of public moneys for the benefit

of a particular religious community or denomination **except** moneys raised for that purpose.

**8. —Safeguards in Relation to Arrest and Detention.**

1. A law authorizing the arrest or detention of persons should ensure that a person arrested or detained under the law—

   (a) is informed of the grounds of his arrest or detention at the time he is arrested or detained or as soon thereafter as is practicable;

   (b) is taken before the nearest Magistrate within a period of twenty-four hours after he is arrested or detained, excluding the time necessary to convey him to the Magistrate;

   (c) is released from custody at the expiration of that period unless further detention is authorized by a Magistrate; and

   (d) is at liberty to consult, and to be represented and defended by, a legal practitioner of his choice.

2. This Principle does not apply to a law authorizing the arrest or detention of enemy aliens or providing for preventive detention, but a law providing for preventive detention—

   (a) should be made only in the interest of the security of Pakistan or of public safety;

   (b) should ensure that (except where the President or the Governor of a Province, in the interest of the security of Pakistan, directs otherwise) a person detained under the law is informed of the grounds of his detention at the time he is detained or as soon thereafter as is practicable; and

   (c) should ensure that a person is not detained under the law for a period longer than three months without the authority of a Board consisting of—

      (i) where the law is a Central Law—a Judge of the Supreme Court, who shall be nominated by the Chief Justice of that Court, and another senior officer in the service of Pakistan, who shall be nominated by the President; or

      (ii) where the law is a Provincial Law—a Judge of the High Court of the Province concerned, who shall be nominated by the Chief Justice of that Court, and another senior officer in the service of Pakistan, who shall be nominated by the Governor of that Province.

**9. —Protection Against Retrospective Punishment.**

No law should authorize—

   (a) the punishment of a person for an act or omission that was not punishable by law at the time of the act or omission; or

   (b) the punishment of a person for an offense by a penalty

greater than, or of a kind different from, the penalty prescribed by law for that offense at the time the offense was committed.

**10. —Regulation of Compulsory Acquisition of Property.**

1. No law should authorize the compulsory acquisition, or the compulsory taking possession, of property except for a public purpose.

2. A law that authorises the compulsory acquisition, or the compulsory taking possession, of property should provide for the payment of compensation for the property, and either fix the amount of the compensation or specify the principles on which, and the manner in which, the compensation is to be determined.

3. These Principles may be departed from—

   (a) for the purpose of permitting the destruction, the acquisition or the taking possession of property in order to prevent or reduce danger to life, health or property;

   (b) for the purpose of ensuring the proper management, for a limited period, of any property for the benefit of its owner; or

   (c) in relation to property which is or is deemed to be evacuee property under any law.

4. For the purpose of these Principles, "public purpose" includes the purpose of acquiring in the public interest, any industrial, commercial or other undertaking which is of benefit to the public, any interest in such an undertaking or any land for use in connection with such an undertaking.

**11. —Protection Against Forced Labor.**

1. No law should permit forced labor in any form.

2. This Principle may be departed from in relation to—

   (a) the punishment of persons for offences against the law; and

   (b) the compulsory service of persons for public purposes or otherwise in the public interest (whether by way of conscription or in any other way).

**12. —Public Educational Institutions.**

1. No law should, on the ground of race, religion, caste or place of birth, deprive any citizen of the right to attend any educational institution that is receiving aid from public revenues.

2. This Principle may be departed from for the purpose of ensuring that a class of citizens that is educationally backward shares in available educational facilities.

**13. —Access to Public Places.**

No law should deny to any person access to a public place (other

than a place intended solely for religious purposes) on the ground of race, religion, caste or place of birth.

14. —**Protection of Languages, Scripts, and Cultures.**

No law should prevent any section of the community from having a distinct language, script or culture of its own.

15. —**Protection Against Slavery.**

No law should permit or in any way facilitate the introduction into Pakistan of slavery in any form.

16. —**Practice of Untouchability Forbidden.**

No law should permit or in any way facilitate the introduction into Pakistan of the practice of untouchability in any form.

### CHAPTER II—PRINCIPLES OF POLICY

7. (1) The Principles set out in this Chapter shall be known as the Principles of Policy and it is the responsibility of each organ and authority of the State, and of each person performing functions on behalf of an organ or authority of the State, to act in accordance with those Principles in so far as they relate to the functions of the organ or authority.

(2) In so far as the observance of any particular principle of policy may be dependent upon resources being available for the purpose, the Principle shall be regarded as being subject to the availability of resources.

8. (1) The responsibility of deciding whether any action of an organ or authority of the State, or of a person performing functions on behalf of an organ or authority of the State, is in accordance with the Principles of Policy is that of the organ or authority of the State or of the person concerned.

(2) The validity of an action or of a law shall not be called in question on the ground that it is not in accordance with the Principles of Policy, and no action shall lie against the State, or any organ or authority of the State or any person on such a ground.

### PRINCIPLES OF POLICY

1. —**Islamic Way of Life.**

1. The Muslims of Pakistan should be enabled, individually and collectively, to order their lives in accordance with the fundamental principles and basic concepts of Islam and should be provided with facilities whereby they may be enabled to understand the meaning of life according to those principles and concepts.

2. The teaching of the Holy Quran and Islamiat to the Muslims of Pakistan should be compulsory.

3. Unity and the observance of Islamic moral standards should be promoted amongst the Muslims of Pakistan.

4. The proper organization of zakat, wakfs and mosques should be ensured.

**2. —National Solidarity.**

Parochial, racial, tribal, sectarian and provincial prejudices amongst the citizens should be discouraged.

**3. —Fair Treatment to Minorities.**

The legitimate rights and interests of the minorities should be safeguarded, and the members of minorities should be given due opportunity to enter the service of Pakistan.

**4. —Promotion of Interests of Backward Peoples.**

Special care should be taken to promote the educational and economic interests of people of backward classes or in backward areas.

**5. —Advancement of Under-privileged Castes, etc.**

Steps should be taken to bring on terms of equality with other persons, the members of under-privileged castes, races, tribes and groups and, to this end, the under-privileged castes, races, tribes and groups within a Province should be identified by the Government of the Province and entered in a schedule of under-privileged classes.

**6. —Opportunities to Participate in National Life, etc.**

The people of different areas and classes, through education, training, industrial development and other methods, should be enabled to participate fully in all forms of national activities including employment in the service of Pakistan.

**7. —Education.**

Illiteracy should be eliminated, and free and compulsory primary education should be provided for all, as soon as is practicable.

**8. —Humane Conditions of Work.**

Just and humane conditions of work should be provided and children and women should not be employed in vocations unsuited to their age and sex, and maternity benefits should be provided for women in employment.

**9. —Well-Being of the People.**

The well-being of the people, irrespective of caste, creed or race, should be secured—

(a) by raising the standard of living of the common man;

(b) by preventing the undue concentration of wealth and means

of production and distribution in the hands of a few, to the detriment of the interest of the common man; and

(c) by ensuring an equitable adjustment of rights between employers and employees and between landlords and tenants.

10. —**Opportunity to Gain Adequate Livelihood.**

All citizens should have the opportunity to work and earn an adequate livelihood, and also to enjoy reasonable rest and leisure.

11. —**Social Security.**

All persons in the service of Pakistan or otherwise employed should be provided with social security by means of compulsory social insurance or otherwise.

12. —**Provision of Basic Necessities.**

The basic necessities of life, such as food, clothing, housing, education and medical treatment, should be provided for citizens who, irrespective of caste, creed or race, are permanently or temporarily unable to earn their livelihood on account of infirmity, disability, sickness or unemployment.

13. —**Administrative Offices to be Provided for Public Convenience.**

Administrative offices and other services should, so far as is practicable, be provided in places where they will best meet the convenience and requirements of the public.

14. —**Entry into Service of Pakistan not to be Denied on Grounds of Race, etc.**

1. No citizen should be denied entry into the service of Pakistan on the grounds of race, religion, caste, sex or place of residence or birth.

2. This Principle may be departed from where, in the public interest—

(a) it is desirable that—

(i) a person who is to perform functions in relation to a particular area should be a resident of that area; and

(ii) a person who is to perform functions of a particular kind should be of a particular sex; or

(b) it is necessary so to do for the purpose of ensuring that in relation to the Central Government, persons from all parts of Pakistan, and in relation to a Provincial Government, persons from all parts of the Province concerned have an opportunity of entering the service of Pakistan.

15. —**Reduction of Disparity in Remuneration for Public Services.**

Disparity in the remuneration of persons in the various classes of the service of Pakistan should, within reasonable and practicable limits, be reduced.

16. **—Parity Between the Provinces in Central Government.**

    Parity between the Provinces in all spheres of the Central Government should as nearly as is practicable, be achieved.

17. **—Service in the Defence Services.**

    Persons from all parts of Pakistan should be enabled to serve in the Defence Services of Pakistan.

18. **—Elimination of Riba.**

    Riba (usury) should be eliminated.

19. **—Prostitution, Gambling and Drug-Taking to be Discouraged.**

    Prostitution, gambling, and the taking of injurious drugs should be discouraged.

20. **—Consumption of Alcohol to be Discouraged.**

    The consumption of alcoholic liquor (except for medicinal purposes and, in the case of non-Muslims, for religious purposes) should be discouraged.

21. **—Strengthening Bonds with the Muslim World, and Promoting International Peace.**

    The bonds of unity amongst Muslim countries should be preserved and strengthened, international peace and security should be promoted, good-will and friendly relations amongst all nations should be fostered, and the settlement of international disputes by peaceful means should be encouraged.

# INDEX*

Administrative organization, 90, 122 n38, 139, 164; decentralization, Ayub on, 10, 43, 46, 115, 154, 182; Mirza on, 14; *Pakistan Observer* on, 129, 136, 138, 139 n40

Administrative Staff College, 165

Advisory Council of Islamic Ideology, 175-176, 193, 200

Aga Khan, 6

Agricultural Development Corporation, 108, 155

Ahmad, Azizuddin, member Constitution Commission, 49

Ahmad, Mohammad, author of *My Chief*, 10

Ahmad, Nazir, welcomes Ayub to lawyers convention, 87-88

Ahmed, Aftabuddin, member Constitution Commission, 49

Ahmed, (Khan Bahadur) Naziuddin, President East Pakistan Lawyers Association, 66-67

Ahmed, M. U., Principal Dacca College, 132

Ahmed, Mahmud, Professor, University of Karachi, 132

Ahmed, Muzaffar, Additional Chief Secretary, West Pakistan; member Cabinet subcommittee (2) on Constitution Commission questionnaire, 123

Ahsan, (Syed) Qamrul, answers Constitution Commission questionnaire, 63

Alavi, Hatim A., Director State Bank of Pakistan, 87

Ali, Mahmud, former East Pakistan politician, 212-213

Ali, Raja Ghazanfar, 179

Ali, (Chaudhri) Mohamad, former Prime Minister, 65; as possible member constitution commission, 50; answers Constitution Commission questionnaire, 69-73, 182; attack on military

regime, 71, 74, 85; interviewed by Constitution Commission, 84; discussion of constitution prohibited because of, 167; comments on, by: Ataur Rahman, 65; Ayub, 74-75; Bhutto, 76-77; *Dawn*, 77-78; *Pakistan Observer*, 78, 81; West Pakistan Governor, 78-79; Ayub's secretary, 79; letters-to-the-editor, 79

Ali, Mohammad, of Bogra, former Prime Minister; Ataur Rahman on, 65; candidate to National Assembly, 1962, 213; elected to National Assembly, 214

All-Pakistan Economic Conference, 100

All-Pakistan Womens Association, and Muslim Family Laws Ordinance, 96; Ayub's speech to, 131

Allocation of resources. See Fiscal policies

Amin, Nurul, rumored as possible member Constitution Commission, 50; before Constitution Commission, 63; on legislatures, 63-64; petitions for release of détenus, 212-213

Awami League, some members arrested under martial law, 158

Ayub Khan. See Khan, Mohammad Ayub

*Azad*, Constitution Commission interviews editor of, 62

Bahawalpur District Council, 81

Bar Association of Dacca, 61, 67, 79

Bar associations, on trial of Suhrawardy, 162

Barori, D. N., member Constitution Commission, 49

Basic Democracies, 40-48; as local government, 23, 198; discussed at Governors Conference, 33, 107; Basic Democracies Order, 40-41, 85; elections to, 34, 40, 41, 42, 44; as electoral college, 41, 120, 125, 141-142, 143, 164, 187; vote of confidence in Ayub, 45, 47-48; conventions: at Lahore, 74-76, 85, 141-142; at Dacca, 137, 154, 155; at Kar-

* When the typical designation of a person begins with a non-English title, it is given here in parentheses.

achi, 138; comments on, by: Manzur Qadir, 31, 42, 91; Ibrahim, 31, 41, 91; Ayub, 32, 42, 45-46, 107, 182, 194; Zakir Husain, 35; *Statesman*, 36, 90; Nurul Amin, 64; Chaudhri Mohamad Ali, 71-72; Bhutto, 77, 164; *Dawn*, 114; Habibur Rahman, 131, 140-141, 157, 164; Constitution Commission report on, 174-175, 194; 1962 Constitution on, 188, 194, 209; and elections of 1962, 214

Basic Principles Committee Report of 1951, 69, 199-200

Bhutto, Zulfiqar A., Cabinet member; member Cabinet subcommittee (1) on Constitution Commission report, 105; warns against political activity, 124; candidate for National Assembly, 213; elected unopposed to National Assembly, 214; speeches: to students of Islamia College, 24; to Law Society in Lahore, 76; to Gordon College in Rawalpindi, 76-77; to Hyderabad Bar Association, 106; to East Pakistan Advisory Council, 131; to Lahore businessmen, 135-136; on speaking tours for Constitution, 211; opinions on: *Pakistan Times*, 12 n.25; unitary form, 24, 77; Chaudhri Mohamad Ali, 76-77, 85; 1956 Constitution, 76; Constitution Commission, 76, 171; failure of parliamentary democracy, 76; presidential system, 76, 77; Basic Democracies, 77, 164; federal form, 77; dictatorship, 77; constitution, 106, 123, 124, 164; Family Laws Ordinance, 106; elections, 124; economic development, 135-136; first meeting of National Assembly, 137; national unity, 164

Brohi, A. K., rumored as possible member constitution commission, 50

Bureau of National Reconstruction, set up, 23; objectives, 23, 85, 115; comments on: by *Dawn*, 23; by Manzur Qadir, 25; by *Statesman*, 90; economic conference in Hyderabad, 100; seminar on national unity in Lahore, 115-116; seminar on national unity in Dacca, 131-134; youth forum in Dacca, 213

Bureaucracy, Ataur Rahman on, 64-65. *See also* Civil Services

Burki, Lieutenant General W. A., Cabinet member; *Pakistan Observer* on, 19; on constitution and constitution commission, 31; on screening of officers, 32; to East Pakistan Union of Journalists, 141

Cabinet, constituted by Mirza, 15; sworn in, 15; *Dawn* on, 16; *Pakistan Observer* on, 18; *Statesman* on, 90; resolution on vote of confidence in Ayub, 45; to study Constitution Commission report, 92; subcommittee (1) on Constitution report, 105, 123; subcommittee (2) on report, 123; subcommittee (3) to draft constitution, 128; economic committee of, 142; considers recommendations of Finance Commission, 145-147; decides to provincialize railways, 164; discusses launching of constitution, 165; resigned, 214; Ayub on first cabinet under 1962 Constitution, 214. For members of Cabinet, *see* Appendix A

Capitals; Rawalpindi to be new location of, 34, 36; moved to Rawalpindi, 98; Rawalpindi temporary, Islamabad permanent, 137; Karachi merged with West Pakistan, 148; Islamabad, principal seat of Central Government, 175; in 1962 Constitution, 187, 195; Dacca to be subsidiary capital, 34, 110, 129, 137, 175, 187, 195

Censorship. *See* Press

Chittagong District Bar Association, 67

Choudhury, Fazlur Qadir, 9

Choudhury, G. W., honorary adviser to Constitution Commission, 49; on Raisman award, 151 n60

Choudhury, Hamidul Huq, owner of *Pakistan Observer*, 7; urges release of détenus, 212-213

Chowdhury, Abu Sayeed, member of Constitution Commission, 49

Chowdhury, Imam Hossain, Chief Justice, East Pakistan, 59

Chundrigar, I. I., former Prime Minister; possible member constitution commission, 50; President Pakistan Bar Association, 56; Ataur Rahman on, 65

Civil Services, screening of, 23-24, 36; bureaucracy, 64-65; should be kept out of politics, 63, 68; Chaudhri Mohamad Ali on, 72; Ibrahim on, 87; equality in appointment to, 129; in 1962 Constitution, 176. *See also* Corruption

Commission on Marriage and Family Laws, recommendations of, 96. *See also* Muslim Family Laws Ordinance, 1961

Commonwealth Press Union, 130

Communists, 86, 158

Constituent Assembly of 1947, 4, 5, 62; of 1955, 5

Constitution, promised by Mirza in Proclamation of 10/7/58, 14; Basic Democracies to be a part of, 41; models for, 51; experts to help draft, 59, 87, 92; warning against publicizing views on, 81-82, 167; date of announcement of, 87, 120, 165-166, 172; Cabinet subcommittee (1) studying report of Constitution Commission, 120, 121, 123; appointment of Cabinet subcommittee (2), 123; administrative aspects of, 123, 124; Cabinet subcommittee (3) appointed to draft, 128; and allocation of resources, 128; Ayub to explain aspects of, 137; to have federal form, 164; Cabinet discusses launching of, 165; broadcast of Ayub's speech on, 166; special briefing by Ayub of newspaper editors on, 166; distribution of 900,000 copies of synopsis of, 166-167; announcement of, 170; "Summary" of, 175; issues of, 4-5; in Constitution Commission questionnaire, 51, 62; sources on, 53 n7. *See also* Elections; Federal form; Fiscal policies; Fundamental rights; Government; Judiciary; Language; Legislature; Parliamentary system; Presidential system; Unitary form; opinions on, by: *ulema*, 5; Iskander Mirza, 14; Ayub, 14, 20, 21, 22, 25, 27-28, 32, 35, 42, 43, 76, 87, 91, 92-93, 107-108, 113, 117, 119, 124, 125, 128, 138, 140, 141, 153-154, 155, 156, 181-182; Ibrahim, 24, 27, 30, 31, 131; Manzur Qadir, 25, 28-29, 41, 47; *Pakistan Observer*, 27, 93-94, 107-108, 120-121, 126, 127, 129, 140, 143, 165, 166, 176, 178, 179; Z. H. Lari, 28, 58; W. A. Burki, 31; Habibur Rahman, 59, 131; *Statesman*, 90, 167; *Dawn*, 92, 129, 176, 177; Bhutto, 106, 124, 164; Zakir Husain, 114, 140, 141, 156; *Morning News*, 138, 140, 141, 176, 177, 178, 179; Hafizur Rahman, 156-157; A. K. Khan, 165; Sardar Habibullah, 174; Nurul Huda, 178; Maulana Maudoodi, 178-179; Azam Khan, 179; Islamic constitution, first need of Pakistan, 4; *ulema* vs. secular Muslims, 5; no representative of Islamic ideology on Constitution Commission, 50; Manzur Qadir on, 25; Ayub on, 32, 47, 75, 107; *ulema* on, 68-69; Habibur Rahman on, 157; Islamic provisions, in Constitution Commission report,

174, 193; in Constitution Commission questionnaire, 192-193; public opinion on, 193; in 1962 Constitution, 193, 199-200; Constitution of 1956, went into effect 3/23/56, 5; abrogated 10/7/58, 6; Ayub on why suspended, 14; fundamental rights in, 20; parts of included in Constitution Commission questionnaire, 51; as model for new constitution, 51; electoral method in, 63; on federal form, 184; division of powers between Center and provinces in, 187; fiscal arrangements in, 194; written under difficulty, 198; compared with 1962 Constitution, 204-205; opinions on, by: Ayub, 53, 75; Munir, 57; Nurul Amin, 63-64; Ataur Rahman, 65; East Pakistan organizations, 67; *ulema*, 68; Chaudhri Mohamad Ali, 70, 72, 73; Bhutto, 76; Zakir Husain, 106; Constitution of 1962, contents of, 176; reactions to, 176-180, 198-206; recommendations of Ayub on, 181-182; gainers and losers under, 198-209; compared with 1956 Constitution, 204-205; and Ayub Khan, 206-209; criticisms of, 208-209; massive publicity campaign for, 211; provisions of: presidential system, 183; modified federal form, 184; National Assembly, 185; reserved seats for women, 185; division of powers between Center and provinces, 187; Islamabad and Dacca as capitals, 187, 195; political parties, 189; politicians, 190; judiciary, 190, 191, 201; fundamental rights, 192; no provision for Basic Democracies, 194; fiscal arrangements, 194-195, 204; allocation of funds between provinces, 195; national languages, 195; transitional, 195-196; Ayub to be first president, 196; repeal of Proclamation, four laws, and all but 5 Martial Law regulations, 196; protection of fundamental rights, 201; intellectuals, 202-203; concessions to East Pakistan, 203-206

Constitution Commission, appointment of, 14, 85, 90; date of announcement of, 34, 35, 45; selection of members completed, 42; members, terms of reference, 49-52, 83; first meeting, 51; plans interview schedule, 52; Shahabuddin on, 58, 84; and martial law, 80; secretary of Commission on work of, 83; holds interviews, 62-64, 83-84; completes work, 94; dissolved, 102;

role of, 170-172; comments on, by: Ayub, 20, 22, 26, 27, 29, 32, 34-35, 42, 43, 46, 52-53, 75-76, 86, 91, 92-93; *Pakistan Observer*, 26; Ibrahim, 31, 34, 41, 91; Zakir Husain, 31, 35, 92; Manzur Qadir, 31, 41, 47, 79; W. A. Burki, 31-32; Sheikh, 32-33; Habibur Rahman, 33; Bhutto, 76; *Dawn*, 77, 78, 80, 92; Nazir Ahmad, 87; questionnaire, released to press, 51; public response to, 61-73; interviews published, 62-66; critical issues in, 62; published replies to, 66-73, 81; Government's reaction to replies, 74-80; public controversy over replies, 80-81; answers from several West Pakistan councils, 81; *Report of the Constitution Commission, 1961*, to be studied by Cabinet, 92; completed, 100; submitted to President, 101, 107; Cabinet subcommittees on constitution, 105-107, 110, 120, 121, 123, 128; considered by Governors conference, 128; to be announced with constitution, 139, 140; released to public, 170; contents of, 173-175; on form of government, 183-184; on East Pakistan's grievances, 183-184; on legislatures, 184-185; on division of powers between Center and provinces, 186-187; on electorate, 187-188; on political parties, 189; on judiciary, 190-191, 201; on fundamental rights, 192; on Islamic provisions, 192-193; on Basic Democracies role, 194; on fiscal arrangements, 194; on capitals and languages, 195; on transitional provisions, 195-196; comments on, by: Ibrahim, 92; Zakir Husain, 93, 100-101; *Statesman*, 101-102, 173; Bhutto, 106; *Dawn*, 172; *Morning News*, 173; *Pakistan Observer*, 173

Cornelius, A. R., Chief Justice of the Supreme Court; speech to Dacca High Court Bar Association, 59; signs Constitution as witness, 170; administers oath of office to Ayub, 215

Corruption, Ayub's determination to clean up, 14; martial law courts and screening committees to deal with, 23; Public Conduct Scrutiny Ordinance, 23-24; of businessmen, 24; results of screening, 36; comments on, by: *Pakistan Observer*, 17, 24; Nazir Ahmad, 87; *Statesman*, 90; *Dawn*, 113-114; examples of, 210 n18. *See also* Politicians

Dacca. *See* Capitals

Dacca District Bar Association, 24, 87, 162

Dacca District Board, 27

Dacca High Court, 190

Dacca High Court Bar Association, 59, 61, 67

Darul Uloom Islamia, 29-30

*Dawn*, history of, 6; editor interview by Constitution Commission, 84; editorials, 16, 26, 29, 30, 32, 77, 80, 88, 113-114, 139, 148, 149, 162, 177, 203

Dawood, Ahmad, 8

Dictatorship, Ayub on, 32; Chaudhri Mohamad Ali on, 71; Bhutto on, 77; *Dawn* on, 78; *Pakistan Observer* on, 129; students on, 160

Disparity. *See* Economic development, East Pakistan; Provinces, disparity

East Pakistan Chambers of Commerce and Industry, 109

East Pakistan Income Tax Bar Association, 67

East Pakistan Lawyers Association, 61, 66, 67

East Pakistan Mukhtears Association, 67

East Pakistan Prevention of Prejudicial Acts Ordinance, 8

East Pakistan Provincial Advisory Council, 86, 131, 137, 154, 155-156

East Pakistan Public Safety Ordinance, 158

Economic development, *Pakistan Observer* on, 18; Hafizur Rahman on, 99; Ayub on, 100; program of National Economic Council, 109; committee on improvement of railway administration, 163

Economic development, East Pakistan; and PIDC, 33, 100, 108, 110, 131, 163; discussion by Cabinet members of, 98-99; decentralization of Pakistan Eastern Railway, 99, 163-164; and Agricultural Development Corporation, 108; and WAPDA, 108; steel mill for Chittagong, 142; Government's steps to improve, 163; newspaper publicity by Government on, 165; comments on, by: Ayub, 33, 108, 124, 125, 126, 145, 155-156; Sheikh, 33, Shoaib, 34, 100, 110, 139, 146-148; *Pakistan Observer*, 98, 109, 125-127, 136-137; A. K. Khan, 98, 110; East Pakistan Chambers of Commerce and Industry, 109; Secretary of Finance Department, 109-110; Hafizur Rahman, 110; Mahmud Husain, 131-132; Bhutto, 135-136; *Dawn*, 139; Habibur Rahman,

157, 165; Abdul Qadir, 163; disparity between provinces, Government's efforts to reduce, 33; Planning Commission's steps to reduce, 34; finance committee set up to reduce, 110; five editors on, 62; Ataur Rahman on, 65; *Pakistan Observer* on, 98, 109; A. K. Khan, on 99; Rehman Sobhan on, 116; "two economies," Ayub on, 107-108, 156; Islamia Academy of Dacca on, 108-109; advocated by Rehman Sobhan, 108-109, 116, 127-128; Shoaib on, 109; *Pakistan Observer* on, 129; *Statesman* on, 130; Israrul Haque on, 134-135. *See also* Finance Commission; Fiscal policies

Election Commission, 120, 142

Elections, opinions on, by: Ayub, 20, 22, 32, 34, 43, 74-75, 87; Constitution Commission questionnaire answers, 62, 63; S. M. A., Majid, 66; East Pakistan organizations, 67; Chaudhri Mohamad Ali, 70; Zakir Husain, 93, 100; Constitution Commission report, 174; to Basic Democracies, preparation for, 41, 42; date of, 44-45; comments on, by: Zakir Husain, 31; Ayub, 32, 40, 42, 45, 74-75; of 1962, preparations for, 137, 142; to Provincial Assemblies, 211; to National Assembly, 211, 213-214; comments on, by: Ayub, 87, 125; Bhutto, 124; *Pakistan Observer*, 137; Akhtar Hussain, 211; electoral college, Basic Democracies as, 120; comments on, by: Ayub, 14, 32, 44, 46, 125; Manzur Qadir, 41; Chaudhri Mohamad Ali, 73; Constitution Commission report, 194; electorate, 187-189

Elective Bodies (Disqualification) Order 1959. *See* Politicians

Family Laws Ordinance. *See* Muslim Family Laws Ordinance

Faridpur Mukhtear Bar Association, 67

Faruqi, N. A., 123

Federal form of government, answers to Constitution Commission questionnaire on, 61-68; Chaudhri Mohamad Ali on, 72; Bhutto on, 77; now being favored by Government, 120; confirmed by Ayub, 131; *Pakistan Observer* on, 140; in 1962 Constitution, 164, 184; public opinion on, 183; Constitution Commission report on, 183-184. *See also* unitary form of government

Finance Commission, set up 8/61, 110; Ayub promises to appoint, 125, 128;

*Pakistan Observer* on, 126-127; Shoaib on, 139; appointment of 12/12/61, 139; proceedings of, 142; chairman, members and terms of reference of, 143-144; first meeting, 143-144; newspapers on, 144; hearings resumed, 144; report submitted, 144-145; *Morning News* on, 144-145; *Statesman* on, 145; Cabinet's agreement on report of, 146; National Finance Commission in 1962 Constitution, 176, 194; report to be part of Constitution, 194-195. *See also* Fiscal policies

Fiscal policies, allocation of resources, Ayub on foreign exchange earnings, 108, 125, 155-156; East Pakistan Chambers of Commerce and Industry on, 109; as part of constitution, 128; Israrul Haque on, 134-135; *Pakistan Observer* on, 136-137; Shoaib on, 139, 146-148; *Ittefaq* on, 149; Zakir Husain on, 156; in 1962 Constitution, 194-195. *See also* Finance Commission

Fundamental rights, discussed by West Pakistan High Court, 20; M. R. Kayani on, 55; Chaudhri Mohamad Ali on, 70; Nazir Ahmad on, 87; *Pakistan Observer* on, 93; deputation of lawyers on, 116; S. Nasiruddin on, 117; Ayub on, 118, 123-124; Constitution Commission report on, 174, 192; public opinion on, 191-192; in 1962 Constitution, 175-176, 192; official delegation on, 192; judiciary on, 200-201; law-makers entrusted with protection of, 201

Gordon College, 76-77, 91

Government, future form of, Ayub on, 26, 43, 44, 46, 53, 182; Anwar Iqbal Qureshi on, 44; *Pakistan Observer* on, 61; public opinion on, 182; Constitution Commission report on, 183; strong Center, Ayub on, 15, 32, 115, 181, 181-182; *Pakistan Observer* on, 179; *Morning News* on, 179; local government, Ayub on importance of *panchayats*, 22; Union Boards to be introduced into West Pakistan, 29; Chaudhri Mohamad Ali on, 71-72; Basic Democracies as, 194. *See also* Basic Democracies; under 1962 Constitution, explained in "Summary of Constitution," 175; Ayub on, 182. *See also* Federal form; Parliamentary system; Presidential system; Unitary form

Government of India Act 1935, 76

Governors Conference, 30, 33, 34, 41, 98,

107, 123, 124, 128, 137, 140, 154, 155
Gurmani, Mushtaq Ahmad, 94

Habibullah, (Sardar), member Constitution Commission, 49; dissenting notes to *Report*, 174
Hamid, (Sheikh) Abdul, 105, 128
Haq, (Qazi) Anwarul, 123
Haq, Fazlul, 7
Haque, Israrul, 134-135
Haripur Tehsil Council, 81
Hasan, K. Sawar, 49
Huda, M. N., Dacca University Economics Professor, 133
Huda, Nurul, President Pakistan Bar Association, 178
Huq, (Syed) Azizul, 212-213
Husain, (Chowdhury) Mohammad, 214
Husain, Imdad, 132
Husain, Sajjad, 132
Husain, Tafazzal, editor, *Ittefaq*, 12 n21, 159
Husain, Zakir, Governor East Pakistan, Cabinet member; possible member constitution commission, 50; warns against publication of views on constitution, 81-82; visits Chittagong, 91; warns students, 95; speaks to Provincial Advisory Council, 114; speaking tours for 1962 Constitution, 211; on constitution commission, 31, 35, 92, 100-101; on distribution of subjects between Center and provinces, 31; on elections to *panchayats*, 31; on Basic Democracies, 35; on unitary form, 86-87; expert constitutional draftsman to be sought, 92, 100; on constitution, 114, 140, 141, 156; on political parties, 92, 93; on presidential form, 93; on general elections, 93; on disparity, 99; on cabinet subcommittee, 106; on allocation of funds, 156; *Pakistan Observer* on, 114-115
Hussain, Akhtar, Governor West Pakistan, Cabinet member; possible member constitution commission, 50; member Cabinet subcommittee on report, 105; speaks to Institute of Islamic Research, 124; named Chief Election Commissioner, 142; on 1962 elections, 211; receives President at first meeting National Assembly, 215
Hussain, Altaf, editor *Dawn*, 6; possible member constitution commission, 50
Hussain, Dr. Mahmud, Vice-Chancellor Dacca University, 99, 131-132
Hyderabad Bar Association, 106

Hyderabad Tehsil Council, 81

Ibrahim, Mohammad, Cabinet member; member subcommittee on report, 105; speaks to: Dacca District Bar Association, 24, 87; Dacca District Board, 27; Karachi High Court Bar Association, 58-59; his comments on: constitution, 24, 27, 30, 31, 131; local government, 27; Governors Conference, 30; Basic Democracies, 31, 91; constitution commission, 31, 34, 41, 91, 92; military regime, 58; Kayani's remarks, 58; independence of judiciary, 58-59, 87, 116; rule of law, 87; politicians, 91; failure of parliamentary democracy, 91
Iftikharuddin, (Mian), 6, 12 n24
*Imroze*, editor of, 8, 84
Institute of Islamic Research, 124
Isa, (Begum) Saeeda Qazi, 213
Islam, as a binding force. *See* National unity
Islam, principles of, Ayub on, 24, 43, 110-111, 113; *Pakistan Observer* on, 97; Habibur Rahman on, 112; Government efforts to modernize Islamic leaders, 111. *See also* Constitution of 1962, Islamic provisions; *Ulema*
Islamabad. *See* Capitals
Islamia Academy of Dacca, 108-109
Islamic Advisory Council. *See* Advisory Council of Islamic Ideology
Islamic Republic of Pakistan, 5
Islamic Research Institute, 193, 199, 200
*Ittefaq*, 8, 9, 62, 149

Jacobabad District Council, 81
Jama'at-i-Islami, 82, 82 n15
Jan, Arbab Ahmed Ali, member Constitution Commission, 49
Jinnah, Mohammad Ali, 4, 5, 6, 16, 21, 44, 53, 57, 66, 133, 134
Judiciary, its concerns, 20, 55; West Pakistan High Court discusses fundamental rights, 20; civil courts reinstated, 20; power of courts to issue writs, 20; power to suspend High Court judges, 22; official delegation on, before Constitution Commission, 190; Constitution Commission report on, 174, 190-191, 201; provisions in 1962 Constitution, 190, 191; Supreme Court, 57, 117, 118, 190; comments on, by: Munir, 57; Z. H. Lari, 58; S. Naziruddin, 117; Ayub, 190, 201; public opinion, 190; *Statesman*, 201; legal

system, opinions by: Ayub on, 19, 22, 116; *Pakistan Observer* on, 19; independence of, opinions on, by: M. R. Kayani, 21, 55, 56; Ayub, 22, 58, 118; Anwar Iqbal Qureshi, 44; Imam Hossain Chowdhury, 59; Habibur Rahman, 59; Ibrahim, 58-59, 87, 116; Chaudhri Mohamad Ali, 70; deputation of lawyers, 116; lawyers and judges before Constitution Commission, 200-201; rule of law, comments on, by: Ayub, 22, 55; Manzur Qadir, 29; Kayani, 55, 56; Munir, 57; A. R. Cornelius, 59; Imam Hossain Chowdhury, 59; Chaudhri Mohamad Ali, 70; Ibrahim, 87; lawyers and judges, 200-201. *See also* Fundamental rights

Karachi. *See* Capitals
Karachi Bar Association, 28-29, 116-119
Karachi High Court Bar Association, 22, 55, 58-59
Karnafuly Paper Mill, 99
Kayani, M. R., Chief Justice West Pakistan High Court, 21; speech before Pakistan Bar Association, 55-56; reactions to speech, 56-57, 58
Khairpur District Council, 81
Khairpur Divisional Council, 81
(Khan) Abdul Ghaffar Khan, 96, 119, 199
(Khan) Abdul Qayyum Khan, 162, 163
Khan, Abul Kasem, Cabinet member; addresses Dacca University Economics Association, 98-99; member Cabinet subcommittee on Constitution Commission report, 105; speaking tours for Constitution, 211; candidate for National Assembly, 213; on price rise, 99; on bifurcation of PIDC, 110, 131; on constitution, 165; on presidential form, 165
Khan, (Malik) Amir Mohammad, 162, 164
Khan, (Maulvi) Ebrahim, 50
(Khan) Ghulam Ishaq Khan, 123
Khan, Liaquat Ali, 5, 53, 63, 65, 66
Khan, Mohammad Ayub, President of Pakistan; named Chief Martial Law Administrator, 6; first Pakistani Commander-in-Chief, 10; subject of biography, *My Chief*, 10; plans for reform of national life, 9-11; and press, 14, 27-28, 29, 32, 87, 123-124, 124-125; appointed Prime Minister, 15; supersedes Iskander Mirza and assumes presidency, 15; visits East Pakistan, 15,

21-22, 33-34, 34, 86, 107, 124-126, 137, 153; promulgates Presidential Cabinet Order, 15; preoccupation with Basic Democracies, 23; refutes idea of one-party system, 26; union board system to be introduced into West Pakistan, 29; Cabinet conferred rank of Field Marshal on, 40; meet-the-people tours, 42-44, 44, 45-47, 47, 85; vote of confidence in, 45, 47-48; inducted into office, 48; appoints Constitution Commission, 49; reactions to Constitution Commission questionnaire replies, 74-76; adds new term of reference to Constitution Commission, 83; plan for Basic Democracies and constitution, 84; visits Southeast Asia, 91; denies interim constitution, 93; promulgates Muslim Family Laws Ordinance, 96; attends Commonwealth conference, 97; statements during summer 1961, 107-108; hears deputation of lawyers, 116; explains important aspects of constitution, 124-126; promises to appoint finance commission, 125; reactions to East Pakistan visit, 126-128; reveals federal system to be provided, 131; appoints committee on decentralization of central institutions, 135; political program for January, 1962, 137-138; Constitution Commission report to be announced with Constitution, 139; names Akhtar Hussain as Chief Election Commissioner, 142; receives report(s) of Finance Commission, 144-145; attempts to remove interwing economic disparities, 145; reviews industrialization in East Pakistan, 155; warns Basic Democrats to avoid politics, 155; promise to raise two more battalions in East Pakistan fulfilled, 157; visit to Rajshahi University postponed, 159; ordinance debarring habeas corpus petition if person held under Security of Pakistan Act, 162-163; to hold special briefing on constitution for newspaper editors, 166; signs master copy of Constitution, 170; Ayub as first president provided in 1962 Constitution, 196; and East Pakistan, 203-206; and the 1962 Constitution, 206-209; attains all but one objective in 1962 Constitution, 209; Manifesto of March 23, 1962, 211-212; granted clemency to all students arrested under Martial Law Regulations, 213; ordinance prohibiting

unregulated political activity, 214; sworn in as President, 215; declares lifting of Martial Law, 215; speeches, on Jinnah's anniversary (Dec. 25), (1958), 21; (1959), 44, 85; (1961), 138-139; on Pakistan Day (March 23), (1959), 25-26; (1961), 97; (1962), 211-212; on Revolution Day (Oct. 27), (1959), 40; (1961), 128-129; to students, 21, 119-120; to union boards, 22; to Karachi High Court Bar Association, 22; to Darul Uloom Islamia, 29-30; in Dacca stadium, 34; in London, 52; to Basic Democracies members, 74-76, 85, 91, 137, 138, 141-142, 155; to East Pakistan Advisory Council, 86; to *ulema*, 97; on receiving the Constitution Commission report, 101; to West Pakistan divisional commissioners conference, 115; to Karachi Bar Association, 116-119; to women's groups, 119, 131; to officers of Pakistan Navy, 119; to Commonwealth Press Union, 130; to Aligarh Muslim University alumni, 131; to a gathering in Campbellpur, 138; to Writers Guild, 154-155; at opening of Fenchuganj fertilizer plant, 155; in Dacca 2/6/62, 156; broadcast announcing constitution, 166, 170, 189-190; addresses National Assembly, 215; his opinions on: decentralization, 10, 43, 46, 115, 182; Islamic democracy, 10; integration of West Pakistan, 10; land reform, 10; powers of president and of provinces, 10; development administration, 10; constitution, 14, 20, 21, 22, 25, 26, 27-28, 32, 35, 42, 43, 47, 53, 75, 76, 87, 91, 92-93, 107-108, 113, 117, 119, 124, 125, 128, 138, 139, 140, 141, 153-154, 155, 156, 181-182, 202, 206, 211; unitary system, 14, 35, 43, 45-46, 46, 183; electoral college, 14, 32, 44, 46, 125; Mirza's ouster, 15; presidential system, 15, 28, 29, 35, 42, 44, 75; national unity, 15, 34, 52, 97, 107, 124, 125-126, 139; students, 15, 162; strong central government, 15, 32, 115, 181; legal system, 19, 22, 116; parliamentary democracy, 15, 20, 28, 52, 74, 86; constitution commission, 20, 22, 26, 27, 29, 32, 34-35, 42, 43, 46, 52-53, 75, 76, 91, 97, 171; elections, 20, 22, 32, 34, 43, 74-75, 87; Pakistan's problems, 20, 21; legislature, 20, 44, 46, 141; rule of law, independence of judiciary, 22, 55, 118; Law Commission, 22; local government, 22; inflation, 24; Islamic principles, 24, 110-111, 113; future form of government, 26, 43, 44, 46, 53, 181-182; political parties, 26, 32, 42-43, 47, 53, 75, 86, 91, 123, 138, 142, 154, 189-190, 213; reforms, 29, 34; Islam, 29-30, 119; dictatorship, 32; martial law, 32, 87, 88; Basic Democracies, 32, 34, 42, 45-46, 74-75, 107, 125, 141, 194; economic development of East Pakistan, 33, 100, 108, 124, 125, 145, 155-156; military regime, 34, 52; politicians, 46, 75, 125; Jinnah, 53; Liaquat Ali Khan, 53; Chaudhri Mohamad Ali, 74; freedom of press, 74; Communists in East Pakistan, 86; military courts, 88; two economies, 107-108, 108, 156; provincial differences, 108, 125; fiscal policies, 108, 125, 155, 155-156; Family Laws Ordinance, 111-112; Supreme Court, 118; fundamental rights, 118, 123-124; women in legislature, 141; Suhrawardy's arrest, 153; WAPDA, 155; Agricultural Development corporation, 155; Karnafuly Dam project, 155; bifurcation of PIDC, 155; judiciary, 190, 201; Islamic Advisory Council, 200; new cabinet, 214; others' opinions on, *Pakistan Observer*, 21, 22, 34, 43-44, 81, 125-126; *Statesman*, 90; Toynbee, 93; *Dawn*, 113-114; S. Nasiruddin, 117

Khan, Lt. Gen. Mohammad Azam, Cabinet member; and vote of confidence, 45; on provincial differences, 132, 164-165; letter to students' guardians, 162; on provincialization of railways, 164; on reaction in East Pakistan to constitution, 179

Khan, Tamizuddin, 50

Khulna District Bar Association, 162

Kurram Agency Council, 81

Kushtia Bar Association, 67

Lahore District Bar Association, 162

Lahore High Court Bar Association, 57

Lahore Resolution of 1940, 4, 26, 186, 211-212

Language issue, 4, 5, 33, 65, 160-161, 175, 195

Lari, Z. H., 28, 50, 58, 201-202, 213

Law Commission, 22, 190

Law Society of Lahore, 76

Laws (Continuance in Force) Order 1958, 184, 196

Legal system. *See* Judiciary

Legislature, distribution of powers between Center and provinces, 10, 31, 63, 72, 186, 186-187; Ayub on, 20, 44, 46, 141; Constitution Commission questionnaire on, 62, 63, 67; Nurul Amin on, 63-64; Ataur Rahman on, 64; women and, 141, 185, 214; Constitution Commission report on, 184-185; public opinion on, 185; official delegation, 185; "Summary of Constitution" on, 175

Lyallpur District Bar Association, 162

Mahmud, (Begum) Shamsunnaha, 49
Majid, A., 49, 83, 120
Majid, H. A., 143
Majid, S. M. A., 66
Manifesto of 3/23/62, 211-212
Manikganj Bar Association, 67
Martial Law, proclaimed Oct. 7, 1958, 6; and the press, 7-9; Regulations, 8, 42, 95, 142, 158, 162, 196, 212; and business, 24; and Constitution Commission, 80; arrests under, 158; public opinion under, 182; comments on, by: *Dawn*, 16, 80; M. R. Kayani, 21, 55-57; Ayub, 32, 87, 88; Ataur Rahman, 65; Chaudhri Mohamad Ali, 73; Nazir Ahmad, 88; Habibur Rahman, 131; *Statesman*, 159-160. See also Military regime
Martyrs Day. See Students
Maudoodi, (Maulana) Abul Ala, 178-179
Mercantile Marine Academy, 110
Military regime, takeover, 6, 16; military courts to deal with corruption, 23, 88; reactions to, by: *Dawn*, 9, 88; *Pakistan Times*, 9; *Pakistan Observer*, 9, 16-18, 19, 21, 22, 27, 88, 127; Ayub, 34, 52; *Statesman*, 36, 89-90; Ibrahim, 58. See also Martial law
Mirza, Iskander, 5, 6, 14, 15, 16, 65, 66, 67, 70, 94
Mohammad, Ghulam, 5, 63, 66, 67, 78, 79
Mohsenuddin, (Pir), 212-213
*Morning News*, 6, 148, 162, 177
Multan District Council, 81
Munir, Justice Mohammad, 50, 57, 214
Murshed, Justice S. M., 132
Muslim Family Laws Ordinance, 96, 106, 107, 111-112, 112, 119
Muslim League, 4, 6, 64, 84, 214
Mymensingh Bar Association, 61, 67

Nasiruddin, S., 116-117

National Assembly, 5, 137; of 1962, 142-143, 185, 211, 213, 213-214, 214-215, 215
National Economic Council, 109, 176, 194
National Finance Commission, 176, 194
National unity (including "sense of nationhood," "national integration," "cultural unity"), Islam as a binding force, 4, 87, 115-116, 132, 133, 134; hindrances to, 4-5; Government's efforts to promote, 33-34; subject of Bureau of National Reconstruction seminars, 115-116, 131-135; comments on, by: Ayub, 15, 34, 52, 97, 107, 120, 125-126, 138-139; Manzur Qadir, 25; Islamia Academy, 108-109; *Dawn*, 134-139; Bhutto, 164; Habibur Rahman, 165
Nawaz, (Begum) Jahanara Shah, 49
Nazimuddin, (Khwaja), 50, 63, 65, 66, 68
*New World*, 8
Nizam, O. R., 49
Noon, Feroze Khan, former Prime Minister, 65

Pabna Pleaders Bar Association, 162
Pakistan, description of, 4
Pakistan Bar Association, 55-57
Pakistan Day (March 23), significance of, 38 n33; Ayub's speeches on, 22, 25-26, 97, 211-212. See also Lahore Resolution
Pakistan Eastern Railway, 99, 163
Pakistan Industrial Development Corporation, 33, 100, 108, 110, 131, 136, 139, 154, 155, 163
Pakistan International Airways, 157
Pakistan Medical Association, 67
*Pakistan Observer*, history of, 6-7; blacklisting of, 9; editorials, 16-19, 21, 22, 24, 27, 43-44, 47, 88, 93, 98, 114-115, 126-127, 136-137, 138, 143, 148, 178
Pakistan Police Service, 72
Pakistan Railway Board, 99
*Pakistan Times*, 6, 8
Parliamentary democracy, 20, 52, 62, 63, 66, 66-67, 68, 71, 72, 86, 93, 94, 174; failure of, 15, 63, 64-65, 66, 67, 70, 74, 76, 91, 173-174
*Pasban*, 62
Pirzada, Shafiuddin, 49
Planning Commission, 34, 98
Political parties, abolished, 6; answers to Constitution Commission questionnaire on, 62, 63, 65, 66, 67, 70; official

delegation on, 189; in 1962 Constitution, 189; Ayub's broadcast of 3/1/62 on, 189-190; opinions on, by: Manzur Qadir, 25, 42, 79, 213; *Dawn*, 26; Ayub, 26, 32, 42-43, 47, 53, 75, 86, 91, 123, 138, 142, 154, 189, 213; Ataur Rahman, 65; Chaudhri Mohamad Ali, 70, 70-71; Ibrahim, 91; Zakir Husain, 92, 93; *Pakistan Observer*, 114-115; Hafizur Rahman, 164; Constitution Commission report, 174, 189. *See also* Awami League; Jama'at-i-Islami; Muslim League

Politicians, 5; disbarment of, 32, 90; disqualified under EBDO, 47, 125, 152, 179, 199, 212n, 213; appeal to President to pardon, 179; 1962 Constitution on, 190; reaction to 1962 Constitution by, 199; request release of détenus, 160, 212-213; in 1962 elections, 214; Lari on, 28; Ayub on, 15, 32, 46, 53, 75, 119, 125; Sheikh on, 33; Manzur Qadir on, 47; newspaper editors on, 62; Ataur Rahman on, 64-65; Bhutto on, 76, 124; *Dawn* on, 80; Ibrahim on, 91. *See also* Khan Abdul Ghaffar Khan; Suhrawardy, H. S.

President, powers of, 206-208, 208
Presidential Cabinet Order, 15
Presidential (Election and Constitution) Order, 1960, 44-45
Presidential system, comments on, by: Ayub, 15, 28, 29, 35, 42, 44, 75; Habibur Rahman, 59; Syed Qamrul Ahsan, 63; Bhutto, 76, 77; Zakir Husain, 93; A. K. Khan, 165; Constitution Commission report on, 174; in 1962 Constitution, 183. *See also* Parliamentary system

Press, history of, 6-7, 11 n8; censorship, 7, 7-8, 96, 159; Press Trust of India, 7; under martial law, 7-9, 12 n24; arrests of newsmen, 8, 12 n21; *Pakistan Times*, seized by Government, 8; Ayub's conferences and interviews with, 14, 32, 87, 123-124, 124-125, 166; *Dawn* on, 32; Ayub on, 74. *See also* Azad; Dawn; Ittefaq; Morning News; New World; Pakistan Observer; Pakistan Times; Pasban; Sangbad; Statesman

Proclamation of October 7, 1958, 5-6, 14, 196

Provinces, 4; distribution of powers between central government and, 5, 10, 186-187; provincial assembly, 1962 elections to, 211; disparity between (other than economic), 4, 9, 15, 97-98,

99, 106, 107, 108, 110, 126, 129, 132, 149. *See also* National unity; Finance Commission; Fiscal policies

Public Conduct Scrutiny Ordinance, 23-24

Public opinion, in newspapers, 9; Kayani on, 56; Chaudhri Mohamad Ali on, 70; and economic discussion, 98; as expressed in *Pakistan Observer*, 98; as revealed under martial law, 182, 198; on form of government, 182; on federal form, 183; on legislature, 185; on division of powers between Center and provinces, 186; on electorate, 187; on judiciary, 190; on fundamental rights, 191-192; on Islamic provisions, 193; and martial law, 198

Qadir, Abdul, named Finance Minister, 163, 214

Qadir, Manzur, Cabinet member; "reaction assessment tour" of West Pakistan, 24-25; speeches, 28-29, 80, 91, 211; rumored as possible member constitution commission, 50; warns against political activity, 79; criticizes views of Dacca Bar Association, 79; press conference, 85; member Cabinet subcommittees (1), (2) and (3), 101, 105, 106-107, 120, 128; to accompany Ayub to United States, 107; and students, 154, 159; tribute to Quayle, 172; comments on: seizure of Progressive Papers, Ltd., 8-9; constitution, 25, 28-29, 41, 47; Bureau of National Reconstruction, 25; political parties, 25, 42, 213; national unity, 25; rule of law, 29; Basic Democracies, 31, 91; constitution commission, 31, 41-42, 47, 79, 171; electoral college, 41; democratic government, 41; political activities, 79; public opinion, 79; Islamic Advisory Council, 200

Qasem, Abul, 63
Qazi, Aftab, 123
Quaid-e-Azam. *See* Jinnah, Mohammad Ali
Quaid-e-Millat. *See* Khan, Liaquat Ali
Quayle, 170, 172. *See also* Constitution, experts to help draft
Qureshi, Anwar Iqbal, 44, 85-86

Radio Pakistan, 84, 94
Rahman, Ataur, 64-66, 212-213
Rahman, Habibur, Cabinet member; member Cabinet subcommittee (1) on constitution commission report, 105; elected to National Assembly, 213,

214; speeches: to religious leaders, 112; to Basic Democracies members, 140-141, 157; to Administrative Staff College, 165; comments by, on: constitution commission, 33; constitution, 59, 131, 157; independence of judiciary, 59; presidential form, 59; martial law, 131; economic development, 157; national unity, 165; elimination of economic disparity, 165

Rahman, Hafizur, Cabinet member; visits Chittagong, 91; addresses Dacca University Commerce Association, 99; on price differentials, 99; on economic development East Pakistan, 110; on constitution, 156-157; on political parties, 164

Rahman, Tufail Ali, member Constitution Commission, 49

Railways, decentralization of Pakistan Eastern Railway, 99; committee to recommend administrative improvements in, 163-164; Lt. Gen. Azam Khan on, 164; Malik Amir Mohammad Khan on, 164; Cabinet decided to provincialize, 164

Raisman Award, 146-147, 149, 151 n60

Rajshahi District Bar Association, 162

Rangpur Bar Association, 67

Rangpur District Bar Association, 162

Rawalpindi. *See* Capitals

Rawalpindi Divisional Council, 81

Revolution (military takeover), *Dawn* on, 37; *Pakistan Observer* on, 37; first anniversary of, 36-37, 40; second anniversary of, 88; third anniversary of, 127, 128-129, 129-130. *See also* Martial law, military takeover

Rule of law. *See* Judiciary, rule of law

Sangbad, 8, 9, 62

Sanghar District Council, 81

Sarkar, Abu Hossain, 212-213

Screening committees. *See* Civil Services

Security of Pakistan Act, 152

Shafi, (Mufti) Mohammad, 112

Shahabuddin, Justice Muhammad, chairman Constitution Commission, 49; on Constitution Commission, 51, 57-58; becomes Chief Justice, 57; *Statesman* on, 90; signs Constitution Commission report, 100; presents report to Ayub, 101

Shahidullah, Dr. Mohammad, 132

Shaikh, Naseer A., 49

Sharif, Justice Muhammad, member Constitution Commission, 49; on Iskander Mirza, 94; on parliamentary

democracy, 94; on anti-Pakistan *ulema*, 112

Sheikh, Lt. Gen. K. M., Cabinet member; "reaction assessment tour" of West Pakistan, 24-25; on constitution commission, 32-33; on developing East Pakistan, 33; as possible member constitution commission, 50

Shoaib, Mohammad, Cabinet member; member Cabinet subcommittee (1) on Constitution Commission report, 105; to accompany Ayub to United States, 107; to become a director of World Bank, 163; comments by, on: economic development for East Pakistan, 34, 100; unitary form, 87; budgeting for elections, 107; "two economies," 109; finance committee, 110; allocation of resources, 139; decentralization of State Bank and PICIC, 139; Finance Commission, 139, 146; announced Cabinet agreement on Finance Commission recommendations, 146-148; newspaper reactions to this statement, 148-149

Sobham, Rehman, advocates "two economies," 108-109, 116, 127-128, 134, 150 n14

*Statesman*, 7, 35-36, 89-90, 94, 101-102, 105, 130, 133, 145, 148, 149-150 n13, 153, 159, 159-160, 161, 198, 199, 201, 208

Students, addressed by Ayub, 21, 107, 119-120; addressed by Bhutto, 24; rioting, 95-96, 154, 157-159, 160; Shaheed (Martyrs) Day, 160-161; unrest of, 161-162; trial of, 161, 212; granted clemency by Ayub, 213

Suhrawardy, H. S., former Prime Minister, disqualified by EBDO; arrest of, 152-153, 159, 168 n5; habeas corpus petition, 162-163; played politics, 199; Ataur Rahman on, 65

Sukkur District Council, 81

"Summary of the Constitution," 175-176

Supreme Court. *See* Judiciary, Supreme Court

Tangail Pleaders Bar, 67

Thanvi, (Maulana) Ihteshamul Haq, 30, 96

Toynbee, Arnold, 93

*Ulema*, opinions on constitution, 5, 178; response to Constitution Commission questionnaire, 68-69; and Muslim Family Laws Ordinance, 96, 107; Ayub to, 29-30, 97; Habibur Rahman to,

112; and sighting of Id moon, 97; Justice Sharif on, 112; conference of, 112-113; and the 1962 Constitution, 199-200

Unitary form, Government campaign for, 85-87, 89; opinions on, by: Ayub, 14, 35, 43, 45-46, 183; Bhutto, 24, 77; Anwar Iqbal Qureshi, 44; Abul Qasem, 63; *Dawn*, 78, 85-86; Zakir Husain, 86-87; Shoaib, 87; Hatim A. Alavi, 87. *See also* Federal form

Wasiuddin, Khwaja, East Pakistan

Martial Law Administrator, 213

Water and Power Development Authority, 98, 108, 155

West Pakistan High Court, 190

West Pakistan High Court Bar Association, 162

West Pakistan Provincial Advisory Council, 78-79

Wint, Guy, 27-28

Women, Ayub's address to, 119; Ayub on role of, 141; reservation of seats in legislatures for, 185, 214

Writers Guild, 154-155